WE WERE MARCHING ON CHRISTMAS DAY

A History and Chronicle of Christmas During the Civil War

by

Kevin Rawlings

To Mike Brown,
Merry Christmas! Enjoy this little known &
written about slice of Civil War History.
May all your days be like your fondest
Christmas memories.
Best Wishes & Warmest Regards,
Kevin Rawlings
Christmas 1995
"Hagerstown, MD"

Toomey Press
Baltimore, Maryland

For information about this and other titles, contact:
 Toomey Press
 P.O. Box 122
 Linthicum, MD 21090
 410-850-0831

Photograph Credits:
 K.R. – Kevin Rawlings
 USAMHI – United States Army Military History Institute

Book Design and Production:
 Cynthia Edmiston,
 Merrifield Graphics & Publishing Service, Inc., Hanover, Maryland

Printing:
 H. G. Roebuck & Son, Baltimore, Maryland

Library of Congress CIP Number 95-061885

ISBN Number 0-9612670-4-6

INTRODUCTION

This book is truly a labor of love. One that started when I began researching a costume to portray the Civil War Era Santa Claus at Antietam National Battlefield during their first illumination program in 1989. I found many details in a centennial reproduction of *Harper's Weekly* which included the front page image of the patriotic Santa Claus drawn by Thomas Nast. As a Civil War reenactor I was hooked on the idea of doing a Santa Claus that no one else had portrayed.

My wife Mimi agreed to help with the project which was vital since my sewing skills did not compare with hers. Together we selected the materials, cut patterns, and assembled what may well have been the first ever Civil War Santa suit.

To add to my Santa Claus impression I began researching the whole concept of Christmas before and during the Civil War. I read through many letters, diaries, and unpublished manuscripts, as well as the few books that addressed the subject. The conclusion I reached was that by the time of the Civil War, the majority of our present day Christmas customs and traditions were already established.

As the number of stories and drawings I found grew, I developed a slide presentation and then, at the urging of my wife, set about to write a book about Christmas in America during the Civil War. In doing so I have allowed the participants to relate their stories to you in their original form. Grammar and spelling are for the most part unchanged.

I would like to thank a number of people who have helped bring this project to fruition. Brian Dankmeyer, who transcribed letters and diaries at USAMHI; Dr. Richard Sommers and his staff at the USAMHI, who took an interest in this project; Kate Jerome, who became so intrigued with my Christmas tales she ended up typing several years worth of research notes; Wanda Dowell and Susan Cumby at the Fort Ward Museum in Alexandria, Va., who gave me a place to hold my lecture and be the Civil War Santa in a real historic setting; Living History Coordinator and Park Ranger Cathy Beeler of Monocacy National Battlefield, who has been my staunchest supporter of the Christmas program done there. To Frank and Marie-Terese Wood, whose treasure trove of 19th century prints I found truly amazing. Their help in supplying illustrations for the book will not soon be forgotten.

Dan Toomey and his wife Carol get my undying gratitude for their persistence and skill in bringing this book to print. Dan believed in the project from the outset and waited years to see it completed.

Last, but certainly not least, I want to thank my wife Mimi and daughter Elspeth for allowing me to steal the time away from my duties of husband and father for the several months it took to complete this book. You two make every day like Christmas and bring joy into my life. I dedicate this book to the both of you with all my love.

Kevin Rawlings
Sharpsburg, MD

"But is Old, Old, Good Old Christmas gone? Nothing but the hair of his good, gray old head and beard left? Well, I will have that, seeing I cannot have more of him."

Hue and Cry After Christmas

From *The Sketch Book of Geoffrey Crayon, Gentleman*
by Washington Irving

tradition: *n.* 1. The handing down of beliefs, legends, and customs from generation to generation, especially by word of mouth or practice. 2. A belief, legend, or custom so handed down. 3. Any long continued practice or custom.

custom: *n.* 1. A habitual practice. 2. Social habits or practices collectively.

legend: *n.* 1. An unverifiable story handed down by tradition from earlier times and popularly accepted as historical. 4. A collection of stories about an admirable person. 5. A person who is the center of such stories.

The Random House Dictionary

"There seems a magic in the very name of Christmas. Petty jealousies and discords are forgotten; social feelings are awakened in bosoms to which they have long been strangers; father and son, or brother and sister, who have met and passed with averted gaze, or a look of cold recognition, for months before, proffer and return the cordial embrace, and bury their past animosities in their present happiness. Kindly hearts that have yearned towards each other, but have been withheld by false notions of pride and self-dignity, are again reunited, and all is kindness and benevolence! Would that Christmas lasted the whole year through (as it ought), and that the prejudices and passions which deform our better nature were never called into action among those to whom they should ever be strangers!"

From *Sketches By Boz*
by Charles Dickens

CONTENTS

Figure 1-1. *Harper's Weekly* Christmas issue for December, 1860. It would be the last cover devoid of military scenes for four years. (K.R.)

1

CHRISTMAS COMES TO AMERICA

On December 23, 1823, the editor with the unlikely holiday name of Orville L. Holley, published two articles in the *Troy Sentinel* of Troy, New York. The first, an editorial written by Mr. Holley, stated. . . "We know not to whom we are indebted for the following description of that unwearied patron of children—that homely and delightful personage of parental kindness—Santa Claus,—his costume and equipage as he goes about visiting the firesides of this happy land, laden with Christmas bounties; but from whomsoever it may have come, we give thanks for it. There is, to our apprehension a spirit of cordial goodness in it, a playfulness of fancy, and a benevolent alacrity to enter into the feelings and promote the simple pleasures of children, which are altogether charming. We hope our little patrons, both lads and lassies, will accept it as a proof of our unfeigned goodwill towards them—as a token of our warmest wish that they may have many a merry Christmas; that they may long retain their beautiful relics for those homebred joys, which derive their flavor from filial piety and fraternal love, and which they may be assured are the least alloyed that time can furnish them, and that they may never part with the simplicity of character, which is their fairest ornament, and for the sake of which they have been pronounced, by Authority which none can gainsay, the types of such as shall inherit the kingdom of heaven."[1] Mr. Holley's plethora of words would not be long remembered.

The second piece began with the now immortal line. . . "Twas the night before Christmas. . . " The then unknown author fired the imagination of children and adults alike with the written visual images of Santa Claus, his sleigh flying through the air from rooftop to rooftop, the eight tiny reindeer with names that pulled the sleigh, and his startling practice of coming down chimneys to leave gifts for good children. Never before had Santa Claus in his many incarnations and names been visualized like that, but Clement Clarke Moore gave rise to that round, jolly little fellow, Santa Claus, a thoroughly American invention that many countries around the world would come to embrace.

The Santa Claus and Christmas traditions we know today were based in the traditions handed down from the first settlers of the New World. Principally, the German, Dutch, and English would be the main founding ethnic groups to bring their Old World Christmas traditions and customs to America. That is not to say the French, Spanish, and other lesser known ethnic influences did not contribute their own Christmas practices to our culture.

The most important contribution the Germans gave to the American Christmas traditions was the Christmas tree. The Christmas tree would originate in Germany, but its popularity would detour through England first. Prince Albert, Queen Victoria's German-born husband, first set up a Christmas tree in Windsor Castle in 1841. The Royal Christmas tree would be mass produced for the public in an etching that appeared in *The Illustrated London News* in 1848, followed by an American version published in *Godey's Lady's Book* in December issues for 1850 and 1860. Editor Sarah Josepha Hale had her illustrator take out all the royal trappings and ornamentation and made the illustration uniquely American for her feminine readers. The rise in acceptance by the British public was sparked by the Royal Consort through his gifts of decorated trees to army barracks and schools. Prince Albert's own palace tree was seven feet tall and, in the European style, made even taller by placing the tree on a table. Towering eleven feet tall, the top was adorned with an angel and its branches illuminated with tapers (small candles),

delighting the Royal family's children with candy dangling from the boughs. Presents were hidden among the innermost recesses of the tree and surrounding base.

It was not the first time English royalty had celebrated Christmas with a traditional "Weihnachtsbaum." King George I of the German-rooted House of Hanover, and Queen Victoria's great-great-grandfather, introduced England to the Christmas tree. By 1789, the first known written reference to the Christmas tree in England was alluded to as "a charming imported German custom."[2] The thirteen-year-old Princess Victoria wrote in her diary on Christmas Eve of 1832 about her aunt's own table-top tree. "After dinner we went upstairs. I then saw Flora, the dog which Sir John was going to give Mamma. Aunt Sophia came also. We then went into the drawing room near the dining room. After Mamma had rung a bell three times we went in. There were two large round tables on which were placed two trees hung with lights and sugar ornaments. All the presents being placed round the tree."[3] Many of her other relatives had Christmas trees erected in parlors and drawing rooms in their palaces and estates.

But the Christmas tree was part of a more ancient custom. The Romans adapted it for their Saturnalia celebrations from the occupied German provinces. St. Boniface was said to have found a small fir tree behind the sacred oak of Odin, which he toppled during his completion of the Christianization of Germany in the eighth century. He dedicated the fir tree to the Holy Christ Child. Fourteenth and fifteenth century German records state that pine trees with apples tied to the branches were customary props in Miracle Plays performed in front of cathedrals. These trees were known as "Paradise Trees" because they represented the tree of Life in the Garden of Eden, the apples being the fruit of Knowledge that Eve plucked and gave to Adam. When these miracle plays were suppressed from performances in churches, the "Paradise Trees" went underground into homes and the custom of adding white wafers to represent the Holy Eucharist began. The people of northern Germany placed figures of Adam, Eve, and the Serpent beneath the family Christmas tree until a hundred years ago.

Figure 1-2. The famous illustration of Queen Victoria and Prince Albert's first Christmas tree in Windsor Castle in 1841. It was first published in *The Illustrated London News* in 1848. Sarah Josepha Hale "Americanized" the same picture in *Godey's Lady's Book* in 1850 and 1860. (K.R.)

According to legend, Martin Luther created the Christmas tree one Christmas Eve after being emotionally moved upon seeing the multitude of winter stars brightly shining through the branches of a fir tree. Wishing to repeat the experience for his children, Martin Luther set up a tree with an abundance of candles. An unknown Strasburg resident made the first historical mention of the Christmas tree in notes written in 1605. The anonymous writer noted,

> "At Christmas, they set up fir-trees in parlours at Strasburg and hang thereon roses cut out of many-coloured paper, apples, wafers, gold-foil, sweets, &c."[4]

The Christmas tree started as a domestic invention, but soon gained a toe-hold in Protestant churches in Germany. Eventually German Catholic churches succumbed to its charms, though it would be known more as a Protestant institution. In a less than affable description written by Dr. Johann Konrad Dannhauer, a Strasburg theologian in the mid-seventeenth century, he scornfully observed,

> "the Christmas- or fir-tree, which people set up in their houses, hang with dolls and sweets, and afterwards shake and deflower. . . Whence comes the custom, I know not; it is child's play. . . . Far better were it to point the children to the spiritual cedar-tree, Jesus Christ."[5]

Slow to gain popularity because of its Lutheran origins, the Christmas tree began to germinate in the Scandinavian countries, Finland, Norway, Russia, France, and England. Candles or tapers became part of the Christmas tree's lore in Germany in 1737, attributed to a country lady acquaintance of Karl Gottfried Kissling, a scholar at the University of Wittenberg. He told of how she set up a tree for each of her sons and daughters, lighting candles on or around each tree, and laid presents beneath them before calling each child into the room to receive the intended tree and gifts. The oldest written description of a tree decorated and illuminated with candles was penned in 1708 by the sister-in-law of King Louis XIV, Liselotte von der Pfalz. By the time the Christmas tree was introduced to England, candles were firmly established as part of the tradition.

German peasants, where the older religious faith still held sway, were slower to adopt the Christmas tree than their more up-scale townspeople counterparts. There also did not seem to be the elitism associated with the Christmas tree in Germany that was much in evidence between the social classes in England, where only the wealthy Victorians of the mid-nineteenth century could afford Christmas trees.

The height of the Christmas tree's popularity in Germany was reached by the turn of the nineteenth century after branching out all across Europe and the Mediterranean. Princess Helene of Mecklenburg introduced Paris to the Christmas tree in 1840, the same year Queen Victoria and Prince Albert set their tree up for their children in Windsor Castle.

German immigrants arriving in America introduced New York, New England, Pennsylvania, Maryland, and countless other areas to their Christmas traditions. A legend that historians are unable to document, maintains that mercenary Hessian soldiers employed by the British during the American Revolution, brought the first Christmas trees to the colonies. It may be a fair conjecture that when General George Washington and his soldiers of the Continental Army crashed the Hessians' Christmas party at the Battle of Trenton in 1776, a Christmas tree may have been part of their short-lived celebration.

Many Germans settling in the Pennsylvania Dutch country made the decorated Christmas tree popular before 1820. Fort Dearborn is known to have had a decorated fir tree as early as 1804. The first decorated tree in Milton, Massachusetts, debuted in the home of a German exile for Christmas in 1832. A German language instructor at Harvard University, Charles Follen's Christmas tree was described in a penny pamphlet published by deaf English social writer and economist Harriet Martineau. As a guest in Follen's home that Christmas, she was enamored with the tree and wrote:

> "I was present at the introduction into the new country of the spectacle of the German Christmas-tree. My little friend Charley and three companions had been long preparing for this pretty show. The cook had broken her eggs carefully in the middle for some

weeks past, that Charley might have shells for cups; and these cups were gilded and coloured very prettily. . . . We engaged in sticking on the last of the seven dozen of wax-tapers, and filling the gilded egg-cups and gay paper cornucopiae with comfits, lozenges, and barley-sugar. The tree was the top of a young fir, which was ornamented with moss. Smart dolls and other whimsies glittered in the evergreen, and there was not a twig which had not something upon it.

It really looked beautiful; the room seemed in a blaze, and the ornaments were so well hung on that no accident happened, except that one doll's petticoat caught fire. There was a sponge tied to the end of a stick to put out any supernumerary blaze, and no harm ensued. I mounted the steps behind the tree to see the effect of opening the doors. It was delightful. The children poured in, but in a moment every voice was hushed. Their faces were upturned to the blaze, all eyes wide open, all lips parted, all steps arrested. Nobody spoke, only Charley leaped for joy. The first symptom of recovery was the children's wandering round the tree. At last a pair of eyes discovered that it bore something eatable, and from that moment the babble began again. . . . I have little doubt the Christmas-tree will become one of the most flourishing exotics of New England."[6]

The German influence soon appeared in the growing metropolitan cities of Boston, Cambridge, Rochester, New York City, Cincinnati, Philadelphia, Baltimore, Richmond, and Williamsburg. Many homesick German newcomers tried to recreate Christmas memories of home with their families in the old country, and introduced the Christmas tree to their neighbors and friends in their adopted communities.

Charles Frederic Ernest Minnegerode, another German political exile, introduced Williamsburg to the folklore of the Christmas tree when he arrived there from Philadelphia in early 1842 to teach the classical languages of Greek and Latin at the College of William and Mary. Minnegerode received permission to set up a Christmas tree in the home of professor Judge Nathaniel Beverly Tucker, whose children

he had befriended as a favorite frequent visitor. After telling the family the many folktales surrounding the beginnings of the humble Christmas tree, he scoured the countryside around Williamsburg to find a suitable fir tree for Christmas of 1842. Having none of the Christmas ornaments of glass and tinsel to decorate the tree his family in Germany had at home, Minnegerode and the Tucker children improvised decorations from many materials found in their home. Word of the mysterious new tree, lighted with candles and decorated with a variety of homemade decorations, circulated among the neighbors in the community and outside Williamsburg, and permission was sought from the family to visit the tree in its decorated glory.

To this day a community Christmas tree is erected each holiday season mere yards from the Tucker house where Charles Minnegerode introduced Williamsburg and many areas of the Old Dominion State to the Christmas tree. Four years after Minnegerode introduced Williamsburg to the decorated and lighted fir tree, another German named August Bodeker made Southern holiday history when he erected his own ornamented and candle illuminated tree before his shop in Richmond. Like Williamsburg, Richmond has never been without a Christmas tree since that day.

German pioneers took the custom with them as they travelled west to settle new lands. Finding no fir trees in St. Clair County, Illinois for Christmas in 1833, Gustav Koerner improvised his Christmas tree by decorating a sassafras tree with candles, apples, sweets, ribbons, bright scraps of paper, nuts, and polished haws, the fruit of the hawthorne tree.

Another German, Reverend Henry Schwann, who had resided in this country less than a year, nearly lost his ministering assignment when he erected the first decorated tree in an American church in Cleveland in 1851. His congregation nearly mutinied and denounced the tree as a revival of a pagan custom.

Churches in the United States played an important part, as they had in Germany, in the acceptance of the public interest in Christmas trees. The first Christmas trees many Americans saw were the simple decorated trees erected in churches for their Christmas season services. So much interest, in fact, that many churches charged admission for people to view the trees. Many churches eventually enlarged the experience by putting on Christmas plays and ceremonies. *The Danville Advertiser* of Danville, New York, reported the Christmas activities in its community churches in 1862.

> "Christmas, with all its bright anticipations, has come and gone. On Christmas eve several of the different Church Societies had provided entertainments for the Sabbath School Scholars. At the Methodist Church a very fine Christmas tree well filled with presents of nearly all varieties, greeted the eyes, and, together with appropriate exercises, the evening passed pleasantly." In the same article the Presbyterian Society had their entertainment at "Osgoodby's Hall. We noticed a very nice evergreen loaded with presents for distribution among the scholars, and a table being spread to satisfy their appetites."[7]

Singer Jenny Lind known as the "Swedish Nightingale," was given a Christmas tree by the women of Charleston, South Carolina. The tree was erected in front of her hotel window when she visited Charleston during her concert tour in 1850. She also arranged a privately decorated tree for her drawing room and surprised the members of her company after an evening of entertaining in her drawing room. The presents hung from the boughs of the tree with the name tags attached to each present for the members of her troupe. P. T. Barnum, who was her manager, recounted in his biography that Lind's presents were little personal jokes for each person wrapped in multiple layers of covering. With a little poke at Barnum's temperance principles, he received a small marble statue of a young Bacchus.

Eleanor Custis Lee, Robert E. Lee's fifth child, mentioned in a journal entry written Dec. 29, 1853, about their table-top Christmas tree at West Point while her father was superintendent of that military academy.

The final act of adoption of the "German toy" into American Christmas tradition came about in 1856 by none other than the President of the United States. New Hampshire born Franklin Pierce set up the first decorated Presidential Christmas tree in the White House. President Pierce entertained and passed out gifts around it to the children of the New York Avenue Presbyterian Church Sunday School.

Most decorations were handmade at home, some edible like dried and sugared fruit and nuts, and popcorn balls and strings, while others were made out of colored paper, ribbon, wax, spun glass, and silver foil. Angels and doll faces were popular ornaments, as were animals, the Christ Child, stars, and Santa Claus after 1849. The well-to-do could afford to import German decorations made of glass in Dresden and Nuremburg. One of the most beautiful German ornaments to top the Christmas tree here in the United States was the Nuremburg angel with out-stretched arms holding a wreath in either hand, stern face, and wings ready to take flight. One American tree described in the mid-nineteenth century had as its theme "little horses, whips and wagons, red shoes, collars and handkerchiefs, as well as nuts, fruits and candies."[8] It would not be until a decade after the Civil War that Christmas decorations would be mass-produced commercially.

The first Christmas tree dealer arrived in New York City in 1851 when Catskills woodsman Mark Carr and his sons procured a spot on the sidewalk corner at Vessey and Greenwich Streets for a dollar. Cutting down the fir trees that grew on his mountainside land, Carr arrived in the city with two oxen carts loaded with his wares. Hoping to corner the market of the large German population living in New York City, Carr and his sons sold out of their merchandise much quicker than anticipated. Returning the next year with a larger amount of holiday trees, the birth of the Christmas tree trade had begun. By the 1880's, more than 600 Christmas tree dealers vied for prime and costly space from which to sell their wares.

The decorated Christmas tree, the German settlers' gift to their adopted home, would overcome prejudice of ethnicity as well as religious intolerance against a pagan symbol, as the editor of *Gleason's Pictorial Drawing Room Companion* in 1852 prognosticated,

> "Already is the Christmas tree established as one of the household gods of New England and a large portion of the states."[9]

Figure 1-3. Gathering Christmas greens in New York for home decorations and fragrance by Winslow Homer. (K.R.)

In 1859, Charles Dickens wrote from England one of the best descriptions of the Christmas tree. Of his Christmas tree observation he wrote:

"I have been looking on this evening, at a merry company of children assembled around that pretty German toy, a Christmas tree. The tree was planted in the middle of a great round table, and towered high above their heads. It was brilliantly lighted by a multitude of little tapers; everywhere sparkled and glittered with bright objects. There were rosy-cheeked dolls, hiding behind green leaves; and there were real watches (with movable hands, at least, and an endless capacity of being wound up) dangling from innumerable twigs; there were French-polished tables, chairs, bedsteads, wardrobes, eight day clocks, and various other articles of domestic furniture (wonderfully made, in tin, at Wolverhampton), perched among the boughs, as if in preparation for some fairy housekeeping; and there were jolly, broad-faced little men—much more agreeable in appearance than many real men—and no wonder, their heads took off, and showed them to be full of sugar plums; there were fiddles and drums; there were tamborines, books, work-boxes, paint-boxes, sweetmeat-boxes, peep-show boxes, and all kinds of boxes; there were trinkets for the elder girls, far brighter than any grown-up gold and jewels; there were baskets and pincushions in all devices; there were guns, swords, and banners; there were witches standing in enchanted rings of pasteboard, to tell fortunes; there were teetotums, humming tops, needle cases, pen wipers, smelling bottles, conversation cards, bouquet holders; real fruit, made artificially dazzling with gold leaf; imitation

Figure 1-4. *The Christmas Tree* by F. A. Chapman. A gift from German immigrants to their new homeland, it was the centerpiece of holiday activities in America by 1850. (K.R.)

apples, pears, and walnuts crammed with surprises; in short, as a pretty child, her bosom friend, 'There was everything, and more.'"[10]

The Dutch immigrants arriving on the shores of the New World would bring with them many lasting customs and traditions. But none would be so endearing as that at Christmas of Saint Nicholas, the patron saint of children and numerous occupations and people. The Dutch settlers of New Amsterdam (later New York), would introduce Sinter Claes, Dutch for St. Nicholas, to early America. The other Dutch variation, Sint Niklaas, would become Anglicized to Saint Nicholas. The Dutch of old New York would build a cathedral in New York City in his name. Sinter Claes would become further "Americanized" by non-Dutch neighbors into Santa Claus.

The ancestry of the Old World Saint Nicholas was based on a fourth century bishop of Myra in Asia Minor, in what is now known as Turkey. Born in 280 A.D. in the port city of Patara to an older, wealthy couple thought childless, Nicholas was orphaned at the age of thirteen when plague decimated the town's population. An uncle who was a priest, took in the orphaned Nicholas. The child was known for his piety and charity, and the uncle had Nicholas educated in a monastery. Six years later, Nicholas became ordained into the priesthood. According to a legend written in an ancient manuscript, Nicholas was nearly shipwrecked during a storm on the Mediterranean Sea. Imploring God to calm the raging sea, the weather cleared and the ship safely arrived in the harbor of neighboring Myra. The elders of the local church in Myra, were meeting at the same time in an attempt to elect their new bishop. While praying for guidance, the elders received a message from God during a vision. They were instructed to appoint the first man named Nicholas arriving in the church at a certain hour to pray. The unsuspecting Nicholas went into the church to thank God for sparing his life. While praying, the elders approached Nicholas and elected him their bishop. Because of his youth, Nicholas was known as the "Boy Bishop."

Shortly after becoming Bishop of Myra, Nicholas ran afoul of the Roman emperor Diocletian. Diocletian decreed all subjects of the Roman empire to worship him as a god. When Nicholas and thousands of followers of the new Christian religion refused, Diocletian imprisoned Nicholas and many of the other revolters. Nicholas spent ten years in a Roman prison before being released by Diocletian's successor, Emperor Constantine. Returning to his duties as the beloved Bishop of Myra in 313, Nicholas served until his death on December 6, 342. At his death, a viscous fluid smelling strongly of myrrh was said to have leaked profusely from his casket while being interred in the crypt in his church. Anyone suffering from sickness and incurable disease, was instantly healed after coming in contact with the mysterious fluid.

Many stories and legends grew up around Nicholas of his granting of secret wishes and gift giving to those especially in need, before he became bishop and after. One story during his reign as bishop, had him raising from death three boys murdered and dismembered by a nasty innkeeper and embalmed in a barrel of brine. Praying over the barrel, the boys arose from the dead intact and the innkeeper made a religious conversion after being forgiven for his sins. Another legend attributed to Nicholas when he was still a child, had him saving three poor daughters of a Patara merchant, who had lost his fortune, from destitute lives by providing dowries, and enabling them to marry respectably. Through the years of travel, he gained the reputation as the protector of children. Another of the many tales that grew around Nicholas's legend had him throwing gifts of bags of gold through windows or down chimneys. Several gold coins falling out of one bag supposedly landed in a stocking hung up to dry before the fireplace. This tale would find use as a traditional holiday custom centuries in the future.

The Catholic church canonized Bishop Nicholas in the ninth century (the Catholic church in 1969 claimed St. Nicholas was never canonized and demoted him and 29 others from sainthood) and he became known as the patron saint of children. Over the centuries he became the patron saint of scholars, thieves, pawnbrokers, the country of Russia, and eventually the city of New York. The list would grow to include sailors through stories told of St. Nicholas appearing in the midst of storms to calm the seas and save the lives of sailors and their vessels.

In 1087 a group of Italian sailors created a huge uproar during the Crusades when they pirated away the remains of St. Nicholas from his tomb in Myra. Concerned by rumors of pirates and the spreading Muslim influence sweeping the Mediterranean area, the Italian sailors brought St. Nicholas's body to the Italian city of Bari. The day the sailors landed, a celebration began and forty-seven people inflicted with incurable diseases were healed. For days afterward, dozens more were also rumored to be healed. The people of Bari built a church named after St. Nicholas to enshrine his remains. To this day a celebration of his body's arrival in Bari occurs each St. Nicholas Day (December 6).

St. Nicholas's stature in the Christian church grew until he was second in popularity only to the holy family of Jesus, Mary and Joseph. Throughout Europe, many towns and cities built churches and cathedrals named in his honor. The deeds, legends, and powers of St. Nicholas also continued to grow. In some countries St. Nicholas would ride on a white horse on the eve of the anniversary of his death in his episcopal garb of red and white vestment, gold embroidered cope, mitre and staff, inquiring of the children he visited about their behavior. Another incarnation gave him the power to fly on a white horse through the sky in his vestments and wearing a long white beard. This St. Nicholas closely resembled the Norse Yule god Odin who possessed many of the same caring, gift bringing, and selfless acts associated with the more human St. Nicholas. Numerous countries across Europe celebrated St. Nicholas Day as a day of feasting, festival and plays re-enacting the saint's secret gifts of gold to the merchant's daughters and raising of the three murdered boys, and in the fifteenth century the ritual mock-elections of the "boy bishop." Even England was not immune to the parade of boys following a child dressed in costumed bishop vestments.

By the sixteenth century, the Protestant Reformation under the leadership of Martin Luther, railed against the worship of the saints as "childishness and falsehood." The feast day of St. Nicholas was a particular target for Luther. Wishing to see a more evangelical observance

on December 25, Christmas Day, the reform-minded Protestants wanted to see the practice of gift giving and mid-winter festival stamped out. While they did not completely succeed, St. Nicholas's Day waned across Europe under Protestant attack. Ironically, many newly converted Protestant families replaced the gifts left by St. Nicholas with those given by the Christ Child. They also succeeded in driving the Dutch to heartily embrace and retain St. Nicholas and his day.

St. Nicholas remained an important figure in Holland, still dressed in his bishop's clothing and keeping some religious overtones. With his helper, Black Peter, trotting on foot beside him, St. Nicholas would ride his white horse and deliver gifts to the shoes of good children. Black Peter's job was to leave switches and lumps of coal for bad and lazy children. The worst of the children were abducted and sent to disagreeable places. Black Peter symbolized the enslavement of the Devil for one night to perform good deeds, and take away those children found with unredeemable characters and shown the error of their ways. Many parents would scold fractious children with the admonition of "Watchout! Black Peter will come and get you if you don't behave."

During the hated Spanish occupation of Holland, Black Peter wore Spanish clothing and was conquered into subservience by St. Nicholas as a form of a political joke. St. Nicholas and Black Peter arrived from Spain by boat in late November visiting local hospitals, shops, and participating in parades until St. Nicholas Eve. At other times, Zwarte Piet (Black Pete) would be a dusky Moorish servant. But the scariest form would be the cloven-footed, horned creature resembling the devil, smeared with chimney soot, and carrying a ledger to record the names of good and bad children.

The Germans would also contribute with Pelsnickel (Saint Nicholas in furs) and Weihnachtsmann, a religious Saint Nicholas traveling on Christmas Eve. Some of the other less well-known ethnic Christmas personages arriving in the United States from Europe, were the Italian good witch Befana riding on a broomstick, the kind grandmotherly Russian Babouscka, or the white bearded Grandfather or Father Frost, the

Spanish Three Kings of the Magi, the German Knecht Ruprecht, Christkind, Kriss Kringle, and the French Papa Noel.

When the Dutch immigrants arrived in America, they set about re-inventing the Holland of their former homeland, transporting their many customs and the traditional lore of St. Nicholas. When New York-born writer Washington Irving wrote under the name Diedrich Knickerbocker and published *The History of New York* in 1809, he set down in print how the Dutch instituted St. Nicholas onto the American cultural landscape. Irving would relate how the Dutch:

> "Thus, having quietly settled themselves down, and provided for their own comfort, they bethought themselves of testifying their gratitude to the great and good St. Nicholas, for his protecting care, in guiding them to this delectable abode. To this end they built a fair and goodly chapel within the fort, which they consecrated to his name; whereupon he immediately took the town of New Amsterdam (New York City) under his peculiar patronage, and he has ever since been, and I devoutly hope will ever be, the tutelar saint of this excellent city."

With the next paragraph, Irving locked in the first of several Christmas customs that Americans would take to their hearts. "At this early period was instituted that pious ceremony, still religiously observed in all our ancient families of the right breed, of hanging up a stocking in the chimney on St. Nicholas eve; which stocking is always found miraculously filled; for the good St. Nicholas has ever been a great giver of gifts, particularly to children."[11] A sketchy description of what would become known as the Knickerbocker Santa Claus emerged.

This Santa Claus was described as a short elfin figure, a clay pipe clenched in his teeth, a short beard, wearing knee-breeches, striped woolen stockings, and buckle shoes. His coat would resemble the frock coat popularized during the colonial era, with large brass buttons on either side, trimmed in fur, with a waistcoat underneath. His hat alternately would be a broadbrim black felt hat, a fur cap, or a woolen knit cap with fur trim resembling the cap many men wore to bed to keep their heads warm. This image would become reality in woodcut panels published in the official 1848 version of Clement Moore's "A Visit From Saint Nicholas." Until the Civil War, there would not be any standard image of St. Nicholas or Santa Claus.

While the Dutch introduced New Amsterdam (or old New York) and the surrounding colonies to their particular form of St. Nicholas and Santa Claus, the Germans would introduce to the bastion of English heritage and the South's first city, Baltimore, their own version of the patron saint. Though the Germans were not at Maryland and Baltimore's founding, they were not far behind as waves of immigrants from the Protestant north and Catholic south settled in the city as craftsmen, weavers, cobblers, bakers, and other trades closely associated with Baltimore's growth. The Teutonic variations visiting the doorsteps and knocking on the doors of children in the seventeenth and eighteenth century Baltimore were the religious bishop Weihnachtsmann (old St. Nikolas) and Pelsnickel in a great cape and fur cap.

The stern St. Nikolas travelled about Baltimore in the elaborate robe, miter, and staff of a bishop, dispensing lectures on the doorsteps of houses about the merits of good behavior to children perilously close to the dividing line, while good children received a present. Pelsnickel walked with a great rod or bundle of switches and heavy bag slung over his shoulder while wearing a chain that dragged the ground clinking and clanking, and bells on his clothes announced his noisy arrival and departure. Upon knocking on doors and entering houses to receive replies to his pointed questions on the manners of the small occupants housed within, the secular and sometimes more frightening appearing Pelsnickel would reach out for the recalcitrant child to administer punishment, always stopping short of actually doing so. Most children were scared straight for the entire next year while receiving a gift for their doorstep conversions. Sometimes the two Christmas figures appeared together on St. Nikolas Eve as a team. St. Nikolas reprieved many guilty children before Pelsnickel could carry out his threats of punishment. Pelsnickel became the spy of St. Nikolas, arriving before the elder gift bringer and checking the year's manners and making threats for negative answers.

Both personages were eventually merged into one figure with attributes of both combined. St. Nikolas Eve died out as Santa Claus began to evolve and gain popularity with the acceptance of the official Christmas Eve on December 24. One other lasting tradition the Germans gave to Baltimore was the Christmas dinner of turkey and sauerkraut.

It is the English customs that seem to influence our Christmas traditions the strongest. From these we get the Christmas Yule Log, the Christmas Feast, the Christmas greens, the Mistletoe Ball and the tradition of kissing beneath the Mistletoe, Christmas caroling, and Christmas cards. Christmas festivities had almost ceased and disappeared at the beginning of the nineteenth century. The roots of this go farther back to the time of Oliver Cromwell, Lord Protector of England. Following the deposing and beheading of King Charles I by Cromwell and his army of roundheads, Cromwell outlawed any observation of the Christmas holidays because many of the rituals were steeped in ancient pagan origins, and because the reign of Charles I was marked by drunken excesses, gambling, theatrical revels, dancing, singing and other secular pleasures and debauchery during the holiday's celebration.

During the early Christianization of ancient England, it was found practical by the early missionaries to combine existing pagan mid-winter festivals and rituals that could not be easily stamped out, with church observances of both the Nativity and Epiphany to keep peace with the populace. After 601, Christmas celebrations were accepted after Pope Gregory I prescribed to the missionary of the Anglo-Saxons, Augustine, to lay claim to the mid-winter "Yule" festival as an official Christian holiday. By the time Alfred the Great ascended the throne, the Twelve Days of Christmas was firmly established as a church holiday. King Alfred decreed it illegal for work to be performed during those allotted days. In strict adherence to his own decree, Alfred refused to do battle during the holy days' observance and lost a strategic town to the Danes rampaging against English coastal towns and inland settlements.

Many of the clergy became unsettled with the gaining popularity of the English Christmas customs and pagan origins of the greens, mistletoe, holly, and "Yule" log. Many of the origins relating to the mistletoe and other greens had basis in Druid mid-winter fertilization rites. Another threat deemed inappropriate to the solemnity of the religious holiday was the secular aspect of feasting and drinking in an atmosphere of good fellowship. Several centuries later, the Christmas and Twelfth Night celebrations in the royal courts of King Henry VIII and his daughter Queen Elizabeth I, became the brightest spot on the court's full social calendar. Gathered together under the palace roof were the finest literary and musical talents of each era for the latest dances, songs, and plays performed after marathon feasts and banquets of holiday delicacies. Even more alarming to the clergy was the Christmas court of James I, where those invited could not attend court unless the mandatory amount of at least 300 pounds sterling was in one's pocket for wagering at the court gambling tables. James I was by no means the only monarch to permit and oversee gambling in the royal court, for each of his several predecessors participated with royal relish.

After Cromwell's seizure of power, the Puritans, both on the European continent and in the Massachusetts Bay colony, decreed Christmas should be a more somber day. The Puritans of Massachusetts passed a law making it mandatory to work on Christmas Day. After nearly ten years of prohibition, the Christmas holiday was restored after the coronation of Charles II in 1661. One writer of verses memorialized the event with the verse:

> "Now thanks to God for Charles' return,
> Whose absence made old Christmas mourn;
> For then we scarcely did know,
> Whether it Christmas were or no."[12]

Even though the banned Christmas traditions and holidays were freed from the underground, they never returned to the raucous and boisterous celebrations of pre-Cromwellian days.

Many clergymen resisted the return of the non-Christian aspects of Christmas. A paler version of the Christmas holidays continued to fade as the onset of the Industrial Revolution began to tear the fabric of the family apart, and with it many holidays ceased to exist. It would be during the Romantic and Victorian Eras that Christmas again would be embraced and turned back into the festive, philanthropic, and yes, the commercial season we now know, love, and sometimes disdain.

Victorians in their family-oriented festive observance of the holiday, would festoon their houses or dwelling places with greenery in a variety of decorations. No house was ready for entertaining unless the fragrance and multi-green hued color of fir, pine, balsam, cedar, holly and ivy were strewn about from mantlepiece, picture frames, and various other furnishings. Many of the Christmas greens the Victorians used had a history from all across Europe dating back a thousand years or more with the ancient concept of nature's continuing rebirth in the cycle of sowing, growing, harvest, fertilization and fallow periods. When Christianity spread across Europe and England, the religion's spiritual concepts of the soul were wedded to the pagan concept of earth spirits. The mutual concepts imbued in the beauty and fragrance of nature's regenerating plants found similarities in Christianity's teaching of spiritual rebirth and immortality. Indeed, the evergreen in its very name was thought to symbolize continuing life, remaining always green in the dead of winter when almost all other vegetation is dead, naked, or brown.

Holly was given as gifts during Saturnalia celebrations in Rome and throughout the Roman Empire. Roman troops occupying ancient England are thought to have introduced England to the thorny leafed plant decorated with red berries when the soldiers celebrated their winter holiday. The red and dark green colors inspired the now traditional colors associated with the Christmas season. Many old Victorian figures of England's Father Christmas and the American Santa Claus were always wearing a sprig of holly on their costumes. Long thought to protect the wearer or decorated dwellings from bad witches or casting of the evil eye, Christianity picked up on its symbolism as that of the burning bush God appeared as to Moses. The holly also became representative of the crown the Roman soldiers made Jesus wear as they mocked his divinity and was crucified in. Further superstitions about the

uses of holly held that it needed to be burned or fed to cattle after the end of Christmas, or that dropping a piece rendered a person unlucky.

Ivy was another greenery associated with the Romans. It played an important part in the mythology of Bacchus as ivy was the wreathed crown the god wore. Worn also by the mortal Roman celebrants at Bacchanalia festivals to pay homage to Bacchus, the sacred plant was linked to the belief it protected against drunkenness and its aftereffects. Priests in the early English church decried its use because of the association with drinking of wine at feasts during pagan celebrations. The pagan holly and ivy later became a Christmas carol of the same name, much loved by the English and accepted and sung by Christian church choirs in respectable institutions of higher learning like Kings College and St. John's College.

"The holly and the ivy,
When they are both full grown,
Of all the trees that are in the wood,
The holly bears the crown."

Pine, cedar, and fir were and still are connected to the Christmas tree. Their use as decorations go back to the Europe of a thousand years past, where it was used for brightening dwellings with their green color in the dark of winter's grip and lending fragrance to perfume the stale air of rooms shut up against the cold and damp weather. Churches made use of pine, cedar, and fir along with fragrant herbs for altar and vestry decorations. After incorporating Christian symbolism to former pagan uses, many churches opened their arms to greenery usage in decorating. One chronicler recorded in the sixteenth century about the "time of Christmas, every man's house, as also their parish churches, were decked with ivy, bay, and whatsoever the season afforded to be green."[13]

Victorians used the feathery foliage in garlands, bunches, and singular boughs to highlight and compliment parlours, brighten drawing rooms, and scent dining rooms. Many of Charles Dickens's novels and short stories written during the Victorian era included many descriptive holiday festivities and decorations, as was his own household of ten children, awhirl with the holiday season of dances, gifts for children and adults, parlor games and tableaux, and parties. From *The Pickwick Papers* Dickens wrote of one Christmas party just prior to the 25th, at a country manor farm with gleeful dancing and merriment.

"At the upper end of the room, seated in a shady bower of holly and evergreens, were the two best fiddlers, and the only harp in all Muggleton. In all sorts of recesses, and on all kinds of brackets, stood massive old candlesticks with four branches each. The carpet was up, the candles burnt bright, the fire blazed and crackled on the hearth; and merry voices, and light hearted laughter, rang through the room. If any of the old English yeomen had turned into fairies when they died, it was just the place in which they would have held their revels."[14]

The most sacred of all pagan greens, and the one Christian clergymen were most disturbed by, was the white berry-bearing mistletoe. A parasitic plant that lives on many varieties of trees such as oak and apple trees, it never touches the ground to root. A native to England, Europe, Asia, and even the United States, one legend accorded it as a link between heaven and earth because of its nature of growing. Many Romans and early Scandinavians considered it a plant of healing and peace because enemies who encountered one another beneath the mistletoe were obligated to lay down their weapons and make peace pacts. One of the more violent myths linked to mistletoe's legend involved the son of Norse god Odin. Baulder was murdered by an arrow made of mistletoe cast by the blind god Hodr. Baulder was raised from the dead when it was learned that Hodr had been tricked by the wicked Loki. Mistletoe was pledged to never bring harm to another soul.

Called the Golden Bough by ancient Druids for its healing powers, the sacred plants growing on oak trees were harvested by white-robed priests with golden sickles on the winter solstice (December 22). Two white bulls were slain in ritual sacrifice during the solstice celebration, while sprigs of the gathered mistletoe were reverently laid upon the altar. Any leftover mistletoe was passed out to the celebrants to hang atop doors. Credited with mysterious powers, mistletoe was acclaimed to remedy against poisoning, acciden-tal or otherwise, produced potency in men and animals' procreative abilities, provided protection against wicked spirits, and protected homes from lightning strikes.

It was the sexual connotations relating to ancient fertilization rites involving mistletoe that caused the most discomfort amongst the early English clergy. Rarely was mistletoe permitted inside English churches over the centuries because of that association. How kissing came to be an accepted secular Christmas tradition under a sprig of mistletoe is not clear, though it was decidedly an English invention. Dickens delighted in participating in the custom in real-life as well as employing it in his literary endeavors as seen in a humorous passage taken again from *The Pickwick Papers*.

"From the centre ceiling of this kitchen, old Wardle had just suspended with his own hands a huge branch of mistletoe, and this same branch of mistletoe instantaneously gave rise to a scene of general and most delightful struggling and confusion; in the midst of which, Mr. Pickwick, with a gallantry which would have done honor to a descendant of Lady Tollimglower herself, took the old lady by the hand, led her beneath the mystic branch, and saluted her in all courtesy and decorum. The old lady submitted to this piece of practical politeness with all the dignity which befitted so important and serious a solemnity, but the younger ladies not being so thoroughly imbued with a superstitious veneration of the custom; or imagining that the value of a salute is very much enhanced if it cost a little trouble to obtain it; screamed and struggled, and ran into corners, and threatened and remonstrated, and did every thing but leave the room, until some less adventurous gentlemen were on the point of desisting, when they all at once found it useless to resist any longer, and submitted to be kissed with good grace. Mr. Winkle kissed, the young lady with the black eyes, and Mr. Snodgrass kissed Emily; and Mr. Weller, not being particular about the form of being under the mistletoe, kissed Emma and the other female servants, just as he caught them. As to the poor relations, they kissed everybody, not even excepting the plainer portion of the young-lady visitors, who, in their excessive confusion, ran right under the mistletoe, directly it was hung up, without knowing it!"[15]

The Yule log was originally a source of light and heat in homes across the countryside from the great fireplaces of manor houses to the smaller modest hearths of local peasants. All across Europe and England, large chunks of wood were coated with fragrant herbs and doused with wine and left to dry for several days. When Christmas Eve arrived, the Yule log was lit with a piece of the previous year's log. Good fortune was thought to prevail on the household where the blazing Yule burned until the Twelfth Night. Early Druids and Norsemen lit blazing fires during the long nights of the winter solstice to drive away evil spirits and welcome back the sun as it slowly began the long ascent to spring. In France children believed the Yule log was the source of their holiday gifts, and performed a ritual that entailed carrying a cloth-wrapped log through the house as the children beat it with sticks while crying, "Come forth!" When the desired gift did not appear, the parents sent the children outside to renounce their year's worth of sins. When they were allowed back into the house, they found gifts strewn before the fireplace where the Yule log awaited the festive conflagration.

As the Industrial Revolution began, the movement of people from the countryside to the wages of factory work in the city started the decline of the Yule custom. City fireplaces could not accommodate the large chunks of wood as coal became the fuel of choice in homes. Despite the disappearing blazing Yule log, the home hearth still retained its focus for holiday warmth. Herbs and fragrant greens were still burned in coal grates to freshen the festive atmosphere Victorians encouraged among family members.

The Yule log tradition immigrated to America with the first settlers. Many of the Virginia manor homes and plantations celebrated Twelfth Night of Old Christmas with scented burning logs of ash and birch. Where masters allowed the ritual, slaves in the southern states reportedly performed no work as long as the wood burned. The slaves searched the woods for the largest, greenest log that could be found. Soaking the log in water for several days prior to the Christmas Eve lighting assured a slower burning time over the holidays. Like their European counterparts, a chunk of the leftover Yule log was kept to light the next year's log.

Christmas caroling had once been popular in the churches and cathedrals of ancient England but was in danger of dying out at the beginning of the nineteenth century. Early carols often had bawdy lyrics to usher in the holiday. That changed in the thirteenth century when St. Francis of Assisi adapted the melodies of the bawdy verses and mixed pagan mirth with Christian devotion. Some of the liveliest carols came out of the middle ages such as "The Boar's Head Carol," the oldest of all surviving carols. The repeated cycle of church bannings of the joyful music caused a gradual disappearance of many tunes only to be found anew when strictures eased. Many people recorded the words and music in notebooks that would occasionally surface after long years in hiding. The Puritan suppression of Christmas during Cromwell's reign nearly killed the caroling custom.

It was the Victorians that came to the rescue as they had for so many other Christmas traditions and customs. Only "God Rest Ye Merry, Gentlemen" was well known. All across Europe music was starting to flow from the pens of songwriters as the nineteenth century got underway. In 1818 "Silent Night" was written by Austrian schoolteacher Franz Gruber. Other songs were written or adapted from numerous sources. These included "O Come All Ye Faithful," "Hark! The Herald Angels Sing," and "Deck The Halls."

Americans got into the spirit prior to and during the Civil War. In 1850 Richard Stoors Willis published his composition to the words of Unitarian minister Edmund Hamilton Sears, "It Came Upon The Midnight Clear." There followed many other songs by American songwriters, "O Little Town Of Bethlehem," "Away In The Manger," "I Heard The Bells On Christmas Day," "We Three Kings," and "Up On The Housetop" that is known today as "Santa Claus."

Figure 1-5. Caroling in church was given an American flavor in 1850 when Edmund Sears composed "It Came Upon The Midnight Clear." (K.R.)

Caroling was popular in the cities and towns after being revived by people such as Reverend Edward Everett Hale. Hale wrote about one such caroling party he organized in the snowy streets of Boston. "I always give myself a Christmas present. And on this particular year the present was a Carol party—which is about as good fun, all things consenting kindly, as a man can have." On Christmas Eve Hale procured a "span of good horses and a sleigh that I could pack sixteen small children into, tight stowed." With the children packed in, the sleigh glided "under the full moon, on the snow still white," and they began to sing outside the frosted and glazed windows of the citizens of Boston that the children picked at random. "The instant the horse's bells stopped, (the children's) voices began singing with all that unconscious pathos with which children do sing, and starting tears in your eyes in the midst of your gladness."[16] The word pictures Reverend Hale's description invokes are the Christmas memories of sleighing, caroling, and the friendliness of strangers, the memories we all like to associate with Christmas and strive to recreate in our own holidays.

The Christmas card was a new British custom that very quickly found its way to the United States. Henry Cole contracted with John Calcott Horsley to design and print a Christmas card for him to send to his friends in 1843. Cole and Horsley sold a thousand copies of the time-saving sentiment at a shilling each by 1846. The first message bore the Christmas salutation "A Merry Christmas and A Happy New Year To You." Cole and Horsley had rivals to the mantle of inventor of the Christmas card. Reverend Edward Bradley and painter W. Dobson mailed hand-painted Christmas cards to their friends in 1844, bypassing the usual method of writing Christmas messages by hand. A third claimant also vied for the same title, but the numbers nor the date claimed was ever clear. The earliest Christmas card printed in the United States was done by a merchant and engraver in Albany, New York, named Richard Pease. By the middle of the Civil War, the postal service was giving free delivery to large amounts of manufactured and handmade cards during the holidays. Mass production was still a few years off.

Here in the United States, Washington Irving wrote and published in 1819 *The Sketchbook of Geoffrey Crayon, Gentleman,* about the old Christmas traditions he witnessed on a journey to England at Christmas time. He found that many of our "American" Christmas traditions and customs mirrored the many English customs settlers transported across the Atlantic.

The traditions and customs of these founding ethnic groups have been assimilated into American Christmas customs by tweaking and fiddling with little nuances to become our own. But not without the help of two individuals who completely re-invented our Christmas traditions and added several new twists.

The first was the only child born to Benjamin and Charity Moore in July of 1779. Clement Clarke Moore was raised in New York on the estate of Chelsea. Moore's father was studying for the ministry when he met Moore's widowed mother on her estate. Eventually becoming the rector of Trinity Church and Bishop of New York, the elder Moore would assist with both of George Washington's inaugurals, and administered the last rites to Alexander Hamilton after his deadly duel with Aaron Burr. Moore would also become the President of King's College (now present day Columbia College).

Clement Moore was born into a scholarly atmosphere where his father oversaw his early education. An apt pupil, Moore graduated early from Columbia College at the young age of 19. He would become Dr. Moore with the publication of *A Compendious Lexicon of the Hebrew Language* published in two volumes in 1809. Later he was appointed professor of Oriental and Greek Literature at General Theological Seminary. Moore would later donate ancestral land to the Seminary that would become Chelsea Square, in the heart of New York City. Clement Moore published many discourses and a translation of poems co-authored with a friend. Moore's interest ran far afield as he translated from the French a treatise on sheep raising, to writing an objection to the War of 1812, and editing two volumes of his father's sermons. Eventually publishing his own poetry in a volume in 1844, Moore would also pen a biography of the King of Albania, George Castriot.

In 1813 Clement Moore married the lovely nineteen-year-old Catharine Elizabeth Taylor, the daughter of the Lord Chief Justice of Jamaica, West Indies. This happy marriage produced nine children before Catharine died in 1830. It was Clement Moore's writing of poetry that would lead him to write his most famous poem in 1822. Having grown up in New York, Moore undoubtedly heard the tales of St. Nicholas and was steeped in the legends surrounding the founding and settlement of Dutch New York.

Six of Moore's children were born at the time *A Visit From Saint Nicholas* was composed and read to the family before the roaring fireplace at Chelsea that Christmas Eve. According to the story told by Moore's granddaughter, Dr. Moore was returning from New York to his estate with his own sleigh filled with Christmas toys for his children. Inspired by the jingle of harness bells on the horse pulling the sleigh, Moore thought of who was to deliver them to his own children. Recalling old stories he had heard, Moore began to visualize an old, portly, "jovial," Dutch workman who labored about the Moore estate doing odd jobs. Exclaiming, "Just the man for the piece," Moore modeled the old workman for his "jolly old elf" and swiftly composed his verses. Though only four of the children were old enough to understand the poem with delighted wonderment that Christmas Eve in 1822, family and friends enjoyed Moore's recitation before the fire.

The next autumn, a family friend enjoyed his poem so much while visiting Chelsea, she requested a copy. In her enthusiasm for Moore's poem, Miss Harriet Butler of Troy, New York, anonymously sent the poem to Mr. Holley at the *Troy Sentinel,* before the Christmas holidays in 1823. When published in the *Sentinel* it was given the title *An Account of A Visit From St. Nicholas.* With the publication of his verses, Dr. Moore was embarrassed with regret. It would be Christmas of 1838 before Clement Clarke Moore acknowledged his authorship of *A Visit From Saint Nicholas* in the rival *Troy Budget.*

Many people wanted to know the writer's identity with each year's Christmas re-publication of the verses. Many more falsely claimed to have penned the poem in many publications before Moore publicly stepped forward as the true and rightful author. In 1829, the editor of the *Troy Sentinel* hinted at the writer's true identity as belonging "by birth and residence to the city of New York, and that he is a gentleman of more merit as a scholar and writer than many of more noisy pretensions."[17] The following year saw the first illustrated publication of Moore's poem by Troy wood engraver, Myron King. King's illustration showed St. Nick flying over housetops in his sleigh with harnessed reindeer.

Moore included *A Visit From Saint Nicholas* when he published his collection of poems in a book simply titled *Poems* in 1844. Four years later, New York City publisher Henry M. Onderdonk wanted to publish the popular holiday poem. He acquired the talents of T. C. Boyd, an old wood engraver, to illustrate the poem in a special published presentation for the Christmas holidays. Boyd as an artist, seemed to have slipped through the cracks of the art world as one of the first American artists to capture the visual image of Santa Claus for Clement Moore's "masterpiece of genre word-painting." An earlier picture of St. Nicholas by R. Roberts in the same vein (no doubt inspired by Moore's poem) appeared in the January 1845 edition of *The Great Pictorial Annual Brother Jonathan.*

When published, Boyd's wood engravings of St. Nicholas complimented the visual imagery created by Moore's words. Showing the miniature sleigh and tiny reindeer driving past houses and a water pump in the middle of a city street, the trundle bed of the parents and children, to the clothes of St. Nick, Boyd's artwork evoked a period reminiscent of old New York before the turn of the nineteenth century. St. Nicholas was removed from the religious-based legend to a clearly secular bringer of gifts, the "Americanized" Santa Claus.

Moore and his family continued to live at his beloved Chelsea, until the urban sprawl of New York City by 1854 had enclosed the once secluded country estate. Selling and donating land and profits for philanthropic causes he espoused, Dr. Moore built houses for himself and a married daughter on the street and avenue literally next door to his former estate. He quietly slipped away from the spotlight he never sought, and in his declining years summered at his house in

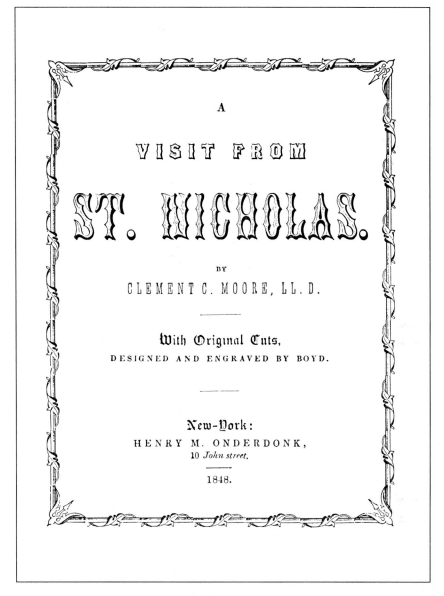

Figure 1-6. Cover page to the illustrated version of Clement Moore's immortal poem *A Visit from St. Nicholas* published in 1848.

Newport, Rhode Island. During the height of the Civil War, Clement Clarke Moore died several days short of his eighty-fourth birthday on July 10, 1863. Moore's body was brought back to New York City to be interred at St. Luke's Cemetery while the draft riots raged. The property for St. Luke's Cemetery was sold in 1890, and Clement Moore's body was reburied at Trinity Cemetery. Every Christmas Eve since the 1930's, children sing Christmas carols and place fresh wreaths at Clement Moore's grave in tribute for his authorship of the world famous verses about Santa Claus and his annual visit each Christmas Eve.

A cartoonist became the second person who transformed Santa Claus and Christmas by making over Dr. Moore's creation. Thomas Nast was born of German parents in a military barrack in Landau, Germany in 1841. The elder Nast sent his family to emigrate to the United States in 1846 before joining them in New York City four years later. Young Thomas Nast showed an early

Figure 1-7. One of several engravings by T. C. Boyd that helped to Americanize Santa Claus. (K.R.)

aptitude for drawing, and was enrolled at the National Academy of Design to study art under Theodore Kaufman. At age fifteen, Nast was hired as a draftsman for *Frank Leslie's Illustrated Newspaper.* Laid-off due to financial problems at *Leslie's,* Nast was 19 years old when he was hired to draw at the rival *Harper's Weekly* and stayed for a year before leaving for Europe. While in England to cover a championship heavyweight boxing match, Nast worked for *The New York Illustrated News* before moving to Italy in the same year as a war correspondent and artist for *The Illustrated London News.* His assignment was to cover Giuseppe Garibaldi's return from exile

to liberate Italy from Austrian control. Enamored with the crusading Garibaldi's ideals to free Italy, Nast stayed with him until the end of his successful campaign. Nast returned to New York City to become a bridegroom to Sarah Edwards on his twenty-first birthday. In 1862, he rejoined the staff of *Harper's Weekly* as a full-time war correspondent in an association that would last twenty-four years.

It was during Nast's tenure at *Harper's Weekly* that he established his reputation as the nation's cartoonist with a social conscience, and achieved his greatest fame as an artist and illustrator. A staunch believer in the Union's cause and the wrongs of slavery during the Civil War, Nast's covers and centerfolds were filled with patriotic messages interwoven into battlefield and political scenes. After the war, Nast turned his sharpened drawing pen on the injustices committed against the black war veterans and civilians during reconstruction; often skewering the Ku Klux Klan and corrupt or ineffectual politically appointed military officials enforcing reconstruction policy. Social ills, graft, and corruption plaguing many of the major cities, especially New York City, were also frequent targets for Nast.

One of his most famous drawing campaigns was against an individual and his political machine, the infamous "Boss" William Marcy Tweed. Nast so infuriated "Boss" Tweed and his Tammany Hall Ring with his scathing caricatures of them plundering the New York City treasury, that Tweed and his cronies issued threats against Nast's life and tried to bring economic and political pressure against *Harper's Weekly*. Attention by an unrelenting campaign of a reform-minded committee of 70 was eventually brought to bear on the Tweed Ring through the investigative disclosures of graft in the *New York Times*, and Nast's biting cartoons, causing "Boss" Tweed to flee the country. Arrested in Virgo, Spain in 1876 when he was recognized by his caricature likeness published abroad, Tweed died in New York's Ludlow Street jail two years later with every one of Nast's cartoons of him found among his personal effects.

It was in 1862–63 that Nast first drew Santa Claus for publication. During the war, Santa Claus made several appearances, in several guises. Late in his administration, President Lincoln commented about Nast and his weekly drawings of the war, and Santa Claus's annual appearance, "as the best recruiting sergeant the North ever had." The Nast Santa Claus made his last appearance in the pages of *Harper's Weekly* in 1886. In financial straits after a series of bad investments and the collapse of the investment house of Grant and Ward in 1884, friends from *Harper's Weekly* suggested he put a collection of his Santa Claus drawings together for publication to try and recoup some of his lost finances. Harper & Brothers published in time for Christmas of 1890, Nast's *Christmas Drawings For the Human Race*.

Following the book's publication, Thomas Nast spent time in his studio at home working in the medium of oil painting which he had originally aspired to as an artist. He painted many canvasses of Civil War subjects he had originally sketched as an artist for *Harper's Weekly*. Many old friends commissioned paintings from him, but Nast was always short of money. One painting he did, entitled "A Jolly Good Fellow," was of Santa Claus standing before a roaring fire raising a tankard of ale with one hand while holding a smoking pipe in the other. Santa Claus was painted in his traditional holiday costume we recognize in the Santa's inhabiting the stores and malls of today. Heavily in debt, Nast reluctantly accepted the appointment as Consul General to Ecuador in 1901 from President Theodore Roosevelt. Roosevelt admired Nast for "his fighting spirit" and wanted to help him out of his financial adversity. While serving as Consul General to Ecuador, Thomas Nast contracted a fever and died December 7, 1902, the day after Saint Nicholas Day.

Thomas Nast was the father of political cartoonists. The many images inscribed by Nast in our political and social history were the Republican Elephant, the Democratic Donkey, Uncle Sam, John Bull, Boss Tweed and the Tammany Hall Tiger, Columbia, and the most famous, Santa Claus.

Thomas Nast would spend most of his life drawing Santa Claus in various poses and situations. It is Thomas Nast's nineteenth century Santa Claus inspired by childhood memories of reading Clement Clarke Moore's poem about Santa Claus, that would become the fixture of our twentieth century holiday image. Nast would give us several other aspects to Santa Claus's American character development of the last two hundred years in the course of his even longer history. In his 1866 annual Christmas number, as *Harper's Weekly* called the centerfolds, Nast would make the North Pole the home of Santa Claus so no nation might lay claim to him as their own. An ironic touch since Nast used the figure of Santa Claus during the recently concluded Civil War for Northern propaganda purposes. It was in that illustration that Nast showed the lore of Santa's workshop for the production of toys, his account book for keeping record of children's

Figure 1-8. Thomas Nast's most famous image of Santa Claus appeared in *Harper's Weekly* on January 1, 1881. It remained nearly unchanged until 1931 when the Coca-Cola Santa made its debut. (K.R.)

behavior, the all seeing Santa Claus keeping watch through a telescope for good children, and forever intertwining Santa Claus to the Christmas tree. In later drawings, Santa Claus would be seen answering mail sent to him by children, rebuking the behavior of remiss and recalcitrant children, and being linked to various figures of children's nursery rhymes. Always, Santa Claus's love for children pervaded each and every drawing done during Thomas Nast's life.

The final adjustment to Santa Claus's image came about in 1931 when advertising artist Haddon Sundblom made minor changes to Santa's costume; making him a full-sized figure, more rotund and jovial, almost grandfatherly, and put a bottle of Coca-Cola in Santa's hand to become a purveyor of the "pause that refreshes." From 1931 to 1966 Sundblom's Santa Claus was either hefting an ice cold bottle of Coca-Cola while making his annual nocturnal deliveries, or accepting the refreshment from some wide-eyed young children lying in wait to glimpse him bounding down the chimney with his bag of presents. Santa Claus's image as drawn by Sundblom for advertisements, graced the pages of *Saturday Evening Post, Look, Life,* billboards, and life-size cardboard cutout displays. Thanks to Haddon Sundblom's recasting of Santa from the Nast Santa Claus, the commercial department store Santa Clauses in this century were spawned and later replaced by the current shopping mall version known to us all.

When the first Christmas came to the American shore at its founding and colonization, it was not the dour, somber day for work and religious introspection most Puritan fathers decreed it should be. It was celebrated in the wooden chapel within the timbered palisades of Jamestown's fort in 1607. The brother Englishmen of New England's future settlers, faced a bleak and dire outlook their first Christmas in Virginia. The men and women surviving famine, disease and Indian uprisings were reduced in numbers of less than forty survivors from an original tally of one hundred. Gathering before the altar of the Church of England, the colonists prayed for arrival of promised supplies and more colonists. They listened to the ancient biblical message of the coming of the new Savior.

The second Christmas in Jamestown was far removed from the first. Instead of privation and despair, that Christmas would set the example for future Southern holiday observances. Receiving the gift of feast from Powhatan's sons and other members of the tribe, Captain Smith and the other Virginia settlers feasted on the rich fare, as one chronicler recorded, "never more merrie, nor feede on more plentie of good oysters, fish, flesh, wild foule and good bread; nor never had better fires in England than in the warm smokie houses."[18] Though far removed from the boar's head feast of old English Christmas repasts, the Virginians set about to keep many reminders of English traditions, but also start new customs as befits pioneers to new worlds.

In the north, some Puritans in Massachusetts colony secretly held onto banished old world observances of festive Christmas traditions by keeping away from the stern eyes of Puritan leaders that wished to stamp them out. In the southern colonies, Christmas flourished as the season for feasts lasting for six days or more, parties, balls and dances in which the lively Sir Roger de Coverly (also known as the Virginia reel) was much stepped to, and hunts to rival those of the Mother country. The holidays were a time for family and friends, and many landowners threw open the doors of their plantation houses for a multitude of people issued invitations for weeks-long celebrations heaped with generous helpings of Southern hospitality. Many of these celebrations were parties of endurance with many attendees partied out before the host was ready to drop. Twelfth Night festivities of the old English Christmas season closely resembled the Virginia revelries.

One distinctly Virginia custom that would appear repeatedly during the Civil War, was the expenditure of gunpowder. While the English at home would ring church bells, many Virginians welcomed the Christ Child's birth with blasts of firearms. Many guests to early Virginia estates brought their fowling pieces and muskets and joined their host in sending a cacophony of explosions echoing across the Virginia landscape as neighbors joined the din and replied to one another. An official proclamation issued by the authorities cautioned against the enthused overuse of gunpowder at festive gatherings. There were still Indians and other contingencies to be prepared for, reminded the authorities.

In 1773, Philip Vickers Fithian, a young divinity student trained at Princeton and tutor to the children of "King" Robert Carter, reported the shattering of the peace on Christmas Eve. "Guns are fired this Evening in the Neighborhood, and the Negroes seem to be inspired with new Life."[19] On Christmas morning, more gunfire erupted around the Carter mansion to welcome the anniversary of the Christ Child's birth.

Virginia would be known as the mother of presidents, and so would she also be known to some as the mother of the American Christmas. Plenty abounded in drink, food, and merriment. Many "groaning boards" laden with the fruits of harvest and delicacies of the hunt were known at Christmas with near-legendary status. Wild fowl such as ducks, geese, turkeys, and partridges from the marshes, fields, and forest competed with the tidewater bounties of fresh and saltwater varieties of fish, oysters, clams, crabs, and mussels. From the hearth came mincemeat pies, plum puddings, fruitcakes, sweetmeats, fruits, nuts, and jellies. The cellars of many houses would also offer up liquid refreshments and beverages of beer, ale, cider, varieties of wine, Madeira, toddies, syllabub, and punches enhanced strongly with rum and brandy. Eggnog, beaten from eggs and whipped with heavy cream, heartily fortified with rum or brandy, would be introduced around the beginning of the eighteenth century and became synonymous with Christmas ever since.

Added to the "groaning" food-laden sideboards, came dancing, games, and entertainments lasting from December 15 through January 6. Mixed with the solemnity of religious services in church and chapel, family members and close friends would reflect on the ancient Christian message and other biblical aspects of Christmas before launching into more secular holiday pursuits and revelries.

A Frenchman travelling through the Virginia countryside during the 1680's, stayed with landed gentleman William Fitzhugh of Stafford County through the Christmas season and remarked that "there was good wine and all kinds of beverages, so there was a great deal of carous-ing. He [Fitzhugh] had sent for three fiddlers, a jester, a tight-rope dancer, an acrobat who tumbled around, . . . they gave us all the entertainment one could wish for."[20]

Williamsburg was the capital of His Royal Majesty's colony, a town that observed Christmas with a certain style. Greens decorated every door and window. The interiors of the inns, houses, and the Governor's Palace were festooned with fragrant evergreens and boxwood cuttings. Fruits from the traditional to the exotic were fashioned into decorative wreaths and fans for doors and above entrances. Pineapples, the traditional symbol of hospitality, apples, lemons, limes, pears, pomegranates, and kumquats all found use in decorations. Other natural materials from holly, bayberry, china berry, magnolia, mistletoe, milkweed, pinecones, and the greens of ivy, cedar, balsam, and pine made for simple to very elaborate decorations pleasing to the senses of sight and smell.

Churches also began to have decorated interiors with greenery from pulpit, altar, and pew. Bruton Parish Church in Williamsburg and many other churches throughout the Virginia colony, as well as other areas, accepted greens into the seasonal observances. One early Virginia newspaper reported in 1712 the main aisle of one church took on the appearance of:

"a very shady walk, and the pews look like so many arbors on each side of it. The pulpit itself has such clusters of ivy holly and rosemary about it that a light fellow in our pew took occasion to say that the congregation heard the 'Word out of the bush, like Moses.'"[21]

Fife and drums of militias paraded around the streets of Williamsburg playing festive airs, while carolers, mummers, and minstrels plied the streets at dusk for coin, refreshments, and libations. The inns, such as the Raleigh Tavern, were gathering places for politicians, planters, and travellers to enjoy the music and dancing of Christmas balls. While the tavern played host to dances, the first theater in America provided more theatrical entertainment of comedies and dramatic plays for well attired women in fine hooped dresses of silk and gentlemen clothed in satin and powdered wigs.

In a Christmas holiday amid a gathering of friends in which billiards were played, wine

Figure 1-9. On Christmas Day 1773, "King" Robert Carter held a ball at his Virginia plantation. Many parties in the South lasted a week or longer and resembled the Twelfth Night festivities of Old England. (K.R.)

Figure 1-10. *Cutting Mistletoe in the South* by Thomas Nast. (K.R.)

drunk, and cards dealt and wagered, William Byrd II jotted down in "secret diaries" the mixing of secular appetites and vices with religious devotions. Breakfasting on boiled turkey Christmas Day 1709, Byrd "received the Sacrament with great devoutness." As evening came on "we were merry with nonsense and so were my servants. I said prayers shortly and had good health, good thoughts and good humor, thanks be to God Almighty." Friends and he "slid and skated on the ice" before retiring to the manor house to replenish appetites with "turkey and chine, roast apples and wine, tongue and udder," and a full menu of meats and seafood.[22]

The Christmas holidays of the kind Virginians indulged in were introduced to the aforementioned Princeton-educated tutor Mr. Fithian in 1773. Having been warned about the "wicked" Virginians, Fithian participated from the sidelines in the festivities, sounds, gossip, and kissing occurring in the Carter dancing room. One can only surmise that he enjoyed himself immensely several days before Christmas.

"There were several Minuets danced with great ease and propriety; after which the whole company Joined in country-dances, and it was indeed beautiful to admiration, to see such a number of young persons, set off by dress to the best Advantage, moving easily, to the sound of well-performed Music, and with perfect regularity, though apparently in the utmost Disorder—The Dance continued til two, we dined at half after three—soon after Dinner we repaired to the Dancing-Room again. . . . When it grew too dark to dance, the young Gentlemen walked over to my Room, we conversed til half after six; nothing is now to be heard of in conversation, but the Balls, the Foxhunts, the fine Entertainments, and the good fellowship, which are to be exhibited. . . ."

Candles lit to banish the dark, a game between young ladies and gentlemen ensued. They played "Button, to get Pauns for Redemption. . . in the course of redeeming my Pauns, I had several Kisses of the Ladies!"[23]

One of the people Fithian was introduced to during the long days and nights of Christmas parties, hunts, and balls was Colonel George Washington and his wife Martha. The Christmas season was an especially happy time for both the Washingtons because their wedding anniversary fell on the old calendar's former observance of Twelfth Night.[24] Married on January 6, 1759, Washington was a man who liked the finest things in life, and parties at Christmas time were no exception. The Washingtons' own Christmas parties were elaborate affairs lasting weeks. Thrown at one of several estates owned by them, though Mount Vernon was generally the site of choice, it included the favored Virginia holiday hunt with Washington presiding as the huntmaster. After accepting the Presidency, Washington held the first of many Presidential Christmas receptions to follow at the temporary capital of Philadelphia. Reserved, dignified, and disdainful of being touched in public, in private Washington showered his step-grandchildren with gifts and heartfelt affection.

While Virginia reveled in its Christmas traditions, many of the other Southern colonies and later states also embraced and evolved their own Christmas customs and traditions. Christmas arrived and moved across North and South Carolina, Georgia, Florida, Alabama, Mississippi, and Louisiana, ever moving westward with the tide of settlers and pioneers. By the turn of the nineteenth century all states and territories had some form of holiday observance.

One Alabama custom pervading parts of the state was the day long romp of "Christmas Riders" or "Fantastic Riders," gaily costumed in a variety of bright colors, hats of multiple shapes and sizes, holiday dress, and clownish behavior. Breakfasting early, the riders went from plantation to plantation of friends, receiving excited stares, applause, and questions from children and adults while merrymaking across the countryside. Keeping their identity supposedly secret, they accepted proffered refreshment from the plantation residents until arriving late in the afternoon at an agreed upon destination for supper, flushed from the glow of the ride or imbibed holiday cheer, none quite knew which.

For plantation wives all across the South, the Christmas season was a festive time, but one of extremely hard work and preparation. Expected to provide a festive air, there were meals to be cooked, entertainments, dances, teas, parties, and servants to oversee. "Guests were served special alcoholic concoctions: songaree (a wine mix), sack posset (sherry, ale, eggs, and milk), and syllabub (white wine and whipped cream). Women cracked nuts, seeded raisins, cut orange peels, washed currants, and prepared fruitcakes, puddings, and mincemeat for their Christmas callers; they also made candy called beene brittle from sesame seeds (called benne seeds by the Africans who first brought them to America). On Christmas Day the mistress of the house provided a huge feast, her home decorated with evergreen and mistletoe, her table crowded with family and friends."[25]

The Negro population in the South would also share in the joys of the Christmas season with the suspension of work for at least a day or two. The more liberal masters granted their field hands a week's vacation from December 25 until after the New Year. Many masters would throw a barbecue for their workers' enjoyment as a way of paying thanks for work exerted from the slaves' backs. James Henry Hammond wrote in his South Carolina plantation record, "On that day a barbecue is given, beef or mutton and pork, coffee and bread being bountifully provided."[26] Other masters provided gifts of hats for the men, cheap jewelry and trinkets for the women, and bolts of jean cloth and other clothing materials at Christmas time to coincide with semi-annual allotments to make clothes.

A former slave commenting on what he described as a life experience in misery, remembered "jolly Christmas times, dances before old massa's door for the first drink of egg-nog. . . "[27] Frederick Douglas remarked that occasional holiday festivities were part of the slave owner's control mechanism to occupy the slaves' minds with thoughts of Christmas holiday pleasures and limited freedoms as a safety valve to bleed off emotions stemming from lives in bondage. One "nervous" white civilian in 1857 thought some slaves in his state of Florida received too much latitude with the "idle, lounging, roving, drunken, and otherwise mischievious [Christmas] week [that] fits the Negro in the least degree for the discharge of his duties."[28]

Christmas goodwill and holiday cheer seemed to be the sentiment between slaveowner and slave to make the holiday happy despite the evil of the institution. One Mississippi slaveholder boasted he endeavored "to make my Negroes joyous and happy,—and am glad to see them enjoying themselves with such contented hearty good will."[29] Another Mississippian gave a gift of five dollars to every family head and unmarried adult, while a third presented a ten dollar amount of molasses, and other staples consisting of coffee, tobacco, calico, and "Sunday tricks" to each adult slave.

While the practice in the South of gift giving did not originate with servants, the rise in the amounts given did. Before the turn of the nineteenth century, most family members exchanged small gifts, while hearty profusions of Christmas salutations were the order of the day. The tradition of "Christmas Gift" centered around servants catching the house residents off guard with the words of "Christmas Gift" and receiving a gift or presentation of a coin or other token. Eventually the practice devolved to family members surprising one another as Agnes Lee described it in her journal entry January 1, 1853.

"I must describe the Christmas holidays. Well twenty mins. before five Manda (daughter of a house servant) rushed in and caught me 'Christmas Gift'. I was up in an instant, examined my stocking, dressed ran upstairs and caught them all there. I spent the whole morning giving and receiving gifts and being as happy as possible."[30]

One of the more unusual events occurring on Christmas Eve happened in Baltimore, a time of Peace on earth, Goodwill to men, did not live up to the angelic greeting between two gentlemen of Baltimore and Philadelphia in 1843. Duels were not holiday occurrences due to the nature of the Prince of Peace's birthday. But the disagreement between William Norris of Baltimore and Philadelphia's David Powell necessitated immediate satisfaction. Seconds were chosen, as were the terms and weapons of choice, rifles at eighty paces. The paces were walked off under count, the signal was given, and both men fired. One bullet missed while the other found its mark, neatly severing the other man's "magnificent whiskers." Both men were horrified at the near

fatality and embarrassing "wound." One witness recorded, "This was such a calamity that both gentlemen were brokenhearted. . . And they embraced and parted, not in anger but in tears."[31] Perhaps a stalk of mistletoe grew in a tree overhead and lent its magical healing powers to the scene.

Before Dr. Moore wrote his poem in 1822, and during the intervening years leading up to the Civil War, Christmas was primarily a religious holiday in some regions of the country. Adults and children worked on Christmas Day. In fact, Christmas was a minor holiday surpassed in importance by such holidays as St. Valentine's Day, George Washington's Birthday, Saint Patrick's Day, and Independence Day/Fourth of July. It would not be until the turn of this century that Christmas would be recognized as a national holiday.

Christmas as a holiday was embraced more in the South than it was accepted in the Northern states. The image of the snow-covered New England countryside at Christmas with sleighs drawn by horses with jingling harness bells, was more myth than the commercially advertised nostalgia foisted on post Civil War consumers of Christmas cards and other products. In an ironic twist, it was a Southerner, James Pierpont, who wrote what is now considered a Christmas carol, "Jingle Bells," in 1850. With the twentieth century, television commercials, magazines, and newspaper advertisements continued to foster the New England Christmas memories of "hearth and home" of more than a hundred years before.

The cold truth was the first three states to recognize Christmas as a legal holiday were the Southern states of Louisiana and Arkansas in 1831, followed by Alabama five years later in 1836. The first Northern state to deem Christmas a legal holiday from work was Connecticut in 1843, eleven years after official recognition in the South. Once begun, the domino of Northern states following Connecticut's example made Christmas a legal state-observed holiday with Massachusetts in 1855, New Hampshire in 1858, and Maine in 1861.

That is not to say the Northern states shunned Christmas before the mid-nineteenth century, because they did not as evidenced in the preceding pages regarding Santa Claus, Christmas trees and other holiday traditions. The Southern states were latecomers to the spreading popularity of the Christmas tree and Santa Claus, while New England traded off by being the last region in the United States to embrace the Christmas celebration. Both geographical regions contributed to our American Christmas culture.

The literary writings of Christmas and its attendant holiday festivities and accoutrements in the novels and short stories of English author Charles Dickens, did much to invigorate the affections of Victorians on both sides of the Atlantic for the holiday. Southerners read and memorized favorite passages from *The Pickwick Papers, Sketches by Boz* and *A Christmas Carol,* and could quote at length the festive scenes out loud at parties. Northerners took to heart the philanthropic messages underlying the moral of *A Christmas Carol* by, in turn, holding holiday fairs to raise money for charity of any city's poor. American printed copies of Dickens's novels sold briskly to an adoring public and the eagerly awaited latest novels and short stories such as *Great Expectations* serialized in popular weekly newspapers like *Harper's Weekly.*

One such passage from *A Christmas Carol,* spoken by Scrooge's nephew Fred, could not help but stir one's feeling about the true meaning of Christmas read by anyone at the time it was published in the nineteenth century. It still rings powerfully today.

"I am sure I have always thought of Christmas time, when it has come around—apart from the veneration due to its sacred name and origin, if anything belonging to it can be apart from that—as a good time: a kind, forgiving, charitable, pleasant time: the only time I know of in a long calendar of the year, when men and women seem by one consent to open their shut-up hearts freely, and to think of the people below them as if they really were fellow-passengers to the grave, and not another race of creatures bound on other journeys. And therefore. . . though it has never put a scrap of gold or silver in my pocket, I believe it has done me good; and I say, God bless it."[32]

The diary of Vicksburg resident Mahala Eggleston Roach, was filled with life's rich pleasures, but also with the painful depths associated with the death of a child. The niece of Mississippian Jefferson Davis, it was the first Christmas without her "little Sophy" on Christmas Day of 1857. While mourning the loss of one child from a recent outbreak of yellow fever, she had to carry on with loving ministrations of her other surviving children and fragile constitution of her husband. Providing the happiness of gifts from "Santa Claus" for her other children, memories of Sophy surrounded her with every little motion she made, including hanging stockings. With emotion in every sentence, Mahala would write,

"The heaviest sorrow of my life has fallen this year. My little Sophy, my bright beautiful child is missing from our little circle. We were all so happy last Christmas. It was hard to bear, but my dearest one, my husband, has been rather unwell all summer, and for his sake, as well as my dear little children, I was forced to bear my loss with composure, and now I am cheerful, yes, happy, contented and grateful; the memory of an angel child has chastened the joy of the day, but not saddened it too much, for we know she is blessed beyond our ideas of happiness, still, I miss that sweet face and joyous prattle; and when I went to hang up the little stockings by the fire for 'Santa Claus', and missed hers, Oh, I thought I could not smile today. . . My presents of oysters, oranges, cakes, etc., were as abundant as usual."[33]

By 1860, most of the Christmas traditions we know today were solidly embedded. Santa Claus was well on his way to ever growing popularity among children and adults alike. Indeed the first department store Santa Claus debuted in Philadelphia in 1849, inspiring Santa Claus ornaments for decorating Christmas trees. The decorated Christmas tree illuminated with candles was at the vanguard of becoming a holiday fixture no house in the twentieth century is without. Stockings were hung with annual regularity and presents exchanged between relatives and friends. Advertising appeared in newspapers touting the latest products suitable for gifts. Christmas cards were becoming popular (but would not be massed-produced until 1875 by Louis Prang). Carolers sang traditional carols while American poets and writers were writing new carols, enlarging the collections of songs.

Figure 1-11. Illustration from Charles Dickens's *A Christmas Carol* first published in 1843 was a favorite with Victorians on both sides of the Atlantic Ocean. (K.R.)

Without Clement Clarke Moore's knowledge, he set the groundwork for changing Christmas and Santa Claus's image to the way we recognize it today, Christmas would have its public side to coincide with the private, family-oriented holiday. Churches and town communities would hold worship services as well as "singing, declamation, dialogues, tableaux—very good and interesting entertainment. When old Santa Claus came marching in dressed in skins, etc. . . . , with lots of presents, he made a nice little speech to children—gave all his presents to be distributed with the rest from the tree, which was most beautifully trimmed, and arranged as usual," stated one man of the local Methodist festivities in 1858.[34]

Christmas of 1860 was a tale of mixed emotions across the country. Storm clouds gathered on the horizon portending the clamor of WAR! December brought the news that South Carolina, the first of the Southern states, had seceded from the Union. Christmas Eve brought forth Governor Pickens's proclamation declaring South Carolina to be separate, independent, free, and sovereign. A diarist from Camden, Arkansas, wrote that Christmas Day, the last peaceful one before war intercedes,

". . . has come around in the circle of time but is not a day of rejoicing. Some of the usual ceremonies are going on, but there is a gloom on the thoughts and countenance of all the better portion of our people."[35]

The Nation was sadly tearing apart. The many Christmas editorials preached of "Peace on earth, goodwill to men," while others rattled the sabers and banged the drums of war. Benjamin Brown French of the "Old Granite State" of New Hampshire, was friend to presidents, and a public servant of long appointment and political patronage. French's journal entry for Christmas Day of 1860 fairly dripped with venom as:

"South Carolina resolved herself out of the Union on Thursday last 20th inst. The earth did not quake, the sun shone on, & Nature did not mark the event with any uncommon convulsion. Still, in reading the 'hifalutin' and bombastical debates of those arch traitors to their Country, who without reason have been guilty of so damning an act as that of endeavouring to break up our Federal Union, one would suppose that this act of secession of an insignificant, nigger-ridden state was really one of the greatest & most sublime events that the World ever witnessed! when in fact it has about the effect in regard to our great Union that the sailing of a jack o' lanthorn [lantern] across a swamp has upon the solar system. . . . "[36]

Jacob Engelbrecht, another staunch Union man and prominent Frederick, Maryland citizen, also noted in his diary about South Carolina's December 20 departure from the Union. "Thank you Gentlemen, You have been Domineering long enough and I do hope you Stay out of the Union." Engelbrecht's notation for Christmas included, "The Christmas Holliday [sic] are over for my part I enjoyed myself very well . . . the "United Guards" had a Parade & the Independent Hose Company had a procession through town with their Engine that they got in Baltimore a few months ago, On top of the Engine there was a man dressed in an Indian Costume who occasionally gave a war whoop—with the exception of a goodly number of Drunken men—I suppose all things passed off quietly."[37] His diary listed the growing roster of senators and government officials resigning and going South to home.

Harper's Weekly's year end centerfold showed a family raising a toast as the hour approaches Midnight and the year its end. The lower corner was graced by a religious scene of repentance and prayer. At the top the old year is carried out, and the new year toddles in. Within the pages of the newspaper was the serialization of Charles Dickens's latest *Great Expectations* as well as the conclusion to his latest Christmas story, *A Message From the Sea.*

HARPER'S WEEKLY

A JOURNAL OF CIVILIZATION

VOL. VI.—No. 262.]   NEW YORK, SATURDAY, JANUARY 4, 1862.   [SINGLE COPIES SIX CENTS.
[$2.50 PER YEAR IN ADVANCE.

Entered according to Act of Congress, in the Year 1861, by Harper & Brothers, in the Clerk's Office of the District Court for the Southern District of New York.

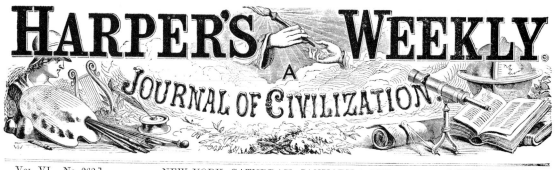

Figure 2-1. Cover page from *Harper's Weekly* entitled *Christmas Boxes in Camp—1861* by Winslow Homer shows soldiers gleefully emptying the contents of three boxes. Note the date January 4, 1862. Special issues came after, not before the event at this time. (K.R.)

2

The Citizen-Soldiers' First Christmas Away From Home

he fortunes of war seemed to have smiled on the fledgling Confederate nation as the year 1861 trickled to a close. South Carolina led the way by seceding from the Union just before Christmas the previous year. Nine other southern states left with domino-falling precision during the first five months of 1861. Three other states, Maryland, Kentucky, and Missouri, never officially left the Union but were given honorary status in the Confederate government. By Christmas Day of 1861, the South had formed the Confederate States of America and forged ahead with the establishment of a nation. A president had been elected, a government formed with its own written constitution, and a capital for the nation selected. On the battlefield, the Confederacy had begun to successfully defend its established borders with its armies raised of volunteers fighting to protect hearth and home. Despite the successes, and a few fumbling fits and starts, all was not rosy for the future life expectancy of the Confederacy.

The northern and western portions of the United States just as defiantly refused to acknowledge the new nation of treasonous states breaching the Constitution. "The year begins with feelings of enmity & apprehensions," an Episcopal minister commented in writing.[1] While Southerners called their efforts a revolution, men of the Union considered the actions of the Southern states to be in rebellion. During the final days of the Buchanan administration, the President washed his hands of the unfolding situation, preferring the incoming President-elect Abraham Lincoln to fix the decades old canker infecting the nation's soul.

On March 4, 1861, Abraham Lincoln became the sixteenth President of the United States. In his inaugural address the new President reiterated his intention to leave the institution of slavery alone in the states it existed in. He further stated he had no objection to a proposed amendment forbidding the interference of slavery by the Federal government with an added rejoinder that domestic institutions could rightfully be controlled by each state as it saw fit. The rub was that the cat was out of the bag as secession was already an accomplished fact. Then Lincoln threw down the gauntlet. The dissolution of the Federal Union of States "is now formidably attempted" but "the Union of these States is perpetual." The Union could not be dissolved and any acts of secession or violence against Federal authority according to Lincoln would be

> "insurrectionary or revolutionary. I therefore consider that, in view of the Constitution and the laws, the Union is considered unbroken; and, to the extent of my ability, I shall take care, as the Constitution itself expressly enjoins upon me, that the laws of the Union be faithfully executed in all the States. . . . In your hands, my dissatisfied fellow countrymen, and not mine, is the momentous issue of civil war. The government will not assail you. You can have no conflict, without being yourselves the aggressors. You have no oath registered in Heaven to destroy the government, while I have the most solemn one to 'preserve, protect and defend' it. . . . "[2]

The country had waited for this moment. Reaction to Lincoln's inaugural speech in the South was seen as "incendiary" and a declaration of war. Support for the new administration's message rang out in newspaper editorials across the North as much as it was denounced as "no Wiser than it was Before."[3] The deed was done with the new President's position stated and presented publicly. More Federal arsenals and forts within the Confederate States declared boundaries were seized by Confederate authorities. The maneuvering now continued in earnest.

Little more than a month since taking office, President Lincoln sent a messenger to the governor of South Carolina to inform him of the government's attempt to resupply Fort Sumter with provisions only. No troop reinforcements were to be involved unless resistance was encountered. The messenger arrived on April 8 and read President Lincoln's message to Governor Pickens. Following the receipt of the message, all Confederate military forces were ordered to their post as tension between the two governments heightened. With Confederate preparations in full swing, a boat bearing a white flag and three Confederate emissaries arrived at Fort Sumter in Charleston Harbor, demanding the fort's surrender. Commander of the garrison, Major Robert Anderson, respectfully declined the emissaries' request after conferring with his own officers.

The official explanation General P. T. Beauregard offered to Major Anderson was the Confederate government "can no longer delay assuming actual possession of a fortification commanding the entrance of one of their harbors, and necessary to its defense and security. I am ordered by the Government of the Confederate States to demand the evacuation of Fort Sumter . . ." After several more inquiries regarding evacuation of the fort throughout the night, Anderson replied he would be forced to evacuate Fort Sumter if he were not resupplied by April 15. On April 12 at 4:30 in the morning, the die was cast and the war began. The guns aimed at Fort Sumter from points all around Charleston Harbor spoke in fiery burst. The Confederate States of America had struck the first blow.

Thirty-six hours after the bombardment began, Fort Sumter surrendered. Terms of surrender were discussed and agreed to and the white flag replaced the stars and stripes of the U.S. flag on the damaged flagpole within the fort. Confederate military men and citizen onlookers cheered their victory. Many people openly expressed sympathy for Major Anderson and the fort's defenders. No casualties were counted among the Federal soldiers during the bombardment. It was during the official surrender ceremony on April 14 that a freak accidental explosion among a pile of cartridges killed one Federal soldier while mortally wounding another. Four others were injured. Charleston was given over to holiday observance and churches celebrated with special thanksgiving services. Governor Pickens told the festive Charleston crowd that "We have met them, and we have conquered." It was Major Anderson's words that would be prophetic. "Our Southern brethren have done grievously wrong, they have rebelled and have attacked their father's house and loyal brothers. They must be punished and brought back, but this necessity breaks my heart." The question was who had out maneuvered whom?

The intervening weeks and months rallied the nation's faithful to the respective causes. Patriotism and duty were the main motivating emotions. Baser motivations were revealed in the business of contractual arrangements for military equipage and clothing for soldiers. Political patronage abounded from bribes paid for buying of material contracts to political appointments of men to military positions regardless of experience or temperament. Neither side was spared.

Riots swept through a number of cities as pro-union or secessionist groups sought to organize militias or block troops from passing through cities, such as St. Louis and Baltimore, on the way to seats of war. Military camps sprang up all over the North and South as the business of training civilians to become soldiers got down to serious work. Agents for both countries sought to purchase from the armories of Europe large stocks of weapons to supply growing armies. Many obsolete weapons were purchased and shipped back to the United or Confederate States. The Navy of the United States put into place a blockade of Southern ports to starve the Confederacy of needed supplies. Through the first two years of the war, the blockade proved to be very leaky as most imported goods reached the Confederacy's ports, though at inflated prices.

Skirmishes and small actions were constantly fought across the breadth of the geographic boundaries of the United and Confederate States with relatively little loss of life. Pressure mounted on both military high commands to take to the field in one major action to decide the outcome of the war. Ninety days was naively thought by many as time enough to decide the deadly contest. The greatest enemy for both armies at this time was death from diseases encountered when bringing together so many people and quartering them in camps where even the simplest sanitary precautions were never implemented. Camp "sinks" (latrines) were often located above water sources and polluted the drinking water of unsuspecting soldiers. Measles, chicken pox, mumps, typhoid, malaria, and a myriad of other diseases considered innocuous today felled large numbers of men in new regiments before they had a chance to experience the horrors of the battlefield.

First Manassas was the largest of the battles fought during the first year of the war. The two inexperienced armies clashed with the Union army having the upper hand pressuring General Pierre G. T. Beauregard's army to give ground all across the battlefield. Late arriving Confederate troops from the Shenandoah Valley launched a counterattack and turned the tide. It was a Confederate victory, but President Jefferson Davis's relationship with the South's new heroes, Generals Beauregard and Joseph E. Johnston, was less than cordial and grew increasingly chilly as the war progressed. The tone of the Federal war effort was set in the East. With the exception of a few scattered successes, a drubbing here and a rout there was the pattern.

Robert E. Lee was a known officer in the regular army, but his first campaign was less than a stellar beginning for a commander known for his audacity. General Lee would end the year in South Carolina improving fortifications against Union forays into the state's interior. More would be heard from him in the coming year.

Federal troops out West were holding their own, winning small victories under commanders like U. S. Grant, Don Carlos Buell, Henry Halleck, and others. The amateur armies of North and South were bloodied and settled in for a long affair little dreamed of a few short months before.

As the holidays approached, the front page story of newspapers in the North and South was not about Christmas, but a diplomatic flap between the United States and Great Britain that would become known as the "Trent Affair." On November 8, Captain Charles Wilkes of the United States Navy seized James M. Mason and John Slidell, Confederate commissioners to Great Britain and France, from the British mail packet *Trent* as it sailed in international waters. Public acclamation rang out all across the North for the naval officer's act of striking a blow at the traitorous Confederacy and foreign intervention. Southern politicians were at first aghast at the treachery of the North against diplomatic personnel on a neutral country's vessel. They soon appreciated the fact that the incident strengthened their hand in justifying secession, and afforded them an excellent opportunity for European recognition. The diplomatic morass the North discovered it was in after cooler heads began to prevail, provided delight and amusement for Southerners. Of equal significance for the North, was the fact that England was sending troops to Canada and the United States might find itself at war with Great Britain for a third time.

Expressions of outrage in the South, threats of war between Great Britain and the United States, and debate on the rights of the United States and the impact on international laws ruling the high seas ensued in the editorial columns of newspapers on both sides of the Atlantic. On the 24th of November, the *U.S.S. San Jacinto* docked at Boston Harbor and the controversial prisoners were ensconced in cells at Fort Warren in the middle of the harbor. By the end of November, news of the "Trent Affair" had reached England with the docking of the *Trent,* igniting howls of official protest and public indignation for the outrage committed on the British flag. British Foreign Secretary Lord John Russell instructed the Minister to the United States, Lord Lyons, that unless the United States released the commissioners Slidell and Mason within seven days with an appropriate apology, Lord Lyons would return to Great Britain and the British Navy was to take measures as circumstances required without

resorting to an act of hostility. Diplomatic tensions were ratcheted up a few notches in an international game of poker between the two powers.

After another incident near the mouth of the Rio Grande in early December, the Lincoln Cabinet had discussions almost daily on the pros and cons of the diplomatic imbroglio since the *Trent's* Confederate passengers had arrived in the United States. Prince Albert, Great Britain's royal consort to Queen Victoria and moderating influence on the hawkish Prime Minister Lord Palmerston and Foreign Secretary Lord Russell, died on December 14. The "Trent Affair" on which he urged a firm policy steeped in moderation instead of a tone of war-like belligerence, was the last piece of official policy the Prince commented on before being incapacitated by his final illness. The official correspondence reaching the desks of President Lincoln and Secretary of State Seward just before Christmas, were the terms Prince Albert had laid out. Couched in language less bellicose than Lord Palmerston's, the Prince's terms requested an explanation of the action that Seward pronounced "courteous and friendly." A door opened by the late Prince provided a way for the United States to back out.

On Christmas Day, Lincoln and his Cabinet met in a lengthy and often heated discussion in which Seward proposed the solution for ending the situation. The United States would not admit any illegality in the boarding of the *Trent,* but the government would be happy to release the Confederate commissioners. Further, the United States expressed its happiness that Great Britain in its protest had finally recognized the rights of neutral vessels sailing at sea. This was a face-saving resolution with a sly tweak of Great Britain's nose over a long simmering problem that caused the War of 1812. Other Cabinet members found it a bitter pill to swallow in yielding to the British. The final decision was delayed until the next day. Lincoln adjourned the meeting and the Cabinet members went off to spend what was left of the holiday with their families. The President, together with Mrs. Lincoln, hosted a Christmas dinner with many invited guests at the White House.

When the Cabinet resumed meeting on December 26, the discussion was again often heated before the members agreed that the seizure of Mason and Slidell while en route to Europe, was illegal. As one cabinet member wrote, "all yielded to the necessity, and unanimously concurred." The United States would release the commissioners forthwith into the hands of the British. Lord Lyons in Washington was informed and both sides peacefully concluded a potentially explosive situation. By swallowing its pride, the United States recognized that in the government's hands, Mason and Slidell had a greater propaganda effect as Southern martyrs than if allowed to carry out their duties abroad. Effectively dimming the Confederacy's hope of foreign recognition, the United States handed over the Confederate commissioners to the British on New Year's Day, thereby dodging a war on a second front.

The Christmas issue of *Harper's Weekly* (published January 4, 1862) featured a drawing by Winslow Homer showing soldiers opening their Adams Express boxes from home with unbridled glee. Charles Dickens's latest Christmas stories are published in their entirety within the pages of the newspaper. The week before, the December 28 issue centerfold contained another Winslow Homer drawing that portrayed the philanthropy of the era as the Great Fair in New York City raised money for the city's poor.

Many letters written to family and friends at home by soldiers in the Confederate armies during Christmas of 1861, reflected an enthusiastic optimism and patriotic fervor for their cause of independence and defense of their right to live lives as they saw fit, unfettered by the restricting hand of the Federal government. For many offi-

Figure 2-2. Centerfold from *Harper's Weekly*, December 28, 1861 issue showing the Metropolitan Fair held in New York to raise money for the city's poor at Christmas. Art by Winslow Homer. (K.R.)

cers and their men it became a holy crusade against Northern aggression, while others fought to maintain a lifestyle they had always known and had no desire to see stamped out. Morale ran high among many regiments that had seen some form of action or tasted victory at the end of a battle or skirmish.

Charles Colcock Jones, Jr. was the former mayor of Savannah and a lieutenant in the 1st Volunteer Regiment Georgia Artillery, also known as the "Chatham Artillery." On Christmas Day Jones wrote a passionately patriotic letter about the ideals he was fighting for to his retired clergyman father at home on their Georgia plantation.

"Christmas Day! Many happy returns to you and my dear mother and precious little daughter! And long before the coming of another anniversary may the storm clouds which now hover about us have been succeeded by the pure light of love, of peace, and of righteousness! This is my hope, but whether it will be realized within the time specified, and by whom, is known only to Him who disposes all things in infinite wisdom and according to His own great pleasure. Of the ultimate success of our cause I have no doubt; but I am persuaded that the struggle will not be without privation and (it may be) great personal danger and perhaps death to many into whose immediate keeping is committed the defense of all we hold dear in life and sacred in death . . ."[4]

Admiral Raphael Semmes commanding the Confederate States Navy *C.S.S. Sumter*, already gaining a reputation as a seaman to be feared as he captured and sank Federal ships in the Atlantic, recorded in his journal the changes wrought by the war on Christmas Day.

"Christmas Day was passed by us on the lonely sea, in as doleful a manner as can well be conceived. The weather is thus described in my journal: 'Thermometer 60 degrees; barometer 29.80. Heavy rain squalls-weather dirty, with lightning all around the horizon, indicating a change at any moment. Under short sail during the night.' The only other record of the day was that we 'spliced the main brace'; that is, gave Jack an extra glass of grog. Groups of idle sailors lay about the decks, overhauling a range of their memories; how they spent the last Christmas Day in some Wapping or Wide Water Street, with the brimming goblet in hand, and the merry music of the dance sounding in their ears. Nor were the memories of the officers idle. They clasped in fancy their loved ones, now sad and lonely, to their bosoms once more, and listened to the prattle of the little ones left behind.

"Not the least curious of the changes that had taken place since the last Christmas Day was the change in their own official positions. They were, most of them, on that day, afloat under the old flag. That flag now looked to them strange and foreign. They had some of their own countrymen on board; not, as of yore, as welcome visitors, but as prisoners. These, too, wore a changed aspect—enemy, instead of friend, being written upon their faces. The two rival nations spoken of by De Tocqueville stood face to face."[5]

Another Confederate soldier named William of an unknown regiment and last name wrote to his mother on Christmas Day while convalescing in Staunton, Virginia, pronouncing it his Christmas gift. As a child, William must have been powerful of argument in defense of any wrongdoing he committed as the silver-tongue language can attest.

"Dear Ma, My Christmas Gift! I shall commemerate this memorable day by writing a few lines to you. With what different feelings do I pass this Christmas Day from what I have spent similar days in the past! It has been my fortunate luck in the past to enjoy the festivities of this day with but few exceptions in the home circle, amid the endearments of home friends. I am now deprived of that blessed priviledge,—a stern and rigorous discipline holds me in galling endurance. —I say galling for such it is, when beckonings of former comfort and liberty invite, but when I reflect that this species of vassalage is but one of the lesser evils of war,—is a necessary feature of the hated institution, I submit to the stern necessity—hoping that there is a time not far in the future when shackles of a military bondage shall no longer fetter the limbs of Southern Free men, when grim-visaged war with its attendant horrors both on the battlefield and in the hospital, the charnel house of the living, shall have fled our borders, and we shall be left the quiet enjoyment of our peaceful homes, none daring to molest us or make us afraid. But, Ma, me thinks this is not the occasion to indulge in high flown declamations,—highly as you appreciate the excellencies of style—I know a plain and practical epistle is best-suited to your taste. You prefer that I discourse in letter just as I would in person, were the glorious opportunity afforded me. But how little can I write you compared to the inummerable things I would say in conversation with you. The events which have transpired during my absence would be productive food for many a long hour's chat. I still hope the opportunity will be afforded me in the future, to rehearse the past, to dwell upon its dangers, its difficulties, and to express my mutual thanks with you, that I have passed through them unscathed—six months of the eventful year on which I entered my military career have wronged their flight into oblivion. How strange and unlooked for has been the experience of many of us who entered upon a soldier's life at their beginning! But how much stranger may the events which shall (change) many a soldier's career ere the earth shall have completed its annual circle! But I am relapsing again into apostrophes. . . . I have been much more highly favored than the generality of soldiers, greatly more so than I at any time anticipated, and in what do you think? Why! I have just risen from the table, and a large, well cooked turkey ushered in the meal.—A turkey for a Christmas dinner. This is something for a soldier to talk and write about too.—Ma, haven't I fared well? It was not only to eat, but I ate bountifully of it. Suffer no uneasiness then in learning that I am at the hospital, for if you had seen me at the table you would have pronounced me far on the convalescent."[6]

For many common soldiers, the beginning of the war was an adventure, a chance to see new places and get away from home. As the newness of the experience wore off, the daily drudgery of drill and other duties took over. Even holidays were not exempt. Guard duty had to be mounted, pickets posted, and the enemy watched for with vigilance in all kinds of weather. Many soldiers grumbled in letters home that their turn at picket duty always seemed to be assigned during inclement weather.

Second Lieutenant Robert Gould Shaw of the 2nd Massachusetts, wrote to his mother from the unit's winter encampment near Frederick, Maryland, about his turn at guard duty on Christmas Day.

"It is Christmas morning, and I hope a happy and merry one for you all, though, it looks so stormy for our poor country, one can hardly be in a merry humor. . . My Christmas Eve has been very much like other eves during the last six months. On the whole, I have passed quite a pleasant night, though what our men call the 'fore-part' of it was principally occupied in taking care of two drunken men (one of them with a broken pate), and in tying a sober one to a tree. After this was over, I did a great deal of reading, and, towards 10 o'clock A.M., had some toast and coffee,—having previously invited my Sergeant to take a nap, so that I might not be troubled by hungry eyes, and made to feel mean, for there wasn't enough to give away. The drummer (who, with the Sergeant of the Guard, for some reason which I never discovered, sits and sleeps in the officer's tent) kept groaning in his sleep; and I couldn't help imagining that his groan always came in just as I took a bite of toast, or large gulp of coffee. This diminished my enjoyment; and when he suddenly said, 'Martha! There isn't any breakfast,' I was certain my proceedings were influencing his dreams! It began to snow about midnight, and I suppose no one ever had a better chance of seeing 'Santa Claus'; but, as I had my stockings on, he probably thought it not worth his while to come down to the guard-tent. I didn't see any of the guard's stockings pinned up outside their tent, and indeed it is contrary to army regulations for them to divest themselves of any part of their clothing during the twenty-four hours."[7]

Boredom and the dullness of Christmas Day was a common complaint of many soldiers. For some, the routine of winter encampments could not compare to Christmases celebrated at home during years past. Once experienced, the dull Christmas was hoped to be traded in by the arrival back home to celebrate the holiday with family and friends, not to be separated from loved ones again.

Samuel J. Alexander of the 62nd Pennsylvania Volunteer Infantry recorded his dull Christmas with a plaintive hope for the next one.

"Yesterday was a rather dull day for Christmas. As far as having fun although it was a pritty day. One of our mess got a box from home on Christmas Eve containing a large roasted turkey and several other good things. So we had the pleasure of eating a very good Christmas dinner but I was not as happy as I was when I ate my Christmas dinner one year ago with my dear wife and I hope before another Christmas rolls around that we may be together never more to part."[8]

Confederate soldier Charles Thurston of the 7th Louisiana Infantry Regiment (Crescent Rifles) wrote a letter to his mother from the "Growler's Den" at Camp Carondelet in Virginia. "My Mother Dear, Yesterday was Christmas and a dull Christmas it was to me I assure you. We had a very jolly time of it. They had 'Egg Nog' and I believe 'Cake,' but the poor private had to content himself with one drink around which was given in the morning. I spent most of the morning in trying to line a blanket coat that was given me by the Government. I made very slow headway . . . My kind friends Mr. and Mrs. Irby of Lynchburg, Va have written me that they would send some Christmas things in a box if I would let them know how to ship safely. I have not written yet and feel somewhat backward in accepting too much of their kindship and generosity . . ." Charles Thurston died in a train accident in July 1862 at Danville Junction.[9]

Another Confederate soldier with the 17th Mississippi Regiment, Co. G, "Confederate Guards" Private Robert A. Moore scribbled his thoughts about Christmas in his pocket diary.

"This is Christmas & a very dull Christmas it has been to me. Had an egg-nog tonight but did not enjoy it much as we had no ladies to share it with us. Several boys a little tight in camp & some have been sent to the guard-house. Spent a few hours very pleasantly at the residence of Swan's. It is the very model of architecture. The situation is very romantic. Several fountains but they are not in operation, beautiful flower vases, lion & deer in front of the house, they are cast iron. Have a guard out. Major a little tight."[10]

Homesickness would infect the letters of many soldiers written to family members and friends at home as the novelty of the adventure wore off. A letter written by James Holloway of the 18th Mississippi on Christmas morning near Dranesville, Virginia, reflected the sadness and melancholy many soldiers on both sides felt as they spent their first Christmas far away from families and home. The unhappy realization that the war would be long began to sink into many thoughts.

"My Dearest Wife and Babies, A healthy Christmas to you all and to father and son and all the rest. I can't say a happy one (though I wish it), for happiness is not ours until we all meet after the war. We may be joyous and gay for the season but joyousness and gaiety is mingled with concern and apprehension for the condition of our beloved country—for our absent loved ones, for our poverty, for the doubt as to the truthfulness of the English news, for the fear that 'Old Abe' and the cabinet will not stand up to the test, etc., etc., . . . You have no idea how lonesome I feel this day. It's the first time in my life I'm away from loved ones at home. Sam is in the regiment and doubtless feels like myself, or will when he wakes up in the morning. I presume you are in New Orleans and in a few hours the house will be astir—the children crazy over their stockings. Were I there, I'd fill them up to the brim with bon-bons—I'd make them think for one day that plenty abounded, that no war existed, and that each was a King or Queen. The delusion should last until they're old enough to appreciate and take in the holy crusade. . . Have six invitations to Christmas dinner today. Jake leaves for town after breakfast and

I'll probably go too, don't know where I'll be tonight. You know how much I like eggnog. I'll write before New Year...Hoping you have written me today, I am still your devoted husband, James M. Holloway."[11]

The letter J. W. Reid penned from the winter quarters of the 4th South Carolina Regiment at Centreville, Virginia, wryly commented on the Christmas festivities the relatives at home were probably enjoying, while wondering if they thought of his situation.

"Christmas Day, 3 O'clock P.M. —Well Christmas is here and in a few more hours will be where eighteen hundred others are, in the past. How often have you and my sisters, and others, perhaps, said, 'I wish Jesse had some of this,' when you were enjoying your little Christmas tricks, but never mind Jesse on such occasions; he is faring very well, considering. In spite of Major-General Law and Gospel, most of the boys managed to get a wee drop today, but all has been very quiet, there being no more noise than three earthquakes and a cyclone, and that is nothing unusual here. For my part I have not tasted a drop. One reason for it is that the stuff is too high, being $5.00 a quart for the worst kind of 'rot skull.' Having drunk none myself I will miss the supreme felicity of the blues and head ache. . . . Before this reaches you Christmas will be over, and then you can look for April and—J. W. Reid."[12]

Robert E. Lee wrote a Christmas letter of parental advice to one of his daughters from his South Carolina command, where he oversaw the building of coastal fortifications and defenses. Reminding his daughter to want only her necessities, he sought to instill in her the discipline and attention to duty he would become famous for.

"My Dear Daughter, Having distributed such poor Christmas gifts as I had to those around me, I have been looking for something for you. Trifles even are hard to get these war times, and, you must not therefore expect more. I have sent you what I thought most useful in your separation from me and hope it will be of some service. Though stigmatized as 'vile dross,' it has never been a drug with me. That you may never want of it, restrict your wants to your necessities. Yet how little will it purchase! But see how God provides for our pleasures in every way. To compensate for such 'trash,' I send you some sweet violets that I gathered for you this morning while covered with dense white frost, whose crystals glittered in the bright sun like diamonds, and formed a brooch of rare beauty and sweetness which could not be fabricated by the expenditure of a world of money. . . . Think always of your father."[13]

In a separate letter to his wife, Robert E. Lee wrote of his appreciation of past Christmases spent with her and their family, and the hope that the future would bring them through the forthcoming trial.

". . . I cannot let this day of grateful rejoicing pass, dear Mary, without some communication with you. I am grateful for the many among the past that I have passed with you, and the rememberance of them fills me with pleasure. For those on which we have been separated we must not repine. If it will make us more resigned and better prepared for what is in store for us, we should rejoice. Now we must be content with the many blessings we receive. If we can only become sensible of our transgressions, so as to be fully penitent and forgiven, that this heavy punishment under which we labor may with justice be removed from us and the whole nation, what gracious consummation of all that we have endured it will be! . . ."[14]

All was not gloom and sadness. Entertainments abounded in camp and field. Competitions from foot races, wrestling, and snowball fights took place between regiments and brigades. Most were fun with cash prizes awarded to first and second place finishers, while some took a harder edge with fierce competition and fights breaking out among the ranks.

A soldier from the 5th New Hampshire Regiment, Co. G, Charles N. Scott described the amusements of the day for his wife Amie. His closing salutation provided a hint of how much he missed his wife.

". . . Tommorrow is Christmas and we are not goin to drill We are goin to keep

Christmas and we are goin to have a little funn to morrow We are goin to have some rasslin and running and jumping and then we are goin to have the greesed pig There is 4 dollars for the best rassler and two dollars for the second best and fore dollars for the best jumper and two for the secon best So I have told you all our funn. . . Yours in lust.”[15]

Captain McCrillis, an officer with the 5th New Hampshire, would provide a further elucidation of the camp's holiday proceedings.

“Wednesday being Christmas, the Colonel said there would be not drill; that he purchased a pig which would be greased and let loose for our entertainment at 10 o'clock. First, a foot race, 500 yards, best two in three. First prize, $4.00; second prize, $2.00. The first prize was won by S. Barton, Company E. We then marched to quarters and partook of oysters and bread. At 3 P.M. we formed in a square, and poor piggy was let loose. After a few minutes he was seized by Pat Rowen, but escaped. Soon he was seized and carried away by a member of Company I. The next was a jumping match with prizes of

$4.00 and $2.00. This closed the day's sport. We had quite a nice time.”[16]

Another soldier of the 5th New Hampshire, James Delmage, alluded in a letter to his wife about the fun time he had on Christmas Day.

“I take pleasure in writing a few lines to you to let you know that I am well and hope this may find you and Eddie the same. . . . I do not expect that we shall have such a good time New Years Day as we had on Christmas. Here is hoping you may enjoy a happy New Year and many soldiers heart will beat high on that day and think of wives and children, brothers & sisters, fathers & mothers, and their sweethearts that they have left behind in the Granite [State]. No more from your Husband, James Delmage.”[17]

Two letters from James M. Williams of the 21st Alabama Infantry to his wife, recalled the hilarity and tasty victuals in camp at Fort Gaines on the Alabama coast on Christmas Eve and Christmas night. The longing for the conjugal affections of his wife are evidenced with a winking eye narrative.

Figure 2-3. Chasing a greased pig was part of the fun and games on Christmas Day in the camp of the 5th New Hampshire. From *Frank Leslie's Illustrated History of the Civil War.* (K.R.)

"A Merry Christmas! I wish my darling! oh! that I had a furlough to share it with you to-morrow we would both get 'tight' on egg-nog wouldn't we? You think you wouldn't do you? but I say if I were home I'd make you take enough to exhillerate you for once in your life well! well! if I am not home with you I won't make a funeral of my Christmas, but will be as merry as can be, we have a merry party in the 'Bazaar' mess and if we only receive a jug of good old rye whiskey by this boat, which we expect confidently, we will make a 'welkin ring' (To make a loud noise or sound) tomorrow; . . ."

On Christmas evening he wrote to her of the day's festivities.

"Christmas began this morning before day-light with me; two glasses of eggnog came for each before we were out of bed, which took away our appetites for breakfast; then the reveille began to beat, when a large party of infantry seized tin pans and everything that would rattle or jingle about quarters and we followed the band all through the regiment singing and tin-panning the tune of 'Dixie'—it has been a long time since I have heard, or made so much racket.

"The grand event of the day was a regi-mental mock parade which came off at ten o'clock; all the companies turned out in full dress, with officers chosen from the privates in the ranks; one of the Infantry boys acted as colonel [Crawford], and imitated him very well, another of our men was dressed as a woman with a cocked hat, to represent the Major—who is nicknamed 'Nancy' you know—I dressed in Lieutenant Cluis' uni-form well stuffed out with Mrs. Turner's pil-lows had command of our company—King was lieutenant every-thing went off in the best manner, the men all acted their parts seriously as though it were a real parade, and the colonel and the officers who took no part in the performance but that of spectators seemed to be very much amused—[Lt.] Colonel Ingersoll seemed to think that the burlesque of the Major was rather too severe and I think he sent word to him he had bet-ter retire from the field; however he was there long enough for every-body to see, reconize,

and laugh at the caricature;—The day passed without anything serious happening to our regiment, a number are drunk, and there have been a few small fist fights, but nobody hurt—The regulars though have had at least one bloody row, and several are laid up with bloody heads, one of whom is reported to be dying to-night—. . .

"I mustn't close my letter without giving you a little description of our Christmas din-ner, Bob Wier who presides over the 'last chance mess' invited us to dine; and a grand dinner it was I tell you!—

Bill of Fare

Cold Turkey	Eggs	Sweet Potatoes
Roast Beef	Bread	Another Kind of Cake
Pigeon Pie	Mince Pie	Sugar Topped Cake
Rice	One kind of Cake	
Salt	Pepper	Vinegar
Pepper Sauce	Turnips	Mustard
Jelly Cake	Sugar	Port Wine
Sherry Wine		

"Every one of the above dishes was there and more than I can eat and remember—then there were toast all around—my toast 'The last chance'—may the 'Bazaar mess' never fare worse than when they took the 'last chance' for Christmas dinner!

'Bob Wier's'

'The loved ones at home', missed to day more than ever—'. . .

"Then there were toast to every one around the table and a little speech in acknowledgement from each,—we drank all our wine in toast and got into the humor of toasting so that when it gave out we com-menced on the pepper vinegar!

"But I must stop—I have worried your patience with the story of my Christmas—...

"May this be the last Christmas that I spend away from your side!"[18]

Private Alfred Bellard of the 5th New Jersey remembered a rather unique reminder of Christ-mas in winter quarters camped on the lower Potomac.

"On Christmas day, Co. H of our Reg. were well supplied with good things as their friends had sent them out about 18 boxes

Figure 2-4. Holiday parade in the camp of the 44th New York State Volunteers. A similar event was recorded in a letter from James Williams of the 21st Alabama Infantry to his wife written on Christmas night. *Leslie's Illustrated.* (K.R.)

containing plenty of poultry and various other good things, making mouths of the less fortunate companys water. As I received a box myself about this time it did not affect me quite so bad as some of the rest. In order to make it look much like Christmas as possible, a small tree was stuck up in front of our tent, decked off with hard tack and pork, in lieu of cakes, oranges, etc. Our band of 15 pieces arrived about the time and the boys were highly elated at the prospect of plenty of music. And it was noticed that when the Regt. marched out to parade with our band at the head of the line, the boys had more rubber in their heels than formerly."[19]

Remarks made in the diary of 8th Michigan Infantry Regiment officer Captain Ralph Ely, was rather different in experience to the majority recorded. His regiment was one of the few that held inspection and drill as other officers, in keeping with the holiday, excused their men from drill.

"December 25th, 1861—Morning inspection and short skirmish drill; in the afternoon attended the Negro Christmas dance, which they performed with energy and delight common to their race."[20]

Eggnog was a much anticipated beverage many people looked forward to during the Christmas holiday; no less so by the citizen turned soldier in both armies during the war. Drunkenness was a discipline problem encountered in the ranks of ordinary soldiers as well as the officer corps on any given day. During Christmas it became almost epidemic as soldiers foraged for the essential ingredients for which to make merry and remember Christmases at home before the war interrupted.

In the Confederate Army in Virginia, the men of the Tennessee Brigade (consisting of the 1st, 7th, 14th Tennessee, 19th Georgia, and 5th

Figure 2-5. The 8th Michigan Infantry still had ". . . inspection and a short drill . . ." on Christmas morning wrote Captain Ralph Ely. (USAMHI)

Alabama Battalion) marched into Strasburg, Virginia, on Christmas Eve and began intently scouring the town for a supply of eggs and whiskey. John Fite of the 7th Tennessee remembered:

> "The boys got hold of eggs and whiskey and had a big time and the next morning they were so drunk that they had a hard time getting started. I have no idea how many of them were drunk. There was a great many so drunk that they couldn't walk. We put the drunkest ones in the wagon and hauled them along."[21]

Fellow member David Phillips with the 7th Tennessee, recorded in his diary with some understatement about the Christmas Day in camp.

> "Christmas morning a fine one. The boys began to take their Christmas last night. A good deal of drunkeness in camp. In the morning the captain gave us a treat of eggnog. One-half the boys very tight by nine o'clock. . . . Never saw so many drunk men before. It might be said with propriety that the 7th was drunk on the 25th."[22]

Robert Mockbee of the 14th Regiment reminisced "Our first Christmas was spent in Strausburg and with much hilarity with which the day was always observed at home was in evidence. More or less old 'Stiple Jack' had found its way into camp and not a few buckets full of 'egg nog' was dispensed by the different messes; and in many instances turkey was indulged in at dinner through the foresight of foragers sent out on the line of march."[23] Marcus Toney of the 1st Tennessee wryly observed, "If there was any whiskey or eggnog left in town, I did not know of it."[24] Many men from Colonel Maney's regiment hastily gulped down their fortified eggnog as the Tennessee Brigade marched north out of Strasburg on Christmas Day to join General Jackson's command at Winchester. The intoxicating effect of the eggnog soon prostrated many men by the roadside. The file closers were obligated to sling the helpless men into the wagons to be hauled for the duration of the march.

The Union Army was not immune to the excesses of Christmas partying as seen in John Beatty's amusing diary entry recounting his

Figure 2-6. The 14th Tennessee Infantry sent out foragers to secure their Christmas dinner while stationed in Strasburg, Virginia, in 1861. This one had chickens hanging from his saddle. (USAMHI)

Christmas experience in the officers' mess of the 3rd Ohio.

> "The Major, Adjutant, and I had a right royal Christmas dinner and a pleasant time. A fine fat Chicken, fried mush, coffee, peaches and milk, were on the table. The Major is engaged now in the heating of the second teapot of water for punch purposes. His countenance is quite rosy; this doubtless is the effect of the fire. He has been unusually powerful in argument; but whether his intellect has been stimulated by the fire, the tea, or the punch, we are at this time wholly unable to decide; he certainly handles the teapot with consumate skill, and attacks the punch with exceeding vigor."[25]

New York infantryman William Blankvelt writing to his brother from camp in Virginia, had one thing only on his mind, whiskey.

Figure 2-7. A well supplied officers' mess. Captain John Betty recorded in his diary "I had a right royal Christmas dinner . . . ." (USAMHI)

"As for Christmas that was nothing to me out here I did not as much as get a drop of wiskey for my Christmas; the weather is getting colder here now the ground is as hard as a brick; . . . About now I suppose you had a happy Christmas and will have a better New Years spree I suppose you remember the little black hoss [his nickname for liquor] we had last New Years eve Well we cant get any out here unless it is sent by express to us from home Quite a number of the boys get boxes of lickour sent to them from home by the Adams Express for you can't buy it out here for no money But I must come to a close for this time but If you like you may send me a box of whiskey It would come myty good out here If you want to send it you may send it by Adams Express and direct it to me the same as the letters you direct to me But if you send it at all be sure and put it up good and strong."[26]

Food was always a welcome care package from home to supplement the less than filling rations provided by the army quartermasters. Foraging in the countryside whenever the armies of both sides encamped, filled the larder and camp cook pots of company messes through purchase or outright liberation. The most welcome sight was delivery of express boxes mailed to soldiers in the respective armies. Sometimes mishaps waylaid packages through theft of errant deliveries. Soldiers were constantly requesting not only food, but clothing and shoes and boots.

Algernon Sidney Wade of the 27th Virginia Infantry received an express box containing boots and a winter coat. It was the edible contents that captured his attention.

"I had a pretty good time this Christmas so far as it has gone. We had a little eggnog yesterday and a good many of the boys felt it a good deal. However the day passed off very quietly. Tell Thomas I am obliged to him for the fine bottle of brandy he sent me, and I did not drink it to excess. We have not cut the turkey yet have been eating the sausage and various other things the boys have been treating me too. Say to little Annie that Uncle Jimmy has not forgotten her yet, and he sees she has not forgotten him, kiss her and cuddle her for me as a Christmas gift, as I cannot get there to give anything. I suppose you had a pretty dull Christmas, no one but the old folks there, and they take very little interest in such things, and especially these war times."[27]

John A. Palmer, a member of Co. G "Salem Light Guard," 36th Regiment Ohio Volunteers, recounted his Christmas in a letter to his parents written just after "tattoo."

"Father & Mother christmas is over and probably a shooting match too out there in the world some-where, and who knows but a Ball is coming off at Pemp, or some other place, with scarcely boys enough to manage the girls.—Well thats nothing to us, for I have just come in from the non-commisioned officers room, where we have been enjoying ourselves immensely in the way of a frolick,—but the query will probably arise among the young folks in the WORLD, where do you get your girls? Well; Soldiers have many things to learn (as you Father) are no doubt aware, and doing without girls is one of them, which by the way is very easily managed by soldiers.—Well I may as well quit that, and tell you that we had 4 Lieutenants here for dinner today, to help us 4 eat stuffed Turkey, with about everything else that can be mentioned, which was finished off with Apples, Nuts, & WHISKY. (Dont let it excite you) And we all partook; 'I mean of the eatables' till we ever nigh unto busting; Well this story I must quit too or I won't finish tonight and I want to send in the morning . . ."[28]

Union soldier John Faller of the 7th Pennsylvania Reserves sent his "Christmas gift" letter home detailing his receipt of a Christmas box and looking forward to a nice holiday dinner. The 7th Pennsylvania had recently been engaged in the Battle of Dranesville on December 20, but was safely bedded down for the winter at Fairfax Courthouse.

"Well to proceed about the boxes in the evening (Saturday) about five o'clock the wagons drove up in camp and you ought to have seen Company A. rolling out to see who got a box and who did't get a box. We shouldered ours and bore it off triumphant to our mansion. We seized an axe and smote it thus. We were very much pleased with all the contents. Tell Barbara the noodles were very nice but we had no time to cook any yet. But if they are as good as the last, they will do. Tell her we are going to cook some and invite some of our friends. The chickens and sausage were very nice and as there was no one home today but George and I, we cut the legs and wings off one and eat them, and when Leo come home we told him that one of the chickens had no legs. We are going to have some sausage for breakfast. Tell Mrs. Weibly we are much obliged to her for those things she has sent us but we have not tasted them yet. We are going to keep the pie for Christmas. Tell Aunt Betsy that was splendid butter she sent, also the pickles. The stockings were very nice but we had just drawn two pairs each, and will have enough of stockings for the winter. Tell her I would like to be up this winter to help to butcher but Uncle Sam has hired me for three years to butcher Rebels and I think I will stay with him. . . . The elderberry jelly is very nice but I don't think we will have much for sore throats. The other crock of Presirves is almost done for we can eat about a pint at one meal... The two big cakes will come in when their time comes and as regards the little cakes, they are gone alas like the many that have bloomed in the summer of our insides. The pepper came very handy. Tell George Foland the cider was elegant and if Mr Harder will take the jug we will send it with him for it is very nearly empty by this time. . . We were very well satisfied with the box and could not expect it better. Tell Cele we aint used to eating pound cake.

"We are going to have a grand dinner on Christmas and if you can make it convenient

Figure 2-8. Soldiers of the 13th Illinois Volunteers waiting for their rations to be cooked. Boxes from home, often sent by the Adams Express Company, supplemented the soldiers fare with good things to eat. *Leslie's Illustrated.* (K.R.)

to come, we would like very much to have you and all the family providing you bring the dishes with you. When any of the boys have company for dinner they have to run around and borrow a plate, tin & spoon. . . . So when you are all eating your big Christmas turkey just think of me standing guard out in the cold. We are both very well and contented and happy as the day is long. I must close by wishing you all a happy Christmas and a merry new year, a big turkey & lots of good things to eat."[29]

Reverend Robert A. Browne, chaplain of the 100th Pennsylvania Infantry "Roundheads" wrote home from Union-held Beaufort, South Carolina, to his own collection of "Round-heads." Browne wrote to his wife from his sick bed within the fortified foothold in South

Carolina about awakening to a beautiful morning of flowers, frost, and birds caroling in the trees.

"A happy Christmas to you and all my precious Round Heads at the Knolls! How I would like to have a line straight thru' from you this morning! But I am content to wait. I trust our Dear Father in Heaven for good news when it comes.

"I wish you could have heard with me the birds carol this Christmas morning, and see the flowers blooming now in the tumbler on my bureau. It is a lovely morning. Out of my window I see the sunshine resting on the waters and shores, the latter lying in blue haze. It is a scene of great beauty. We had this morning a good, sound, healthful white frost. Our regiment enjoys this as a holiday and have no drill.

". . . . A fine fire of pine billets blazes on my hearth, and as Sam is out at present I enjoy all alone this little interview with you on paper. I had out all my daguerrotypes, and I scanned them all with a great deal of satisfaction. After the 6 in the case I had Dr. Young and Mr. Kipick; and then Emma and Mary to look at-quite a fine collection, and among my most important treasures.

"I am now going to be permitted to express some books. I will make but a limited package, hoping to send more again. It will simply consist of something suitable for Christmas gifts, it will be valued all the more as being 'old, sesesch things.' When I get about I will see what I can buy from the negroes and send."[30]

On the civilian homefront many families were feeling the absences of loved ones, though the full import would not begin to be felt for another year. With the exception of families that knew losses through battle or sickness, Christmas would be a time of loneliness and concern for those away at the front. Occasionally, a moment of gaiety would brighten one's life. While soldiers faced daily drudgery in camp, life continued despite the war for civilians. Jobs had to be performed, as did the regimented routine of tending to domestic duties.

Civilian diarist and Southern wag J. B. Jones wrote sarcastically of an incident regarding a passport while working Christmas Day as a clerk in the Confederate War Department in Richmond.

"Mr. Ely the Yankee member of Congress, who has been in confinement here since the battle of Manassas, has been exchanged for Mr. Faulkner, late minister to France, who was captured on his return from Europe. Mr. Ely smiled at the brown paper on which I had written his passport. I told him it was Southern manufacture, and although at present in a crude condition, it was in the process of improvement, and that 'necessity was the mother of invention.'. . . He smiled again, and said he had no doubt we should rise to the dignity of *white paper*."[31]

Northern civilian Elizabeth Blair Lee wrote daily letters to her husband Commodore Samuel Phillips Lee. Elizabeth was a member of the Blair family that had had a hand in politics since the days of Andrew Jackson's "kitchen cabinet." Her husband was a less prosperous relative of the Lee family and himself a Virginian. On the 18th of December Elizabeth wrote to her husband who was commanding the Navy's North Atlantic Blockading Squadron.

"Blair is by me & sends Papa (X) a kiss just where he put it—I must go to the city to morrow for Christmas gifts—for Blair & the other children—I do hope you will get back here to spend Christmas with your boy & your affectionate Lizzie."

On Christmas Eve she would tell him of a special invitation for dinner.

"I went to finish my Christmas gifts up & to my amaze found invitations for Father Mother You & I—to dine at the White House I do wish you would come as I have to go—Mother has some rhumatism & will & indeed cannot go so Father insist that I must particularly since you are post Captain—That will force you to return here—as two post Captains will be too much in one expedition wont it?

". . . But I'll confess myself a lonesome woman this even[ing] when fixing out my boys Christmas pleasure—so many of my joys in him are lonesome—but he is getting stronger & better daily & you were well when I last heard—so I must & ought to be thankful—

"Nelly is very joyous over her little tribe & her preparations for them—Julia Turner is to spend Christmas with her—& they hope for a merry time—& as our little darling will rouse me early I must say good night & God bless you Ever your devoted Lizzie."[32]

Southern civilian diarist Mary Boykin Chestnut jotted down her melancholy feelings with a bit of a sarcastic edge. She was married to former U.S. Senator James Chestnut, a recently commissioned officer in the Confederate army who was serving on the staff of President Jefferson Davis.

"The servants rush in—'Merry Christmas,' &c&c&c—I covered my face and wept.

"Mr. C in good spirits, he is trying a new horse. As long as he has a dollar left in the

Figure 2-9. Santa Claus has delivered his gifts to this good child. Picture titled "Santa Claus and his Presents" from *Harper's Weekly.*

world it will go in horseflesh. If fate will leave him a fine horse to ride, she can never utterly depress him otherwise.

"At our Christmas dinner . . . There was everything nice to eat at that table. Romeo is a capital cook—and the pastry looked as good, with his plum puddings and mince pies. There was everything there that a hundred years or more of unlimited wealth could accumulate as to the silver, china, glass, damask—&c&c."[33]

Comic writer "Orpheus C. Kerr" (a play on the words office seeker), was the less famous contemporary of humorists Artemus Ward and Miles O'Reilly published in weekly newspaper installments.

"A Merry Christmas and Happy New Year, my boy, and the same to yourself. The recurrence of these gay old annuals makes me feel as ancient as the First Families of Virginia and as grave as a churchyard. How well I remember my first Christmas! Early in the morning, my dignified paternal presented me with a beautiful spanking, and then my maternal touched me up with her slipper to stop my crying. Sensible people are the women of America, my boy; they slap a boy on his upper end, which makes him howl, and then hit him on the other end to stop his noise. There's good logic in the idea, my boy. That first Christmas of mine was memorable from the fact that my present was a drum, on which I executed a new opera of my own composition with such good effect, that in the evening, a deputation of superannuated neighbors and old maids waited on my father with a petition that he would send me to sea immediately.

"But to return to the present, suffer me to observe that last Wednesday was celebrated by the Mackeral Brigade in a manner worthy of the occasion. Two hundred turkeys belonging to the Southern Confederacy were served for dinner, and from what I tasted, I am satisfied that they belonged to the First Families. They were very tough, my boy. . . ."[34]

Retired Presbyterian minister Reverend Charles Colcock Jones of Georgia, wrote to his son in the 1st Volunteer Regiment Georgia Artillery at Camp Claghorn. Feeling a sense of foreboding over the deepening conflict this Christmas Day, he called into question the salutation of the day.

"With the shadow of God's judgement and displeasure still resting over our beloved country, and no ray of absolute light breaking from any quarter, I do not know that we can greet each other with a 'Merry Christmas.' But the Apostle bids us 'rejoice in God always,' and this is the privilege of His people. Hoping we are such, we can rejoice that He reigns, that His ways are just and true, that His judgments are right, that we can commit ourselves and all that concerns us into his merciful care, and so rest upon Him to keep and sustain and bless us. We can rejoice in His mercies to our country in her struggle thus far, in His mercies to us and ours, and even see His tender mercies mingling in the cup of His severe afflictions put to our lips the past year. We can greet each other with 'Happy Christmas in our ever blessed God and Savior.' What vanity is all earth without the present favor of God and the hope of glory with Him hereafter!

"Our waking eyes have been saluted with the light of as brilliant a sun and as beautiful a day as this world ever saw. Your dear little one put her hands together and said her prayers as the sun arose; and soon after, the servants came with their 'Merry Christmas,' and our venerable old man wishing us and all ours 'peace all the days of our life, without difficulty or trial in the way; the Blessed Jesus was Lord and Master, in whom was all power and grace, and He was and would be to us the only Giver of all peace.' Next followed your sister's two sweet children, rejoicing in

their stockings stored with all manner of things pleasing to their eyes and ears and their taste."[35]

Benjamin Brown French, a Northern "yankee" political officeholder from New Hampshire, lived in Washington since 1833. An interested observer of the famous and influential policy makers in the Nation's capital, French recorded in his diary his Christmas tinged with melancholy.

"I have recd. as Christmas, from Mr. Forsyth a gallon of excellent brandy and a box of prime cigars. From Mary Ellen two silver labels for decanters, on which are engraved 'Whiskey' & 'Brandy.' From Ben two silk pocket handkerchiefs, from Mrs. Russell a beautiful Prayer Book, & from Mrs. Adams, a Backgammon Board. And so my Christmas of 1861 has passed away, and just at this moment it seems to me as if I little care whether I ever see another. . . .

"My eyes are heavy. I am lonely & sad—sad—sad. 'Is there no balm in Gilead and no physician there?' I think there is, & by & by the balm will come and the physician too, and I shall be healed..."[36]

Farther to the north in Dansville, New York, the *Dansville Advertiser* reported the holiday activities around the town from Christmas pageants held at the town churches to ice skating on the frozen Dansville pond. One article mentioned:

"St. Peter's Church was opened on Christmas Eve for divine services, its Rector, the Rev. Mr. Spaulding, officiating. After the usual service for the evening, he preached an appropriate and deeply impressive sermon, which was listened to with great attention by an appreciating audience. The church was decorated in a new and elegant manner. The decorations over the chancel exceeds anything of the kind we ever saw. From the pinnacle of the high-chancel window a graceful canopy was formed of wreaths of evergreens, drops to within ten feet of the altar; each side of the canopy is suported by triumphal arches, tastefully trimmed with evergreens, which were thrown over each lectern, or reading desk, the open space below the point of each arch, being tastefully relieved by elegant festoons of evergreen wreaths. We are unable to give a detailed account of the various decorations which graced the church. Suffice it to say everything corresponded with the description we have already given, and reflects great credit upon the Ladies of the congregation. The church was also opened on Christmas day and evening."[37]

Southern civilian Sallie Brock Putnam captured the emotions of many Southerners the first Christmas of the war in Richmond.

"Evenings at home, formerly spent in gayety and social amusement, were made pleasant and useful in the labors of love and duty which prepared comfortable hose for the soldier, or a warm visor or a fancy colored scarf, under the patronage of kind old Santa Claus, found their way to the Christmas-bag in the soldier's tent.

"Although it had become expediant to curtail numerous expenses, to retrench in this necessary, or to abstain from that, kind friends at home could not permit the sacred festival to pass by without some evidence of the former delightful manner in which it had been observed. If we sat down at a board less cheerful, or less bountifully provided with creature comforts, care was taken that our own dear ones in the field should not realize it.

"An extra turkey, a rosy ham, a jar of pickles, a jug of egg-nogg, or a large golden pound-cake were carefully prepared, secured in a strong box, into which found their way nameless other articles of cheer and comfort, and intrusted to the patron saint of Christmas, who rarely failed to make his way amid whizzing balls and crashing, bursting shells, to the white tent, with the luxurious dinner for the young soldier who was debarred from taking it at the homestead board.

"The Christmas season in Virginia has ever been one of the most genial hilarity and delight. After the church services of Christmas Day the remainder of the old year is devoted to merry-making. Dull care is thrown to the winds, and old hearts grow young, and young hearts grow glad at the happy festival. The faithful domestics are absolved from regular employment, and come in for their share of the Christmas bounties. An extra shawl, a bright plaid kerchief, a pair of gloves, or the cast-off clothes from the abundant wardrobe of the masters and mistresses, showed they were not forgotten when this delightful time came around for the interchange of presents; and many times the heart of the faithful slave, from the hoarded-up savings of months, to purchase for her the 'Christmas gift.'

"Never before had so sad a Christmas dawned upon us. Our religious services were not remitted, and the Christmas dinner was plenteous as of old; but in nothing did it remind us of days gone by. We had neither the heart nor inclination to make the week merry with joyousness when such a sad calamity hovered over us. Nowhere else could the heart have been so constantly oppressed by the heavy load of trouble as in Richmond, and the friendly congratulations of the season were followed by the anxious inquiries for the dear boys in the field, or husbands or fathers whose presence had ever brought brightness to the domestic hall, and whose footsteps were music to the hearts and ears of those to whom they were so dear." [38]

Among the ranks of the Orphan Brigade of Kentucky in the western army of the Confederacy, a mysterious scribe in the 4th Kentucky rendered his loyal and patriotic feelings on Christmas Day in the clothing account book of Co. C.

"Dec 25th, 1861, The birth of Christ our redeemer finds our country Struggling in the holy cause of liberty with the vile horde of Robbers & assasins sent to burn and destroy by their master Abraham Lincoln who occupies the chair at Washington."[39]

HARPER'S WEEKLY.

A JOURNAL OF CIVILIZATION.

VOL. VII.—No. 314.]   NEW YORK, SATURDAY, JANUARY 3, 1863.   [SINGLE COPIES SIX CENTS.
[$2 50 PER YEAR IN ADVANCE.

Entered according to Act of Congress, in the Year 1862, by Harper & Brothers, in the Clerk's Office of the District Court for the Southern District of New York.

Figure 3-1. Thomas Nast's first and least known Santa Claus was drawn for the year 1862 but appeared in the January 3, 1863 issue of *Harper's Weekly*. In keeping with Nast's efforts to support the war effort he is closely aligned with the Union Army. (K.R.)

3

A FESTIVE HOLIDAY FOR KILLING

he year 1862 fast running down to its conclusion had been a very bloody time. Battles had raged with increasing ferocity and savagery. The bloody clash of arms would inscribe battlefields at Shiloh (Pittsburg Landing), Jackson's Shenandoah Valley campaign, the Peninsula campaign, Second Manassas (2nd Bull Run), Antietam (Sharpsburg), Iuka, Corinth, Perryville, Prairie Grove, Fredericksburg, and Stones River (Murfreesboro) in the annals of American military history. Antietam would have the dubious distinction of being the bloodiest single day battle in American combat history with over 23,000 casualties.

The year also saw the beginning of a technological revolution when ironclad battleships dueled one another to a draw in the waters of Hampton Roads near Norfolk and Fortress Monroe. The end of the era of wooden-hulled ships was signaled in a practical demonstration when the *C.S.S. Virginia*

(*Merrimac*) attacked the Federal Naval Fleet on March 8 sinking the *U.S.S. Cumberland*, burning the surrendered *U.S.S. Congress*, and running the *U.S.S. Minnesota, Roanoke,* and *St. Lawrence* aground. The future of naval warfare had arrived with startling results. During the night the Union Navy's answer to the *C.S.S. Virginia* arrived in the guise of the turreted *U.S.S. Monitor* after a harrowing trip down the Atlantic coast.

The next morning the two ironclad ships were joined in a water-bound brawl that in the end produced no winner. Neither ship sustained serious damage—only dents to the iron plates and sheared heads from the bolts that kept them in place. The Union fleet continued to guard the exit to the Atlantic Ocean and waited anxiously for the Rebel monster to reappear. The career of the *C.S.S. Virginia* was cut short by Union forces advancing on Norfolk Naval Yard. To avoid capture the ship was blown up on the eleventh of May. By the end of the year the *U.S.S. Monitor* was swamped in a storm off the coast of North

Figure 3-2. The sinking of the *U.S.S. Monitor* during a storm off the coast of Cape Hatteras at midnight on December 30, 1862. From *Leslie's Illustrated.* (K.R.)

Carolina and joined her adversary in a watery grave on December 30. By then many more iron-clad ships were being built or already in service. A submarine named the *C.S.S. Hunley* would appear in the near future and change the face of naval warfare yet again.

The North would endure the first invasion by Confederate troops on its soil when Lee's Army of Northern Virginia crossed into Maryland seeking to rally Marylanders to join the Southern cause. Lee also hoped to relieve the Shenandoah Valley of pillaging Union troops so farmers could harvest needed crops to fill the army's larder, and there was the possibility of winning European recognition if the enemy could be defeated on his own home soil. Suffering a strategic defeat, Lee's vastly outnumbered army retreated back into Virginia, allowing President Lincoln to issue the Emancipation Proclamation in the wake of General McClellan's victory. The focus of the war would change on New Year's Day 1863. In addition to the preservation of the Union, the Federal Government was now determined to abolish slavery in the seceded states.

Christmas Day was between engagements for the main armies in the East and those in the West. On December 13 at Fredericksburg, the Army of the Potomac dashed itself against the stone wall of Marye's Heights in disjointed and ill coordinated attacks against the formidable position held by Longstreet's I Corps of Confederates. On the right flank of Lee's army, the Union troops breached Stonewall Jackson's line of the II Corps temporarily in the swampy lowland of Hamilton's Crossing before reinforcements and rallying troops plugged the gap. Most civilian inhabitants had evacuated the town and became refugees by the eve of battle. Those that stayed behind cowered in basements and saw the battlefield become a part of their front parlors. Houses suffered the indignities of shot and shell from the artillery of both armies, combined with the wanton looting and destruction by Union troops using the town for staging areas and snipers' nests. Many Fredericksburg families spent homeless Christmases and returned to badly damaged dwellings. Others moved in with relatives safer distances away from the path of the armies.

The other battle would barely take place outside the Tennessee town of Murfreesboro on New Year's Eve day and continue on into the new year. The inhabitants of Murfreesboro would play welcoming host and open their homes to Confederate officers and be celebrants of the holiday season on the eve of battle. Celebrations ran from the festive society wedding of cavalry hero John Hunt Morgan on December 14 till after Christmas. Following the culmination of battle west of town in the new year, Murfreesboro would become a vast hospital complex as every usable public building and many private homes cared for the wounded. The Confederate army of General Braxton Bragg evacuated Murfreesboro and left the town in the hands of the badly damaged Union army. The Confederate army had managed to repeat its earlier performance at Shiloh of badly mauling the Union army the first day, and then letting its enemy have time to regroup and administer a severe battering to the Confederates when they took the offensive a day later on January 2. The happy festive town on Christmas Day would become the sad charnel site of suffering and death seven days later.

Amid these two great battles, Confederate cavalry went calling on the Federal army in what became known as the Christmas Raid. The object of the raid was to disrupt General Ulysses S. Grant's overland campaign against the city of Vicksburg. Major General Earl Van Dorn was ordered to break Grant's supply line which would in turn force the advancing Yankees to retreat back to the state line for the remainder of the winter. Van Dorn's point of attack would be the new Federal supply base at Holly Springs on the Mississippi Central Railroad.

In mid-December, three brigades of cavalry numbering 3500 men left Grenada, Mississippi, in weather so harsh that some men wore half a dozen shirts under their coats to keep warm. The Confederate raiders stopped a few miles short of their destination on December 19. Van Dorn sent a scout familiar with the area to study the approaches to the town and the disposition of enemy troops. The scout returned before dark with the welcome news that the only activity planned by the Yankees was a Christmas Ball.

At dawn the next day Van Dorn launched a two pronged attack against the town, which succeeded in capturing most of the 1500 man garrison. A newspaper correspondent who accompanied the raiders later wrote. "The scene was wild, exciting, tumultuous. Yankees running, tents burning, torches flaming, Confederates shouting, guns popping, sabers clanking, women . . . frantic with joy, crying 'kill them, kill them'. . . ." By 8 o'clock in the morning Holly Springs was in the hands of the Rebels and with it enough supplies to feed and equip an entire army—much more than the swift moving raiders could hope to carry away.

Van Dorn ordered every building searched. That which was needed by the raiders was to be taken and everything else burned. Christmas came early for the hungry Rebels who picked their way through the warehouses and sutler's shops looking for hats, boots, and bolts of cloth to carry back to their wives and sweethearts. Van Dorn was surprised to find Mrs. Grant staying in the town at the time of the raid. He made sure that no harm came to her or any of the civilian population during his brief stay.

Van Dorn knew that even without the general's wife in the town, Grant would be sending every available man to block his escape. He quickly paroled his prisoners, ordered the railroad wrecked, and by 4 o'clock in the afternoon marched out of Holly Springs with a million dollars worth of Federal property flaming in the cold winter sky. For the next few days his men were constantly in the saddle. On Christmas Day his rear guard fought a delaying action at the town of Ripley, which allowed the main body to make good their escape. Three days later Van Dorn and his men returned to Grenada, having given Grant a Christmas present he was not happy to receive.

The 1862 *Harper's Weekly* Christmas edition (published January 3, 1863) showed a wondrous sight, as an illustration of Santa Claus gotten up in patriotic garb of red, white, and blue, visited with the soldiers handing out delectable goodies to young and old soldiers alike. An article called "Santa Claus Among Our Soldiers" appeared on the second page describing the illustrative visit.

"Children, you mustn't think that Santa Claus comes to you alone. You see him in the picture on pages 8 and 9 throwing out boxes to the soldiers, and in the one on page 1 you see what they contain. In the fore-ground you see a little drummer-boy, who, on opening his Christmas-box, beholds a jack-in-the-box spring up, much to his astonishment. His companion is so much amused at so interesting a phenomenon that he forgets his own box, and it lies in the snow unopened, beside him. He was just going to take a bite out of that apple in his hand, but the sight of his friend's gift has made him forget all about it. He has his other hand on a *Harper's Weekly*. Santa Claus has brought lots of those for the soldiers, so that they, too, as well as you little folks, may have a peep at the Christmas number.

"One soldier, on the left, finds a stocking in his box stuffed with all sorts of things. Another, right behind him, has got a meerschaum pipe, just what he has been wishing for ever so long.

"Santa Claus is entertaining the soldiers by showing them Jeff Davis's future. He is tying a cord pretty tightly round his neck, and Jeff seems to be kicking very much at such a fate.

"He hasn't got to the soldiers in the background yet, and they are still amusing themselves at their merry games. One of them is trying to climb a greased pole, and, as he slips down sometimes faster than he goes up, all the others who are looking at him have a great deal of fun at his expense. Others are chasing a greased boar. One fellow thought he just had him; but he is so slippery that he can't hold him, and so he tumbles over on his face, and the next one that comes tumbles over him.

"In another place they are playing a game of football, and getting a fine appetite for their Christmas dinner, which is cooking on the fire. See how nicely the soldiers have decorated the encampment with greens in honor of the day! And they are firing a salute to Santa Claus from the fort, and they have erected a triumphal arch to show him how welcome he is to them.

"But Santa Claus must hurry up and not stay here too long; for he has to go as far south as New Orleans, and ever so far out West; so he says, 'G'lang!' and away he goes through the arch like lightning, for he must give all our soldiers a Merry Christmas."[1]

Within the pages of *Harper's Weekly* was the story of "Santa Claus's Ball," an anonymously written tale of dolls spying and reporting to Santa Claus on the welfare of his young charges, their good or bad behavior that decided on who was worthy of presents or switches, and the special feeling soldiers' children had in Santa Claus's heart and thoughts. Dolls young and old danced and complained of ill-treatment at the hands of children, reporting who was left with little motherly attention, who died, and who was wanting. Santa Claus was saddened by the lack of playtime many children were receiving on account of the war forcing many to help with the supplying of aid societies with needed articles for the soldiers' welfare.

The Christmas centerfold for the year titled "Christmas Eve" showed a heartfelt scene of a mother praying at the moonlit window of her babies' room for the safe return of her husband in the army. Her husband meanwhile is looking at a photograph of his family in the cold winter camp beside a fire with solemn reflection bordering on homesickness.

An article titled "Christmas Eve" related the emotions many families on both sides of the conflict were feeling this sad holiday season with the exception of Union sentiments evoked in some passages.

"The clearly cherished anniversary of so many hundred years comes back again in all its sacred beauty and antiquity, kept by some with the time-honored custom of gathering together all the members of the family, near and distant, and distributing among them welcome tokens of affection, of which kind old Santa Claus is supposed to be the donor. The happy few may, perhaps, again this year celebrate their annual festivities; but oh! to how many will it be a season of sad, sad memories! On the left hand of our picture, on pages 8 and 9, we see the fond wife with the

Figure 3-3. Santa Claus's Ball. Story printed in the January 3, 1863 issue of *Harper's Weekly* in which dolls came from all parts of the country to tell Santa how they were treated by the children during the year. (K.R.)

Figure 3-4. Christmas centerfold entitled *Christmas Eve 1862* from *Harper's Weekly*, January 3, 1863. Reproduced courtesy of The Picture Bank, Alexandria, VA.

likeness of her brave soldier clasped to her heart, looking up to the moon and thinking that it is also on him, if indeed he is still above the sod, of which she, poor soul, has never-ceasing and bitter misgivings. The gentle moon shines just as brightly as it did last Christmas when he sat lovingly by her side, and they talked with delighted anticipation of the children's joy, when, on waking in the morning, they would find that Santa Claus had more than realized their fondest hopes in the gifts he had prepared for them. Notwithstanding the anxiety so painfully weighing on the mother's heart, it shall still be 'Merry Christmas' with the little ones; and as they lie nestling so sweetly in their little crib, she fills the little stockings, which have been expectantly hung in the chimney, with all they have so eagerly desired. Then she decks the room tastefully with greens, and hangs a wreath below the dear absent father's portrait, which greets the little ones with loving eyes as they awake. Meanwhile the vision of Santa Claus showering his gifts down the chimney comes to them in their merry, happy, little dreams, while his sleigh, laden with gifts, is impatiently waiting to jingle off to the next of his favorites.

"On the right of the picture sits the subject of these tender recollections. By the light of his campfire he can plainly see the loved faces looking up at him from the likeness he holds in his hand. As he gazes he fancies he is again with the dear ones at home; it seems as if the children's merry tones would momentarily ring out with gay laughter. He thinks he feels the clasp of his wife's hand, the slender fingers twined so caressingly round his own; but he raises his eyes, and his own dreary Christmas comes back to him in all its loneliness. The moon is shining down on a beautiful river, and plainly reveals the forms of two comrades on sentry duty. Quite near him is another, who, basking in the warmth of the fire, has fallen quietly asleep, the snow lying on the ground sparkles in the moonlight, and all is very still. But there is somebody who remembers the soldiers' Christmas. Behold Santa Claus driving along with merry speed, and as he goes he rapidly throws out boxes filled with good things by the thoughtful

hands at home, wherein the soldiers shall find enough to make them a jolly feast, and to drink the health of those they love so dearly.

"On the lower right-hand corner we see one of the many of our noble ships struggling with the storm; their duty this Christmas time is to be as active as ever on the watch for privateers, while others blockade rebel ports. There is no merry-making for them this holiday season; only to be tossed about the wild deep, while the great waves seem to toy with their strong vessel.

"On the lower left-hand corner our troops are marching along despite the snow which lies deep on the ground, and is still falling. 'Onward to Victory!' is the word, and they continue to press forward. Rains can not damp their martial ardor, snows can not chill those spirits, cold can not freeze the warmth of their love for freedom, peace, and Union.

"At the top is the Northern Light glowing behind Washington's tomb,....

"Below this are the peaceful graves of those who have numbered all the Christmases they will ever spend on earth. There they lie, side by side, buried on the field where they fought their last battle. The sad hearts of their mourning mothers, sisters, wives, and children can only find comfort in knowing that they nobly responded to their country's call, and that they yielded up their lives to its glory in as true a cause as ever made hearts beat with patriotic emotion. And so let them not mourn, but HONOR THE BRAVE!"[2]

Murfreesboro on a balmy Christmas Eve was the scene of the social climax of a long festive holiday season. A gala ball jointly hosted by the 1st and 2nd Louisiana was danced in the courthouse on the town square to a backdrop of magnificent cedar and evergreen decorations forming the initials of four of the army's generals. The regiments' lists of victories were hung over the windows and festooned with cedar boughs. One eyewitness described:

"the decorations of the hall were magnificent, and constructed with much taste and ingenuity. And if 'bright lamps' did not shine over 'fair women and brave men,' at least many candles did-behind each one a bayonet, which brightly reflected the light on the festive scene. . . . There were trees of evergreen with colored lanterns in them in the corners of the hall, and . . . flowers contributed by the Murfreesboro ladies, on the window-sills. There were two 'B's' entwined in evergreen, on one side of the hall, representing Bragg and Breckenridge, while just below it hung a magnificent regimental flag, and also, in different parts of the hall, a good many splendid trophies from the different battle fields—Yankee flags, captured by General John Morgan."[3]

The officer corps of the Confederate army was able to attend the ball in town and dance with the single women in attendance, the common soldiers camped across the countryside were not so lucky in their choice of company for Christmas. Many knew that a battle was imminent and many lived for the moment knowing with a battle soon due, the future was a dicey prospect at best. The officers of the 20th Tennessee gave to their men as a Christmas gift, a barrel of whiskey for merry-making. The purpose of the gift differed with the end result as one of the regiment's participants witnessed. "We had many a drunken fight and knock-down before the day closed."[4] With the exception of a few bloodied noses and assorted bumps and bruises, nobody sustained a serious injury or hurt feelings upon sobering up. But the pump was primed for the upcoming battle.

The men of another Tennessee regiment, the 154th, had similar problems as their sister regiment. One member stated, "Eggnog was fashionable and Captains, Lieutenants, and Privates was drunk and very troublesome."[5]

In other camps around Murfreesboro, the fun took a more constructive release of energy. James Hall of Manigault's Brigade of Alabamians and South Carolinians wrote to his father about the Christmas Day recreations in which the officers also joined in.

"We have tried to make a Christmas of it here. We have had foot races, wrestling and base[ball] playing. All the officers in our brigade . . . ran a foot race . . . and a rare time we had of it." After

the foot races were run, Hall reported the colonels "chose sides from among their officers and men to play base[ball]."[6]

Many of the troops in the Army of Tennessee were raised in Murfreesboro and the neighboring areas, and many Christmas furloughs were issued for periods of twelve and twenty-four hours. Others slipped away for an unsanctioned visit as knowing officers with a touch of Christmas spirit looked the other way. Spencer Talley of the 28th Tennessee went home to visit his mother in nearby Lebanon. Not only did he get a Christmas gift, but he got to play Santa Claus on his return to camp for his comrades that had stayed behind. His Christmas gift from his mother was:

"a goodly supply of heavy jeans and wool socks that reached well near the knees. Many of our neighbors had clothing ready for their sons and we had a full load of good clothing and other things to bring back to the boys in camp."[7]

Another adventuresome soldier named W. E. Yeatman of the 2nd Tennessee slipped home to Union occupied Nashville. Risking capture and a Yankee Christmas ticket to a Northern prison, Yeatman raked in the bounty of Christmas food and clothing. His mother gave him a special present that would prove to have an unhealthy attraction for Yankee target shooting.

"I remember that my mother decorated my felt hat with a lot of her old fashioned black Ostrich plumes, and the boys thought I was a General when I rejoined them."[8]

Johnny Green of the 6th Kentucky, part of the Kentucky regiments known as the Orphan Brigade, wrote of his Christmas dinner preparations of trial and tribulations outside Murfreesboro.

"Christmas was drawing nigh with all its sweet memories & longings. We had hoped this joyous season would find us on Kentucky's soil, with the invaders of our state driven north of the Ohio River.

"We had tents & each mess had built a chimney to their tent. Genrl Rosecrans was gradually drawing nearer & cavelry skirmishes were of daily occurance but we prepared to enjoy ourselves as long as we might; guard duty & dress parade were the extent of our daily duties and we prepared for a good Christmas dinner.

"A supply of liquor had been captured at Hartsville & from this source or some other those who wanted whiskey had it & some of the boys were good naturedly full I regret to say. I had gone to some farm houses in the neighborhood & bought some eggs & onions. I made a long hunt for a turkey but I was too late; all the turkey in the country had been sold, but I bought a goose & we proceeded to prepare mr goose. He was reported to be young but we were suspicious of his age so David Caruth who undertook to cook him first par boiled him, then stuffed him & roasted him. I made & cooked the biscuit & thought I was about to establish a reputation as a pastry cook for I made a pound cake which looked to be a complete success until I took it out of the oven & let it cool, then it sank in the centre & had a very depressing sadness in it, but we enjoyed it very much & talked of the loved ones at home & the pleasure we would have in recounting our experience to them when this cruel war was over."[9]

Sadly, it would be a memorable Christmas as the Orphan Brigade would be called out to witness the execution of their fellow soldier in the 6th Kentucky, Asa Lewis, for desertion. Feelings for the commanding general, Braxton Bragg, would be murderous and would be made of bad blood throughout Bragg's tenure as commander.

For Captain Jim Womack of the 16th Tennessee, the Christmas he experienced was depressing and solemn. A week before Christmas, Womack had gotten permission to ride to McMinnville to visit his ailing sister only to find she had passed away shortly before his arrival. Confessing in his diary the feelings that weighed heavily on his mind and keeping him from joining the merrymaking going on in his regiment's camp.

"Another Christmas is past and gone! How differently spent from that of '61! That I passed in Charleston and Fort Sumter, where I was delighted and plesed; this I have spent in my tent by the fire near Murfreesboro, attending to many of the duties of the soldier. May the coming Christmas in '63 find our now distracted and unhappy country reposing in the lap of . . . peace."[10]

The many soldiers in the Union army under General Rosecrans spent their Christmas in Nashville or the surrounding countryside in preparation for marching at any moment towards the Confederates at Murfreesboro. For some it was a solemn day in preparation for the inevitable battle to come, and for others it was a dreary day of routine duty. Many men were just trying to stay healthy from the diseases that spread through the camps felling many men, killing some while others spent long recoveries in camp hospitals. The troops tried to find some Christmas cheer and fun but were at a disadvantage being away from homes that many Confederates themselves were near.

A reporter for the *Cincinnati Commercial* and personal friend of General Rosecrans, W. D. Wickham filed his written account of the Christmas Eve bustle of activities and preparations taking place in the camps of the Union army scattered around Nashville.

"Orders for an advance of the Fourteenth Army Corps were issued Wednesday, the 24th December [1862]. The columns would move at daylight Christmas morning. Presently the camps blazed with excitement. The sturdy troops greeted the announcement with shrill clamor, which swelled its cheerful volume far along the ridges and down into the valleys, as musket volleys roll along a line of battle. There was glorious assurance in that manful uproar. The populous hills blazed with sparkling fires. Thousands were cooking rations for the march. The commissariat labored under manifold requisitions . . . Busy pens swiftly indited fond adieus, perhaps the last, to loved ones at home, and it was not long before the mails groaned under the weight of affectionate testimony from those brave hearts. The horseman carefully brushed his equipments, adjusted his last strap, looked well to his holsters, and patted his faithful charger kindly on his shining neck, as if soliciting his last proof of endurance and fidelity. The cannoneer burnished his trusty piece until it glistened, sighting it at imaginary foes, so soon to assume stern substantial form. Aides and orderlies thundered over the highways and through bustling camps, swiftly bearing messages. Here and there were tableaux of soldiers, earnest and animated, standing by the old flag at headquarters, talking of battles and of victory. Picturesque groups of officers in eager colloquoy, clustered about brigade and division marquees, now and then one swiftly mounting and away with orders. And the surgeon, in his tent, drew from his case the glittering blade at which the bold heart shrinks in fear which no mortal enemy can inspire."[11]

Jotting in his diary his thoughts of the contrast between camp and home, John Chilcote of the Ninetieth Ohio Infantry would ruminate;

"This is Christmas, and what a contrast between our Christmas and those who are home in good, comfortable houses, with plenty to eat and good beds to sleep in, and good nurses when sick. . . . The measles, mumps, chicken pox, small pox and about everything else has broken loose and taken hold of the boys. . . ."[12]

Another Ohio soldier with the 15th Ohio described his routine despite the holiday.

"Christmas day was no holiday for us. After breakfast we received orders to march with another foraging expedition at 8 o'clock. We took a road leading south from the Nolensville pike . . . and filled our wagons by 3 o'clock. Near the place . . . was a house where Christmas dinner had been prepared for some of our enemies, and some of our men either confiscated it or paid for it with counterfeit Confederate Script."[13]

Command and countermand were the orders of the day as David Lathrop explained in his diary the foolishness of the march endured by the 59th Illinois.

"Here we are in camp again. After loading our traps in the wagons we lay around promiscuously until yesterday noon, when we marched about five miles toward Nolensville, right about faced, and marched back again to the very spot we started from. 'Strategy, my boy!'"[14]

A soldier named George with the 1st Wisconsin, sent his sister a letter after the Battle of Murfreesboro from a camp near there, and detailed the presentation of a set of colors by the 4th Indiana Battery to his regiment on Christmas Day for gallantry in action in a past battle.

"I suppose you think I am lost but I am not. I am enjoying good health and hope you are the same. Christmas morning we was ordered to march at day light but the order was countermanded and during the day we had a set of colors presented to us by the 4th Indiana Battery which was inscribed on them the following words Presented to the First Regiment Wis Vol by the 4th Ind Battery for Gallant Conduct at Chapalin Hills Oct 8, 1862. Some of the officers of the 24th Wis was over to see the presentation drunk as fools. . . ."[15]

Henry Freeman recorded his Christmas reflections upon the preparations for a movement by the army and echoing a wistful thought heard throughout the war.

"Last night was Christmas Eve. It brought to my mind a thousand recollections of the past. The contrast is great. I sat up late in the evening at the fire, after attending to drawing rations, for we were under marching orders for this morning at five o'clock. A grand movement seems to be at hand. About eleven o'clock at night I heard heavy firing in the front. Where will the next Christmas Eve find me?"[16]

Mead Holmes, Jr. of the 21st Wisconsin Volunteers wrote letters to his hometown paper, the *Manitowoc Tribune,* for publication. From his camp outside Nashville on Christmas Day, Holmes wrote a description about the campsite the 21st inhabited while decrying the use of tobacco among his regiment.

"We are now in a beautiful wooded slope; fronting southward is our parade ground, forty acres, bounded on the south by a small creek, which affords plenty of good water for man and beast. This is in delicious contrast to some parts of Kentucky, where we drank water covered with slime so thick that a strong wind would not ruffle its surface, and water too, full of 'wrigglers,' went down the same channel.

"By the way, I am glad I never used tobacco. It is a serious inconvenience to the soldier. You would be amused to see the shifts to which the boys are driven. They chew it several times, then dry it for the pipe; some go to head-quarters and pick up the cigar buts, precious as pearls to them. This I consider equal to our droughts from the Licking River. Oh, the tyranny of appetite!

"It is Christmas; the grass is green, the birds are flitting from bough to bough, the squirrels are chirping, and so it is a 'merry Christmas' even in our camp. We march tomorrow a.m. Bragg's army is near, and we go to meet them with 'war's stern strength upon our souls' and the God of battles on our side. More anon."[17]

Colonel Hans Heg of the 15th Wisconsin attended a Christmas party where hilarity reigned in a schoolhouse near the 15th's camp. Much of the hilarity was provided by Heg when he and the brigade surgeon outfitted two soldiers in women's clothes and made a grand entrance at the door with their "dates." Colonel Heg arrived at the party "just as if I had a lady on my arm. . . . We kept the house roaring for a good long time."[18] Impervious to the rumors of an impending advance, Colonel Heg considered his men to be merry as the free flow of intoxicants distorted the reality of the countenances of many soldiers that Christmas.

Another officer with an Ohio regiment saw first hand the failure of many soldiers to keep their true emotions from showing while trying to celebrate Christmas spiritedly. Colonel Manderson of the Nineteenth Ohio saw the homesickness that tugged at many soldiers while they tried to party until it became an:

"all-pervading complaint . . . The men gathered about the camp fires during the evening hours with abortive attempts at merriment, soon to be given up, and then to talk in whispers of friends and family and home. The bugle calls, holding out the promise that balmy sleep might bring forgetfulness, were welcomed; although tatoo seemed a wail, and lights-out a sob."[19]

Private B. Francis Nourse of the Chicago Board of Trade Battery, an artillery battery raised and financed by stockbrokers in Chicago, was to see hard service in the upcoming battle, detailed his culinary and laundry attempts in his diary.

"25th. Christmas last night the order to march was countermanded after taps. This pleased us muchly. Nothing unusual today except that I cooked a mess of baked beans.

The second meal I ever cooked. Cooked them in a thin iron pan with a sheet of iron on top covered with coals (hot of course) then after din[ner] I mashed my C[offee] and threw too many things into the kettle. So when I took out my blue shirt it was yellow where ever it struck the sides of the kettle. Pleasant. Wonder where I be next C[hristmas]."[20]

Colonel John Beatty of the 3rd Ohio Infantry summed up his past twenty months of service in the army on Christmas Day while judging his holiday dinner for its lack of side dishes.

"About noon there were several discharges of artillery in our front, and last night occasional shots served as cheerful reminders that the enemy was near.

"At an expense of one dollar and seventy-five cents, I procured a small turkey and had a Christmas dinner; but it lacked the collaterals, and was a failure.

"For twenty months now I have been a sojourner in camps, a dweller in tents, going hither and yon, at all hours of the day and night, in all sorts of weather, sleeping for weeks at a stretch without shelter, and yet I have been strong and healthy. How very thankful I should feel on this Christmas night! There goes the boom from a cannon at the front."[21]

In Ripley, Mississippi, C. M. Cole's Christmas was anything but a pleasant holiday for him and his family as Union troops demanded food and quilts from them. Cole's mother described their family's holiday ordeal in a letter sent to her cousin Blanche in Franklin, Tennessee. Yankee troopers chasing after General Earl Van Dorn following a destructive raid by the Confederate officer and his troops, decided to make the civilian populace pay for any assistance given to the raiders.

". . . They, as usual, took our scanty supply of food and made us cook it, Christmas Day as it was. They came and demanded quilts and comforts. I told them I had none that I could spare. They answered insolently: 'It makes no difference about that; go and get them too.' I almost cried that I had to give my nice comforts to such swine, and I had none but nice ones. The officer with this party told papa that he had understood there was not a Union man in town. Papa told him: 'Not one that I know of.' "[22]

Artilleryman Jenkins Lloyd Jones spent his Christmas with the 6th Wisconsin Battery at Lumpkin's Mill, Mississippi. His battery had provided assistance to the infantry expedition deep into the Mississippi countryside and was returning to their base in Tennessee at a leisurely retreat.

"Christmas! Christmas! resounded through the camp this morning: everyone turning the gay reminiscence of the past in their minds and hoping again to enjoy. Laid quiet during the day. Ate a Christmas dinner of dumplings and unleavened bread. The howitzers ordered to prepare to march, going in charge of a provision train to Memphis. Troubled with bad cold."[23]

Lieutenant Henry A. Kircher of the 12th Missouri illuminated his Christmas of toasting on board the steamboat *Thomas E. Tutt* in a letter to his mother from the Yazoo River where Kirchner would see action several days later at Chickasaw Bayou.

"So we arrived on December 25, 1862, at 4 o'clock in the afternoon at the mouth of the Yazoo, and threw anchor here during the night. We spent Christmas night like all other evenings, days and hours on the boat; one snored, most played cards, others read or chatted about the past. If one compared this pitiful evening with the preceding ones, which was awaited so beautifully, so desirously with impatience, this talk did not help anything at all. Finally, with great effort and might, so that everybody would not stretch his dwindling purse too extremely and rob it of its last few coinlets, because before Christmas everyone could at least see what his fate in this world was, it was possible to get a bottle of brandy from the bow of the boat. So everybody could greet his distress with a not any too great sip of the noble juice of the grain and in this way to soften his sufferings a little, and you can imagine that the rebels were damned and cursed.

"I was the only one who was consoled, for I received a Christmas present, and it was you again who thought of me. The chaplain had given me the 2 pairs of socks and the chocolate the evening before, so I had cause to be more contented than the others, except I would very much have liked to have had a letter from you with pictures of you all in it. I keep thinking the chaplain had a letter for me and that it got lost while he was performing his office and proud duties.

"In short, I comforted myself with the hope that there will also be good times sometime again."[24]

The 1st Missouri Battery had seen recent action in the Battle of Prairie Grove in Arkansas. Camped on the Arkansas River near the town of Van Buren, Captain S. T. Ruffner related a humorous tale about the "Christmas alarm."

"An amusing incident occured here on Christmas Eve. About dark a squad of men came to the river bank to bury a comrade, a noncommissioned officer, who had died in camp. Having interred the body, they fired the customary volley over the grave. The troops up the line, thinking it was a Christmas salute, commenced firing their muskets, and the contagion spread until there was a roar of firearms along the whole line, the battery joining with two guns. Presently a mounted orderly from headquarters dashed up and put the battery men under arrest. We were marched half a mile through the brush and darkness and rain to Frost's headquarters. One of Parson's infantry regiments was filing out, having received their lecture, when we arrived. The General was standing on an empty dry goods box before a blazing fire, apparently feeling good, for he had been to town, and it was Christmas. This was his speech: 'Soldiers, before I say anything I will read you an order which I have just received from General Hindman at Van Buren. A courier has just arrived with his horse all afoam, saying: "General, heavy firing has been heard in the direction of your camp since an early hour this evening. Has the enemy engaged you? I hope you are not permitting Christmas firing." And what should I hear on the receipt of this order but a salute from Ruffner's Battery. Now, this has been done without the command or consent of the captain by one man or a few men; and if the man or men who did it will make themselves known, I will do nothing further than turn them over to General Hindman. Otherwise the whole company will have to suffer; and any man or set of men who will permit others to suffer for what they have done is a dog.' This was not consoling, for Hindman had men shot by the wayside. To the surprise of everybody, one man, Jim Kelly, stepped to the front, saying, 'I am one of them;' then another and another (three), at which Dr. Small, a German staff surgeon, standing by, exclaimed: 'Prave men, pravemen!' The company was ordered to quarters, and the three men held under arrest. The next day at meal time they come walking into quarters, saying that their guards had left them and gone to dinner and they thought they would do the same."[25]

In Lexington, Kentucky, David Humphrey Blair of the 45th Ohio Volunteers, wrote to his wife about the music and other entertainments in Camp Ella Bishop and the prohibition of whiskey.

"We have had a prety Merry Christmas today and it made me think of home We had a brass band in camp which almost charms one that has not heard any sich musick for 5 or 6 months and we had several darkies with their fiddles. And the boys danced and played ball and pitche horse shoes etc. etc all day and the sutler gave a treat of a barrel of apples to each Co. in the morning and the officers gave us all the oysters and fresh sausage we could eat for supper so if old Humphrey Marshall comes in tonight or in the morning we will be able to attend him There is one good thing for Christmas They would not allow any whiskey sold in town for a few days If the boys could have got whiskey there would have been some confusion. . . ."[26]

Colonel Thomas Wentworth Higginson commanded one of the first regiments of former slaves and a number of freedmen along a foothold on the South Carolina coast. An ardent abolitionist, Higginson's career included riding with the fervent John Brown in Bloody Kansas during the 1850's and was a member of the Secret Six that helped to underwrite Brown's invasion of Harper's Ferry. The 1st South Carolina went from a ragtag outfit to a disciplined regiment of soldiers freeing other slaves from former plantations, fighting skirmishes with Confederate irregular forces, and providing pride and contributions of sacrifice for those which the war was soon to become the main focus of the war.

On Christmas Day Colonel Higginson noted in his diary the meaning of the day for the former slaves under his command in a tone of paternalism.

"Christmas Day.
'We'll fight for liberty
Till de Lord shall call us home;
We'll soon be free
Till de Lord shall call us home.'

"This is the hymn which the slaves at Georgetown, South Carolina, were whipped for singing when President Lincoln was elected. So said a little drummer-boy, as he sat at my tent's edge last night and told me his story; and he showed all his white teeth as he added, 'Dey tink "de Lord" meant for say de Yankees.'

"Last night, at dress-parade, the adjunt read General Saxton's Proclamation for the New Year's Celebration. I think they understood it, for there was cheering in all the company-streets afterwards. Christmas is the great festival of the year for this people; but, with New Year's coming after, we could have no adequate programme for to-day, and so celebrated Christmas Eve with pattern simplicity. We omitted, namely, the mystic curfew which we call 'taps,' and let them sit up and burn their fires, and have their little prayer-meetings as late as they desired; and all night, as I waked at intervals, I could hear them praying and 'shouting' and clattering with hands and heels. It seemed to make them very happy, and appeared to be at least an innocent Christmas dissipation, as compared with some of the convivialities of the 'superior race' hereabouts."[27]

In Augusta, Georgia, where military movements and fighting were non-existent, Ella Gertrude Clanton Thomas had as prosperous a Christmas in the South as civilians could muster. But the war was always close at hand as Augusta was the key center for producing gun powder. The blockade was beginning to take effect, although essential supplies and extra material items that made life a little more pleasant could still be gotten. Santa Claus had once more breached the blockade to bring Christmas joy to the children of the South, at least at the Clanton household. A Christmas tree would be set up for the first time in the family's Christmas observance.

"I gave Jeff a wheelbarrow at $1.50 and a whistle. His Aunt Anne gave him a jumping Jack, Aunt Co, a jointed dog—I, a dog knife and his Pa, 50cts. I had forgotten two of Turner's toys—a balloon from Uncle Jimmie and a triangle from Uncle Holt. To Cora, Mr Thomas gave the subscription for the *Field & Fireside* for this year, to Holt a dollar, to Joe and Cate 50cts. I gave Joe a dancing Jack, but could not find the whistle I bought for him. To little Mary [Vason] I gave a doll, dressed, and to Kate a sett of graces. Ma gave me a hansome Valenciennes [lace] pointed collar.

"For the first time, we had a Christmas tree which Mamie, Cora and Lizzie arranged in the girls' room and did not exhibit until the next morning after breakfast very much to the delight of all concerned. Turner was very much afraid Santa Claus would not bring him anything as he has a shrewd suspicion who Santa Claus is. Ma gave us an elegant dinner. For the first time in six years we all assembled around the table together and if Pinck had been able to have joined us the party of sons in law would have been complete. To form some idea of the extravagant prices of things and to compare them with the better times which I hope are coming, I will mention that the apples for the dessert were 10 cts. apiece, the oranges 30 and 40 cts., the icing of the pound cake, &1.50. As to the expense of the various items forming the Charlotte Roose, syllabub and &c, I can only conjecture. The baked and boiled turkey would alone have cost 8 dollars. . . . 'Where I shall be this time next year?' How little I imagined that this Christmas would find me at Belmont—my husband at home, my children all well—my father's family in happiness and health and with the exception of Pinck's illness nothing but prosperity. . . .'"[28]

Christmas before Fredericksburg was a somber affair for the most part for the troops in the Union army as many had lost comrades and friends in the recent battle. Confederates also were not as boisterous as the lack of supplies made Christmas dinners wanting in amount and quality. General Lee found nothing to celebrate in his recent victory as it was a hollow victory to him. The Union army was still encamped across the Rappahanock River, European recognition of the Confederacy's right to exist was all but dead, and even though the Army of Northern Virginia had been victorious, they were still not as well supplied as the beaten foe across the way. But as all soldiers are want to do in times of hardship, they made the best of the situation and found something with which to make merry the day.

John Lee Holt writing in a letter to his wife from camp near Fredericksburg, told her of the loneliness and hope for a furlough while the regiment endured the loss of soldiers, not from battle, but desertion. A member of the 56th Virginia ("Charlotte Greys"), it has been sixteen months since he has been home to see his wife and family.

"Today is Christmas eve Tomorrow is Christmas agin & here we are around our camp fire again instead of being at home enjoying ourselves with the ones we love best as we were want in days gone by to spend the Merry Christmas Holy days Oh how much happier I would feel today were I with you all to spend the Christmastide even if I could stay but a short time I was greatly rejoiced Tuesday at the reception of your most precious letter of the 13th inst It had been so long since I heard from you Thus I was more anxious than usual to hear from you I was truly glad to hear you were all well & hope the Lord of love & mercy may continue to bless you with good health & all other needful blessings 5 of our company deserted a few nights ago &

went home to spend the Christmas. There are a good many leaving the army in the same manner some 25 or 30 in all from our Regt & They have sent out squads of cavalry to arrest them & bring them back It will be very apt to go very hard with them deserting as they did in the face of the enemy Jno Smith & Pete are among those that left our company I wish to go home very much indeed but not in that way. Col Stuart says that no effort will be liking [lacking] on his part for those who have faithfully stuck up to their duty to go home this winter if there is any chance It is thought the Yankees will have to move into winter quarters & if they do the Col thinks we can get the chance to go home. The latest papers state there is a terrible stir in Washington on account of their late defeat Members of the Cabinet resigning etc. I hope things will change for the better before long. . . . As I believe I have written all the news I can think of at present, Wishing you all as Merry a Christmas as possible I must bid you good bye for the present."[29]

Journal entry of Franklin Lafayette Riley with the 16th Mississippi, described the destruction of Fredericksburg during the recent battle. His view of the loss in the city matched his feelings of loss and homesickness being in the army and away from his loved ones.

"Weather continues moderate. Changed camp about a mile to obtain wood. Spent the day chopping poles and building a bunk. Began bringing the comforts of home from our old camp. Went to town. The city is badly damaged from the shelling—and looting—by the enemy. Bits of china and pieces of furniture still lie in the streets. Some of the residents have returned, but they are in pitiful condition. The children won't have much of a Christmas celebration. Nor will we. I miss Bal very much. There is some comfort (not much) in knowing that, if she is looking at the heavens to-night, she sees the same stars I do. So we are not so far apart after all."[30]

Captain Henry A. Chambers penned in his diary about the dispensing of drill for his regiment of the 49th North Carolina for the holiday on an unusually balmy day for December.

"Christmas! What a crowd of bye-gone associations crowd upon the mind upon this almost universal holiday! It seems to be a mile post to mark the intervals as we travel back to the days of infancy.

"*Christmas in Camp* was for a holiday an extraordinarily dull time. It reminded me of a quiet Sunday. Our commanders were kind enough to dispense with all but necessary duties to-day. It was a warm and beautiful day. Nature seemed to smile upon this war afflicted land of ours."[31]

Another North Carolinian, Constantine A. Hege of the 48th, wrote home to his parents about the search for his Christmas box and the loneliness contrasting with his Christmas from the year before. Hege in his religious upbringing was a Moravian. Captured the following year at the Battle of Bristoe, Hege spent time in Old Capital Prison in Washington before signing the oath of allegiance and going home to his folks in 1864.

"There is a great deal of sickness here in camp such as pneumonia, panders and various other diseases. . . I have not yet got my box and I expect never will get it because I got Capt Michel to go to Gordonsville and Hanover Junction to search for my box, but he could not see nor hear anything of it and therefore I expect it has been stole because it is a very common thing for boxes to be robbed about here and there fore I think it is useless to depend upon getting that box any longer. . . . Christmas has come once more and it is very a beautiful morning here, but O! how changed the scene to what it was last Christmas, here I am in the army to day and to day twelve months ago I was home where I could enjoy the blessings of a comfortable house and home of parents and friends and of religious worship, but this Christmas I am surrounded by warriors, cannons, guns, and all kinds of unusual sounds and actions to which I never was accustomed to. . . But I hope and pray that the good Lord in his tender mercy may soon bring this state of things to an end and restore Peace and prosperity to our beloved Country again and turn the hearts of the rulers to peace for ever instead of war. . . . Be assured dear parents I remain your affectionate son until death."[32]

Samuel Pickens of the 5th Alabama Regiment listed in his diary the rations received by him and his messmates. Disappointment was the order for the day as Pickens looked forward to a taste of eggnog.

"Wednesday December 24th: Christmas Eve & a dull prospect for to-morrow. We moved camp about a mile & 1/4 to where there is plenty of wood. We may stay here a month or more if not called away by the Yanx . . . I rec'd no letters but a nice lined blank. & havelock Mama sent. Thursday December 25th: Dull Christmas less like one than any ever saw—Ed, Pasteur & I are to spend it in the delightful way of standing guard. A fiddle which has been introduced into camp & which some one is jerking at is only thing that reminds of what Christmas formerly was— This clear mild day & most pleasant weather we've had for a good many Christmases. This evening Ellison came & brot a little Christmas. Never saw such crowd as collected round him. Our mess got 12 doz-cakes (sugar) & some ginger bred, $2 candy, $5 sugar, bundle Confed. coffee, $2 pepper & lb. butter. He was to bring us the materials for an Egg Nog—but he sorely disapointed us in that—about the first Christmas ever spent without nog. . . ."[33]

Reverend James B. Sheeran, Catholic priest for the rough and tumble Louisianians of the 14th Louisiana of Starke's Brigade (led by Colonel Pendleton since Starkes death at Antietam), nixed a Christmas gift he caught wind of, and had the men donate a nice Christmas present to an orphanage.

"Having heard some intimations that the boys were about to make me a Christmas present, I took occasion to inform them that I did not stand in need of it but if they wanted to honor our Infant Savior they might bestow their charitable gifts to his representatives, the poor orphans of St. Joseph's Asylum in Richmond. They acted on my suggestion and during the following week made up among themselves a very handsome sum of $1,206."[34]

Homesickness filled the otherwise quiet Christmas John Welsh of the 27th Virginia re-lated by letter to his wife. ". . . Yesterday was Christmas and a very quiet one it was the day was very fine and everything quiet I should liked very much to have been at home to have eaten that turkey but I couldent and it is no use to fret so I set down and eat our bread & beef and was satisfied. . . ." The colonel of the same regiment, James K. Edmondson, nearly despaired the state of his Christmas until Christmas morning arrived "a box of very nice eatables." Packed lovingly by his wife in Lexington, the victual contents included a turkey.[35]

The Christmas Corse's Brigade encountered was considered a dull one with the exception of good cheer provided by the Brigade sutler. George Wise remembered the second Christmas:

"to us was a dull one; very few extra edibles were handed around, and only a sprinkling of liquor was to be had outside of the joyous group that encircled the table spread by the energetic and gentlemanly caterer, Mr. Jonah White, our worthy Brigade sutler; his good things were well received and much enjoyed by his numerous friends."[36]

The 13th Virginia left the environs of Fredericksburg and marched to Port Royal where they went into winter camp. Fraternizing with the Yankee pickets across the Rappahannock River, members of the 13th talked, gossiped, and traded plentiful Southern tobacco for very rare coffee and sugar from the Yankee's haversacks. Even "occasionally a nice drop of whiskey" was obtained from the curious foe. One sergeant decried the holiday as "most unpleasant," while the chief musician logged it in his diary as a "Poor Christmas! Not even a drop of spirits." Another soldier, Private Reuben E. Newman had a decidedly more enjoyable Christmas when he joined the family of Parson Price, whose home he had been detailed to guard. The daughter played the piano and with a grand dinner under his belt, Newman proclaimed, "What soldier can boast a better Xmas than this!"[37]

The lack of liquor for making eggnog or just for imbibing was a common complaint among Confederate soldiers this Christmas. Whether from lack of money or availability, alcohol and even provisions were sharply in contrast to the abundance that abounded in Christmas of '61'.

One soldier of the 12th Virginia scribbled a letter home lamenting that the fare on "Christmas day [was] the poorest ever spent, no egg nog, no turkey, no mince pie, nothing to eat or drink but our rations. We all talk of home today and wish to be there."[38] The pull for home had a stronger attraction for others as many men left on leave without permission to spend Christmas with their families. The consequences suffered by those unlucky to be caught by Lee's provost guards, and a strong sense of duty kept many others toiling in the ranks.

The men of the 4th South Carolina had a rather unique way of obtaining the fundamental ingredient for which to make merry frivolity during Christmas week. Lieutenant Richard Lewis narrated the tale of the impersonation of an officer and its consequence in a letter to his mother.

> "We had a terrible spree in camp one night during Christmas week, the boys nearly all getting drunk and kicking up a terrible hurrah! Earle Lewis, of my company, organized a so-called provost-guard, and, after I lay down that night, slipped my sword and uniform out of my tent and doffed himself off with it, and went around the different stations that night, where he knew some men in the Virginia brigades had whiskey to sell, and captured it and brought it into camp that night, under the pretence that he was a provost guard from Longstreet's headquarters, arresting the men, but turning them loose, all being glad to get liberty rather than go, as they thought, to headquarters. Such a day of reckoning and judgment we have never had, and I hope will never have again. General (Micah) Jenkins had us all ordered out, and an address read to us reprimanding us very severely for our drunken and disorderly conduct."[39]

General Robert E. Lee was in no mood to feel joyous this Christmas. He was not happy over the trumpeting of the victory at Fredericksburg by the press and the politicians in the Confederate Congress. He had written to one official that though the army had won a victory, it had been a hollow one and no reason for rejoicing. The enemy still sat on the opposite side of the river despite the pummeling it had received, reasoned Lee.

Amid the regular routine of his day, Lee dashed off a Christmas Day letter to his daughter Mildred in Raleigh, North Carolina.

> "I have pleased myself in reminiscences to day, of the many happy Xmas' we have enjoyed together at our once happy home [Arlington House]. Notwithstanding its present desecrated & pillaged condition, I trust that a just & merciful God may yet gather all that He may spare under its beloved roof. How filled with thanks & gratitude will our hearts then be! But in the meantime let us not forget how abundantly He has blessed us in our condition & should it please Him eventually to establish our independence & spare our lives, all will be well. I cannot tell you how I long to see you. When a little quiet occurs & my thoughts revert to you, your sisters & mother, my heart aches for our reunion. Your brothers I see occasionally. . . . Confined constantly to camp & my thoughts occupied with its necessities & duties, I learn little of what is occurring beyond its confines. I am however happy in the knowledge that Genl Burnside & his army will not eat their promised Xmas dinner in Richmond to day. I trust they never will. You must write to me sometimes you precious child, without waiting for me to reply. I have little time for writing to my children. But you must be sure that I am always thinking of you, always wishing to see you."[40]

Across the Rappahanock River opposite Fredericksburg, the camps of the Union army were trying to recover from the recent battle enough to raise some festive holiday cheer. The gamut of emotions ran from one of boredom and dullness to drunkenness and sporting recreation. Major and regimental Adjutant Frederick L. Hitchcock of the 132nd Pennsylvania Volunteers remembered the Christmas his regiment spent in sporting games and Christmas gill of whiskey per man. Trouble was, many men knew the secret of the old poll trick of vote and vote often. Hitchcock wryly noted the festivities in camp and shed some light on an old army delicacy.

Figure 3-5. Edwin Forbes captured the loneliness of a soldier away from home in *A Christmas Dinner*. Reproduced courtesy of The Picture Bank, Alexandria, VA.

"My diary notes that on Christmas Day we actually had a little sunshine, and that by way of adding good cheer to the occasion a ration of whiskey was issued to the men. The ration consisted of a gill for each man. Each company was marched to the commissary tent, and every man received his gill in his cup or drank the measure, as he preferred. Some of the men, who evidently were familar with the intricacies of repeating in ward elections, managed in various ways to repeat their rations of this vile stuff until we had a good deal more than a gill of whiskey's worth of hilarity in camp. However, the noise was winked at, believing it would soon subside and pass off. All drills were suspended and the men allowed passes freely out of camp, being required to be in quarters promptly at taps. The officers passed the day visiting and exchanging the compliments of the season. The wish for a 'Merry Christmas' was about all there was to make it such. I remember our bill of fare for Christmas dinner consisted of boiled rice and molasses, 'Lobskous' and stewed dried apples. The etymology of the euphonious word 'Lobskous' I am unable to give. The dish consisted of hardtack broken up and thoroughly soaked in water, then fried in pork fat. I trust my readers will preserve the recipe for a side dish next Christmas. One of the boys, to show his appreciation of this extra fare for Christmas dinner, improvised the following blessing:

'Good Lord of love
Look down from above
And see how a soldier's grub has mended,–
Slushed rice, Lobskous, and shoat,
Where only hardtack and hog were intended.'

"The day was not without its fun, however. Among other things, an impromptu footrace was gotten up between the Fourth New York and our regiment."[41]

There followed a footrace with the members of the "Bloody Fourth" New York regiment between the Pennsylvanians and a professional racer for the New Yorkers. The race went off with the 132nd's racer starting off "like a frightened deer, literally running away from the professional from the start and beating him leisurely in the end by more than a dozen feet." The New York fix lost to a Pennsylvania country boy.

Colonel Charles B. Haydon of the 2nd Michigan fondly remembered Santa Claus filling his stockings in years past. On Christmas Day, dinner consisted of a bill of fare a touch more lively than he or his messmate bargained for. On Christmas Eve his homesickness showing through, wrote,

"... If I knew the exact state of affairs around the old fireplace at home I might feel more at ease. Father has long been sick & though now reported better I half suspect that is more from regard to my feelings than the facts. I will hope cheerfully for the best. May Santa Claus to night fill the stockings of all the little ones as he used to mine in days of old & may 'Merry Christmas' be no idle words but full of truth & meaning and good health & good cheer make glad the house hold."

On Christmas Day, dinner consisted for Haydon what he hoped would be palatable beef and hardtack.

"Weather warm which is fortunate for our fireplace smokes wonderfully. We made Christmas dinner on beef, hard tack & coffee. I had fortunately completed my meal when Moore made a discovery which checked him midway in his, viz that the hard tacks were full of bugs & worms. This is no uncommon thing of late but his wry face was the most laughable thing of the day."[42]

John Haley of the 17th Maine of General O. O. Howard's Division, spent Christmas Day in a state of anticipation while on a work detail. When he got back to camp, he was disappointed about the arrival of his Christmas box when his tentmate played a practical joke on him. On Christmas Eve Haley projected that,

"It is rumored that there are sundry boxes and mysterious parcels over at Stoneman's Station directed to us. We retire to sleep with feelings akin to those of children expecting Santa Claus. We have become very childish in some matters—grub being one of them.

"Christmas Day. Went on a detail making corduroy roads. It was a dismal day but rendered quite endurable by the anticipation of what was in store in our boxes. On returning to camp, I was informed by my tentmate that there was no parcel at the station bearing my name. My mental thermometer not only plummeted to below zero, it got right down off the nail and lay on the floor. Seeing this, my tentmate made haste to dive under the bed and produce the box, which he had brought from the station during my absence, and in but a few minutes we were busy discussing the merits of its contents. Most of the men have been remembered, and any that have not received something from home are allowed to share with their more unfortunate neighbors."[43]

Dullness and routine was the experience of the balmy holiday for Thomas Aldrich and the men of Battery A of the 1st Rhode Island Light Artillery recovering from the recent losses of casualties.

"On the 25th [December 1862] my diary says: 'A Merry Christmas!' That sounded well but it was what the people at home would call a very dull one. There was nothing but the regulation hard-bread and pork for breakfast, dinner, and supper. It was quite warm and a fine day, with no duty except the regular camp duty, and a general day of visiting among the other batteries. I went over to Battery B and saw some of them, and found them feeling well after their terrible losses in action."[44]

John C. Williams from the New England regiment of the 14th Vermont, was hearing rumors of a compromise settlement with the Confederates. Despite his claims of not believing it, this camp gossip really bothered him and brought out an abolitionist and ardent Unionist streak in his Christmas diary notation.

"There are various rumors afloat concerning our future movements, none of which I credit. News has come that a compromise is to be effected with the rebels, which is not creditable. No compromise with treason, is my motto. Nothing short of a vigorous prosecutions of the war, until treason shall yield unconditionally. This strife can never be ended permanently, but by the sword and bayonet. Now is the time, if ever, to end this unholy war. Slavery, the wicked fomenter of this horrible strife, should die, so that it shall never again be the cause of a rebellion like this, and ravage the most beautiful country on earth.

"This is Christmas, and my mind wanders back to that home made lonesome by my absence, while far away from the peace and quietude of civil life to undergo the hardships of the camp, and may be the battle field. I think of the many lives that are endangered, and hope that the time will soon come when peace, with its innumerable blessings, shall once more restore our country to happiness and prosperity."[45]

For members of the 1st Minnesota who had been in the firestorm of lead at Fredericksburg, Christmas was anything but a happy time. Except for a little Christmas fare, Minnesotan James Ghostley saw "nothing to put me in mind of its being Christmas except to be eating the cake Sister Emma sent." Another member of the regiment, Mathew Marvin, complained about his lack of Christmas spirit. "Christmas but cant see it. . . . No luxeries of any kind to be had."[46]

Infantryman Frederick Pettit from the "Roundheads Regiment" of the 100th Pennsylvania, described the refugees and destruction of Fredericksburg. He then went on to tell his mother and sister in separate letters about his Christmas day and dinner.

"This part of Virginia was inhabited by much the same class of persons in regard to wealth as those about New Brighton and New Castle. No doubt their children were dissatisfied with their old fashioned parents and homes, and complained because they did not live in style like the fashionable in Fredericksburgh. But look! How changed is their condition now. The most of them have left their home and are now wandering through the South in a naked condition; while those that remain are but little better. Everything of value has been taken from them not even their personal clothing and household furniture being left. I have seen young women here who were once comfortable, dressed in clothing made of old grain sacks and blankets. These sights do not make the feeling soldier very contented when he knows that his own sisters may be in the same condition in a few years if the war continues. And then hear that they are discontented with their present comfortable house makes me fear that God may yet bring them to see the road of need.

"I have nothing now to write. I am still in good health. The weather is quite warm for the season. Christmas passed very quietly. I procured a pint of beans and boiled them with a piece of pork for my Christmas dinner. They were excellent."

To his sister Mary, Pettit would jot a few words similar, but with a subtle difference, to those written to his mother.

"Since we returned from the other side of the river nothing of importance has taken place. You wished to know how I spent Christmas. Doing nothing. Emphatically nothing. It was as quiet a Christmas as I have ever spent in my life. For my dinner I had a mess of beans and pork boiled, which were equal to any-thing I have eaten lately. We now have good rations and plenty of them."[47]

Edward King Wightman of the 9th New York Hawkin's Zoaves, found something to be happy about and listed all the victuals and prices the sut-lers had laid in stock for the soldiers to relieve their pockets of script received during the pay-master's visit at Falmouth, Virginia.

"We enjoyed Christmas hugely here. There were multitudes of sutlers around with every-thing that nobody wanted to buy. Some, though, had eatibles [sic], as for instance, butter at $.75-1.00 per lb; cheese, $.50 or $.75 per lb; sausages, $.50 per lb; apples, 6 for a quarter, etc. On Wednesday I got a pass and went to Falmouth but could get nothing for a Christmas dinner but a haversack full of meal at $.05 per lb. and 3 small papers of black pepper at $.08 each. Next day we were lucky enough to get a bottle of pepper sauce for $.40, which made our pork very palatable.

Figure 3-6. Sutlers were the Civil War equivalent of the Post Exchange. Edward Wightman, a mem-ber of Hawkin's Zoaves, wrote "There were a multitude of sutlers around with everything that nobody wanted to buy." *Leslie's Illustrated.* (K.R.)

Our dinner consisted of fresh meat boiled and spiced with pepper sauce, crackers buttered and crowned with toasted cheese sprinkled with black pepper, boiled pork cut up in pepper sauce, 2 onions in vinegar, and a pan full of warm mush. The whole was washed down with 1/2 a bottle of what was called port wine, the 1/2 bottle costing $1.00. In the evening, some of the boys having received boxes, one of them made a mess pan full of punch and was pressed by invitation to 'smell the mug' and look on at the proceedings. The usual stories were told, songs sung, etc. . . ."[48]

Farther away from the fields of Fredericksburg, staff officer Henry Kyd Douglas related an amusing Christmas dinner that General Jackson held and invited Generals Lee, Stuart, and a host of other guests. This was out of character with the usually taciturn Jackson. General J.E.B. Stuart had also given Jackson a new uniform as a Christmas gift.

"On this Christmas day, I paid my respects of the season to General Jackson and was again asked to remain to dinner—I had received the invitation before. I was anxious to do so, as Smith, aide-de-camp, was giving especial attention to that dinner. It was to be spread in that decorated office of which I have spoken, and Generals Lee, Stuart, Pendleton, and others were expected as guests. They came, it was said, and made it a lively dinner for the General. General Lee rallied him on his style in having a real dining room servant with a white apron on, and when Jeb Stuart discovered a fighting cock stamped on the 'pat of butter' which Mrs. Corbin had sent him, he bemoaned such an indication of moral degeneracy. Randolph and I dined with Mr. and Mrs. Corbin and the guests at the Hall and the evening was not slow."[49]

Walter Phelps, Jr., an officer in the 22nd New York Infantry, ticked off the large Christmas dinner menu the officers of the First Corps enjoyed at their camp near Belle Plains. Phelps asked his wife about the reception the new holiday fad had gotten from their daughter.

"Christmas passed very quiet with us here at Head Quarters. I had a fine flagstaff raised during the day and in the evening Gen. Dobleday and staff and Gen. Wadsworth and staff called upon me. Gen. Wadsworth took dinner with me and passed the evening. We had some very nice hot rum punch, our dinner was excellent—for instance, salmon, roast beef—roast turkey, chicken, ham, celery, sweet potatoes, onions, cranberry jelly, mince pie, apple pie—nuts, raisins, apples, coffee—whiskey, hot rum punch—champagne, cigars & c. quite a good dinner I assure you. I presume Christmas must have been quite an occasion with you, more particularly as the Christmas tree was in vogue—did Annie enjoy it—and how did the matter pass off pleasantly I have no doubt—I thought of you all as we sat over a cheerful fire in my tent with a flowing bowl of punch & fragrant cigar. Such is life—I am very comfortable indeed."[50]

The only Christmas turkey Maryland staff officer McHenry Howard saw was hanging from someone else's saddle while traveling to his camp in the Shenandoah Valley.

"At Luray we turned West on the Newmarket Road, and I think it was Christmas Eve when we crossed the Massanutton Mountain at this picturesque gap, the only road crossing in the fifty mile stretch of this lofty range, for I remember seeing, while climbing over the mountain pass, Captain Emack of the Maryland cavalry with a Christmas turkey hanging to his saddle."[51]

Randolph McKim of the 2nd Maryland Infantry found comfortable quarters in which to enjoy his Christmas in Staunton. The following year McKim would apply to take his vows and become an Episcopal priest.

"We are just through the 'festivities' of Christmas and Duncan and I have been wondering how you all enjoyed yourselves on the day. I said 'the festivities' of Christmas; they consisted only of a very nicely prepared and beautifully set out family dinner. We had everything that you could think of, except ice-cream and iced fruit, etc. Our plum-pudding too did not have any raisins in it, but cherries made a very good substitute. Shall I

Figure 3-7 Children gazing at their first Christmas tree from the *London Illustrated News*. Many soldiers like Walter Phelps of the 22nd New York Infantry wrote home for details of Christmas morning. ". . . did Annie enjoy it . . ?" (K.R.)

give you our bill of fare?—Oyster Soup—Roast Turkey, Ham, Round of Beef, Fresh Beef, Fried Oysters, Lobster Salad—Hominy, Potatoes, Beans Salsafy, Rice, Dried Fruit—Plum-pudding, Charlotte Russe, Jelly, Pound Cake, and Jelly Cake, Puffs, etc., and Java Coffee! That will do for the Southern Confederacy, where everybody is starving! You must not suppose people generally, however, are so fortunate. Mrs. Phillips is a capital housekeeper, and had large supplies of everything on hand when the war broke out. I only make this enumeration to show you how well Duncan and I fared on Christmas Day. The day was a very happy one to me."[52]

From his camp near Fairfax Court House, George Grenville Benidict was another soldier writing for a hometown paper. Rising in the ranks from private to lieutenant during his two year stay in the 12th Vermont Volunteers.

"Dear Free Press: We have had a very fair Christmas in camp. The day was as mild as May. By hard work the day before our mess had 'stockaded' our tent and it is now a little log house with a canvas roof. We have in it a 'California stove'—a sheet of iron over a square hole in the ground—and as we have been confined of late to rations of hard tack and salt pork, we decided to have a special Christmas dinner.

"We got some excellent oysters of the sutler, also some potatoes. Two of the boys went off to a clean, free-negro family, about a mile off, and got two quarts of rich milk, some hickory nuts, and some dried peaches. I officiated as cook, and, as all agreed, got up a capital dinner. I made as good an oyster soup as one often gets, and fried some oysters with bread crumbs—for we are the fortuate owners of a frying-pan. The potatoes were boiled in a tin pan, and were as mealy as any I ate.

Figure 3-8. When an army went into winter camp it would strip the countryside of trees to build log huts with tented roofs. (USAMHI)

We had, besides, good Vermont butter, boiled pork, good bread, and closed a luxurious meal with nuts, raisins and apples, and coca-nut cakes just sent from home. For supper we had rice and milk and stewed plums. Now that is not such bad living for poor soldiers, is it? But we do not have it every day; though we have had many luxuries since our Thanksgiving boxes came.

"We have a pleasant camp ground just now, and if allowed to remain, shall make ourselves quite comfortable."[53]

Charles Moulton of the 34th Massachusetts Volunteer Infantry had a most unusual Christmas Day when he attended a Negro dance and wedding close to Camp Lyons in Virginia. Moulton always wrote chatty letters to family members on the activities of the regiment and camp gossip.

"Christmas passed off with me the same as did Thanksgiving and probably New Year's will 'ditto.' Our grand dinner was fried bacon and boiled onions, which is called 'something extra' for such occasions here in camp. The

officers, however, managed to pass off the day very agreeable with the officers in the Fort. They had a grand supper in the Colonel's tent, where jokes and stories were plenty in store, and toasts freely drank, and a merry time enjoyed all around by a jolly crew. To render the affair complete the Regimental band made its first appearance and serenaded the officials milicatus!

"You have probably read accounts and seen pictures in *Frank Leslie's,* representing the numerous pleasures indulged in by negroes during holidays, when they are allowed the time to spend to their own satisfaction, in dancing, visiting, etc. Well, hearing that such an occasion was to take place on a small scale about 2 miles from camp, and wishing to see how it was passed off, I concluded to attend. I went. The scene of dance and festivities was a large hut, and we arrived there about 10 o'clock, starting away from camp right after roll-call. The room was pretty comfortably filled with the 'culled

Figure 3-9. *A Contraband Ball.* Captain Moulton of the 34th Massachusetts Regiment attended a Negro wedding and dance near Harper's Ferry on Christmas night. *Leslie's Illustrated.* (K.R.)

gemman' and their 'ladie lubs' to the accompanying music of the banjo. A man calling 'all hands around,' 'change partners,' 'form circle through the center,' etc., were the order of the evening and gaily did the merry voices resound through the room. As we arrived at the happy assemblage, the joyful ceremony of the rites of marriage was being performed. The happy couple stood there with their bright rows of ebony glancing in every which way. After remaining a while we wended our way campwards and with sleepy 'peepers' and wearied forms, we laid ourselves down to rest—and so must I now as I hear the bugle sounding for 'taps.' "[54]

Edwin Franklin Palmer and the 13th Vermont spent Christmas touring the battlefield of Chantilly where Generals Kearney and Stevens fell earlier in the summer of 1862.

"In all the brigade there is no drilling. The chaplains preach to the various regiments. Then many visit the Chantilly battle field. A citizen points out the spot where the brave Kearney fell; where the lines swayed to and fro. Here, side by side, are the graves of friend and foe. The enemy held the field. Their dead are buried very decently; but shocking to say, only a few sods were thrown over ours, and frequently, feet, hands and skulls are sticking out, flesh still on. But we found men from the twelfth regiment covering these heroes that fought so bravely. We lose another of our soldiers. Oscar Reed dies suddenly of typhoid fever."[55]

Charles Francis Adams, Jr. of the 1st Massachusetts Cavalry, wrote to his diplomat father from Warrenton, Virginia, on Christmas Eve. Describing how happy he was in the field, Adams detailed how comfortable he was after some adjustments to his winter quarters his messmate despairingly called a "dirty kennel." Adams's father was the U.S. Minister to Great Britain, and both were members of the esteemed public service-minded Adams family that included the second President of the United States, John Adams.

"Anyhow, the next three days until Sunday passed uncomfortably enough, clear and bitter cold, the water in our blankets freezing even at noon. They drilled us Friday and Saturday, and that was a bore; but on Friday

my patience gave out and I resolved to be comfortable if only for a day. So I set men to work and had a fireplace built behind my tent, of rough stone. The seam in the rear of the tent was then opened and closed around its mouth, and lo! in one corner of my tent was a mean, ugly little open fireplace. Then I had a shelf put up on one side, on which I am now writing, and a bed of fir-tree branches on the other side on which I spread my blankets. Thus I become more comfortable than I had ever been before and, though the wind sweeps and the rain drips through my tent, and Davis in abject despair calls it a 'dirty kennel,' in it I can be comfortable and I can write in the coldest weather, and there I am writing now, and tomorrow in it Davis and I will have our Christmas dinner, if we can raise one, which seems doubtful; but your dinner in London and John's in Boston will not taste better than ours, though we do eat tough beef and drink commissary whiskey out of battered and campaign worn old tin plates and cups. And even if it does, I am very sure that my health will be drunk and I will be remembered in Newport and Boston and London and that if it lay in the power of my family, I should eat and drink of the fat of the land."[56]

A letter from James A. Garfield, future President of the United States, Ohio politician, and officer, spent part of the winter in Washington away from the Union army in the West. In a letter to his wife Crete, Garfield related the social activities of the day.

"Yours of the 22nd came to hand this morning as I returned from a Christmas trip across the Potomac. The Ohio people here in the city gave a Christmas dinner to the Ohio soldiers (about 800) who are located in a convalescent camp at Fort Gaines about four miles out of the city, so a large party went out to cheer the boys. There was a fine dinner given them and after it speeches made by Judge Spalding, John Sherman, Governor Chase, Mr. Hutchins, myself and others.

"After the dinner was over I went to the Chain Bridge and over to the Virginia shore to visit Captain [Joseph H.] Allen of the 169th New York. He is Brother Allen of

Figure 3-10. Soldiers used a variety of chimney designs when adding fireplaces to their tents. While in camp at Warrenton, Virginia, Charles Francis Adams, Jr. wrote his diplomat father that he had used rough stone to improve his accommodations with an "...ugly little open fireplace..." just before Christmas. *Leslie's Illustrated.* (K.R.)

Millville, New York, whose wife visited us in Hiram in 1860. He has lately raised a company and come into the service. I was pleasantly surprised to find his wife there, and also to find some half dozen old college acquaintances. The colonel [Clarence Buell] was at Williams a few years before me, and the major [Alonzo Alden] was a class-mate of Harry's. I knew several others. They had a fine Christmas supper concluding with speeches and songs. I staid over night and came into town this morning."[57]

On Christmas Day President and Mrs. Lincoln spent part of the holiday visiting wounded soldiers in Washington hospitals. One Union soldier spending time in a hospital in Washington, D.C., was the convalescing James L. Clark of the 149th Pennsylvania Volunteer Infantry. Writing to a female friend, Clark told her of the Christmas dinner the Columbia College Hospital fed the recovering soldiers.

"Well I must tell you what a Christmas we had here, the Ladys of Washington gave us a grand dinner on that day such as roast turkey and oyster soup pies and cheese and cranberry preserves apples and oranges and ale and wine, it was a grand dinner and I enjoyed it well the day was very pleasant and it is pleasant ever since yesterday. . . ."[58]

Isaac W. Scherich was camped with his company of the 18th Pennsylvania Volunteer Cavalry, across the Anacostia River from Washington, D.C., in what is now Anacostia. Scherich noted in his diary about a chicken that followed him back to camp on Christmas.

"Ordinary camp duties. Some drilling mounted and on foot with the saber. The Anacosta River is very narrow at this place and flowed only a few rods back of our camp. The boys got some drift logs and made a foot bridge so we could go over to a farm house to get milk. I frequently went over into the timber and strolled along the river. One evening a chicken followed me into camp and got into the mess pan....During the evening we had a chicken dinner. After we were filled up and feeling good we got to scuffling in the tent and had a large time."[59]

Elizabeth Blair Lee, daughter of Francis P. Blair, wrote to her husband in the navy every day telling him all the news, political, family, and gossip making the rounds. In a series of letters from December 20 to Christmas Day, Philip's "affectionate Lizzie" informed him of all the Christmas news.

"Blair is very well & merry out gathering laurels—Some of which I will take in to deck St John's tomorrow for Christmas Blair is busy putting some around Papa's picture—He & Becky will I expect deck all my pictures—God bless you . . . I wish our Christmas could be happy together—which is fondly echoed by our loving boy—but he is still joyous & happy—'like a little child—' so often that example is given me by him—God bless you both—& in each other— . . . . So far as we can share Blair's joys this has been a merry Christmas. He was awake before daylight—& had to take a look at his gifts by candle light—it was six—but you know that is not daylight in my room—Of all the toys nothing so pleased him as the Engine & railway Cars & Mary Blair skates—he told me—to say to Papa this is the best Christmas yet—& I do wish Government would just let him be here to this time—."[60]

Longtime Washington resident and public servant Benjamin French Brown, whose career started when Andrew Jackson was President, knew many important figures on Capitol Hill shaping the unfolding events during the Civil War. French is the contrast and contemporary of Confederate War Department clerk J. B. Jones. Commenting in his diary on the generous gift giving in his household, French peeks in on the enjoyment one child in his family takes in a present received.

"Christmas has come and gone since last I wrote. Mrs. F.'s birth anniversary has also come and gone. Dec. 23d she was 31 years of age. I gave her a Prayer Book as a birthday present, and a sewing machine and diamond ring as Christmas presents. She gave me Folk Songs—a superb book—and the 2 first volumes of Pierre Irving's life of Washington Irving. I value them beyond price. My friend Wm. Forsyth sent me a gallon of brandy, six bottles of Champange, and a box of cigars. Harry French gave me a gutta-percha ring, which he made on purpose for me, and being a little too small for my smallest finger I shall wear it on my watch chain, where it now is. I value it very much because he made it expressly for me. These are all the Christmas presents I have rec'd...

"We spent our Christmas very soberly. All the morning I was engaged about house fixing up things. After getting regularly shaved, bathed, & dressed for the day, I wheeled a barrel of apples round to Duff Green's row, partly, and the remainder to the Casparis Hospital. I remained at the latter place and saw the sick soldiers eat their Christmas dinner. Came home at 1/2 past 1, and at 2 dined. We had an admirable Christmas dinner, and Lem. Barker and Taggart as guests. Ben, an unmannerly cub, did not come to the table at all, but ate at his workbench where he was working on his steam engine...."[61]

Winchester resident, Cornelia Peake McDonald, lived through a harrowing Christmas Eve when Union troops flooded her yard to take all available wood for campfires. The plundering Yankees nearly made off with the Christmas dinner she was lovingly preparing for her family.

"In the kitchen all day making cakes for the children's Christmas, labour by no means light with only a young servant to assist, but as Aunt Winnie was there to direct and retrieve errors, all went on rightly smoothly.

"In the afternoon I saw from the door a cavalry regiment ride in and take possession of Mr. Wood's yard and beautiful grounds, attracted no doubt by the grass which is still green in many places. I was pitying them from my heart as Mr. Wood and his sisters are such old people and have always been accustomed to quiet and comfort; but my pity for them was suddenly displaced by anxiety for myself, for I beheld two cavalry men on their way through the yard stop and take the Christmas turkey that had been dressed and hung on a low branch of a tree for cooking on the morrow.

"He had walked with it a few steps before I realized what had taken place, and with the consciousness of the loss came the remembrance of the straits to which I was reduced before that turkey could be obtained; how I had spent six dollars, and sent a man miles on horseback to get it rather than have nothing good and pleasant for our Christmas dinner. With the recollection of all that, came the inspiration to try and recover it, so I flew after him, and in a commanding tone demanded the restoration of my property.

"The man laughed derisively and told me I had no right to it, being, 'secesh' as he expressed it, and that it was confiscated to the United States. 'Very well,' said I, 'go on to the camp with it, and I will go with you to the commanding officer.' He gave it up then and I returned triumphantly to the kitchen with it. Just as I got back I looked and saw a regiment of infantry, 'foot people,' as old Aunt Winnie calls them, filing into our orchard. In five minutes the garden fence had disappeared and the boarding from the carriage house and other buildings was being torn off. Some were carrying off the wood that my poor little boys had cut and hauled. It made me almost weep to see the labour of their poor little hands appropriated by those thieves. How thankful I was that they were far away. I permitted them to go to their Uncle Fayette's some days ago to spend the Christmas with his boys.

"They went off so happily, both riding on Kit, with ammunition enough for a good long meet of shooting. While I was trying to arrest the work of destruction, someone told me the robbers were in the kitchen, carrying off the things. In I went, and found it full of men. One took up a tray of cakes and as I turned to rescue them, Mary, the servant, pulled my sleeve to show something else they were carrying off, and when I turned to him

another seized something else till I was nearly wild. At last Mary said, 'Miss Cornelia he's got your rusks.' (Those rusks that I had made myself and worked till my wrists ached, the first I ever made.)

"A man had opened the stove and taken out the pan of nice light brown rusks, and was running out with them. A fit of heroism seized me and I darted after him, and just as he reached the porch steps, I caught him by the collar of his great coat, and held him tight till the hot pan burnt his hands and he was forced to drop it. An officer was riding by, and beholding the scene stopped and asked the meaning of it. Explaining, I lost my gravity, and so did he, and there we laughed long and loud over it. It was so perfectly ridiculous that I forgot for the time all the havoc that was going on. The officer went away, and soon a guard came and quiet was restored, at least near the house, but all night long the work of demolition of buildings went on...."

On Christmas Day, Mrs. McDonald was too tense from the dinner's near abduction to enjoy the fruits of her labors.

"The day has been too restless to enjoy, or even to realize that it was Christmas. All day reports of the advance of the Confederates, and our consequent excitement. Just as we were sitting down to dinner, we heard repeated reports of cannon. We hurried from the table and found the troops all hastily marching off. They expected a fight, I was told by one, as the Confederates were near town. We could eat no more dinner, the girls and myself, so it was carefully put away till we could enjoy it.

"In the evening I went over to Mr. Wood's to see how the old people were bearing their burden, and to take them something nice from the dessert we could not eat. Found them all very quiet, but sad enough. The poor old gentleman's head looks whiter, had his forehead more wrinkled than before they came to intrude on his sweet, quiet home. As I returned home I saw the troops marching back again, like the King of France. The guard was withdrawn at night, which was rather singular, but all is quiet, and so 'I will lay me down to sleep and take my rest, for it is Thou, Lord, who makest me to dwell in safety.'"[62]

Confederate War Department Clerk J. B. Jones reported in his diary the false rumors of resignations in Washington of Lincoln's Cabinet officials. Happy over the news from different military fronts, Jones could not hide his astonishment at the rising rate of inflation on the prices of goods in Richmond. The children of Richmond continued the Virginia tradition of firecrackers and explosions to welcome Christmas.

"Northern papers show that there is much distraction in the North; that both Seward and Chase, who had resigned their positions, were with difficulty persuaded to resume them. This news, coupled with the recent victory, and some reported successes in the West (Van Dorn's capture of Holly Springs), produces some effect on the spirits of the people here; and we have a merrier Christmas than the last one....

"The boys are firing Chinese crackers everywhere, and no little gunpowder is consumed in commemoration of the day.

"But turkeys are selling at $11 each! Shoes for $25 per pair. Salt, however, has fallen from $1.50 to .33 cents per pound. Fresh meats sell at from 35 to 50 cents per pound.

"A silver (lever) watch, which had been lying in my trunk for two years, and which cost me $25, sold at auction yesterday for $75. This sufficed for fuel for a month, and a Christmas dinner. At the end of another month, my poor family must be scattered again, as this house will be occupied by its owner. I have advertised for boarding in the country, but get no response. It would require $300 per month to board my family here, and that is more than my income. What shall we do? Trust in God!"[63]

Sallie Brock Putnam observed the melancholy atmosphere surrounding many families in Richmond. Prices were climbing on everyday necessities as the blockade bit a little more deeply into the pockets of citizens. Chairs were starting to become vacant as many of the young men anxiously wanting to get into the war became casualties of the war.

"Again the cycle of time had brought to us the Christmas season. But with sadder remembrances still was the festival observed than that of one year before. Aside from the usual religious observances of the day—the joining in the chorus:

'Shout the glad tidings, exulting sing—
Jerusalem triumphs, Messiah is king,'

there was little to remind us of the festival of yore.

"The Christmas dinner passed off gloomily. The vacant chairs were multiplied in Southern homes, and even the children who had so curiously questioned the cause of the absence of the young soldier brother from the festive board, had heard too much, had seen too much, and knew too well why sad-colored garments were worn by the mother, and the fold of rusty crape placed around the worn hat of the father, and why the joyous mirth of the sister was restrained, and her beautiful figure draped in mourning. Congratulations were forced, and tears had taken the place of smiles on countenances where cheerfulness was wont to reign."[64]

Kate Mason Rowland spent her Christmas in one of personal sacrifice and patriotic duty tending to the care and feeding of wounded Confederate soldiers on Christmas Day in a Richmond hospital.

"We spent Christmas Eve with Mother at the Hospital, and the next morning, Christmas Day, helped to make good things for the soldiers, stewed oysters and made egg-nog and then superintended the preparation for the Christmas dinner for the Convalescents. It was delightful to see their enjoyment. Four hundred men were served with chickens, ducks, pies and cider; and the wounded and sick in the wards had turkey, oysters etc. M. had forty-eight hours leave which expired today and he has left us. . . ."[65]

Janet H. Randolph kept in mind her Christmas while living in Warrenton, Virginia, and the kindness of a Union officer that made her holiday memorable.

". . . Well, I have made a long preface to a short story. As I said, the troops had gone into winter quarters; no more dashing in of 'our men' to cheer us up by telling of how things were going on 'across the lines,' and we children looked forward to a dull Christmas. To give us a little pleasure, Mrs. Gen. P., whose husband was in Richmond, formed a dancing class, and twice a week we would meet in her parlors and she would play on the piano for us to dance. There were about eight girls and as many boys. The old-fashioned lancers, the quadrilles, and the waltzes were learned. When Christmas came, we wanted to send a little Christmas present to Mrs. P., to show how we appreciated the pleasure she had given us, but what could we do? There were no stores to sell and no money to buy. The Yankees had their sutlers, who were sometimes allowed to sell to the citizens; but they were not then allowed to do so, for it had been reported that we bought provisions to save up for the 'Rebels.'

"You will recall what I have just said, that 'we had no money;' but when the Yankees came to stay, they used to buy homemade bread, and would furnish materials for the ladies to make pies and cakes, and our mothers were willing to do anything to get some Yankee money, or 'greenbacks,' as we called the paper money. So each of us determined to get a little money from our parents. We collected three dollars, which was a 'whole heap' for us, but how were we to spend it? Recess each day found us consulting on this important question. It was at last decided that we would buy some sugar and tea and coffee, but where we to get it? Again came the consultation, when one of the girls, Lillie P., said: 'Why, there is a very nice Yankee who has his headquarters in the lot next to our house, and I believe he would let us buy it if we asked him.' Then came the question: 'Who is going to face the enemy?' We determined that five of the girls should go, so Mollie S., Florie T., Jennie P., myself, and sister were chosen. The girl who proposed it was to introduce us.

"You can hardly imagine a more scared set of little girls; but we must get our present,

so down we marched and asked the sentinel who walked in front of the officers' tent if we could see Col. Gardener (I remember the name and wish I could remember the regiment) on 'important business.' In a few minutes we were ushered into his presence. I was to be the spokesman, but I am sure if the Colonel had not been so gentle and kind my mouth would never have been able to open. Well, after a fashion, we made known our errand and offered our pitiful little three dollars, which meant so much to us, asking if he would let his sutler sell us that amount in sugar and coffee. Why, certainly; it should be sent to us that afternoon. You can hardly think how glad we were and how we thanked the Yankee colonel.

"Now the pleasant part of my story comes: That afternoon up came the Colonel's orderly with twenty pounds of sugar and a large package of coffee and tea (I suppose five times as much as our money would have bought) and a nice letter with three one-dollar greenbacks, saying that he was glad to contribute to the brave little girls who wished to give a Christmas present to the wife of a Confederate general who had given her time for their amusement. Our delight can hardly be described to the little ones of to-day who have all they want for their comfort and amusement, and I believe that everybody who takes the trouble to read this little story will be glad to know that even in those hard days there were kind Yankees who did feel sorry for the little Confederate girls; and it is just as nice, as the years go by, to remember these kind acts, while it does good also to tell them. And always remember that the old-fashion name of gentleman or gentlewoman belongs to the person who so behaves, and not to any locality or country."[66]

Miss Mary E. Roberts of Marietta, Georgia, penned a thank you to her cousin Mrs. Mary Jones for an increasingly rare Christmas gift as the war continued. In the precious fruit she saw a metaphor for missing loved ones, and wished to

". . . say how much we thanked you for the oranges. I stole some sugar out the closet and preserved them for Mother. She enjoys them so—takes them when she coughs. We had a

Figure 3-11. Winter camp of the 12th Massachusetts Volunteers "Camp Hicks" near Frederick, Maryland. Lithograph by L. N. Rosenthall. From the collection of D. C. Toomey.

saucer of them on the table Christmas Day, and we thought of the dear friends they represented and the now-deserted garden where they grew."[67]

On the high seas of the Caribbean aboard the Confederate raider *C.S.S. Alabama,* Christmas Day was just another day with the exception of the men being excused from work. Boarding officer George Townley Fullam recorded the day's activities and the reveries of an English Christmas.

"Nothing to mark the difference between this and any other day, save the men being exempt from work, and in the evening all hands spliced the main brace. O for a good old English Christmas with its merry associations and innocent pleasures. The three islands were of coral formation, and with the exception of a few gulls, no signs of life either animal or vegetable were seen."[68]

On the eve of the Battle of Murfreesboro, the clothing account book of the 4th Kentucky's Company C, once again became the holiday diary for the mysterious scribe's fervently patriotic and hopeful message.

"Another Christmas has come and still we are engaged in the Bloody Struggle to be free . . . for more than two years we have been combating with the Vandal horde—to Day our army is stronger and more thoughroly [sic] equipped than ever before."[69]

Figure 4-1. *A Visit from St. Nicholas* by Thomas Nast. From *Poems*, 1863-1864. (K.R.)

4

SANTA CLAUS BECOMES A PATRIOT

The Emancipation Proclamation became law on January 1, 1863, linking the war to preserve the Union with the abolition of slavery. It was greeted with mixed emotions by the white soldiers in the Union army as former slaves enlisted to help bring an end to the institution that had enslaved them. The 54th Massachusetts Regiment became one of the better known units of black soldiers when its attack on Fort Wagner dispelled the notion that ex-slaves would not fight and die for their freedom. During the first four days of July, twin disasters at Gettysburg and Vicksburg marked the beginning of the end for the Confederacy. The tide of war was turning in favor of the North as the year came to its conclusion without the bloody strife that surrounded December, 1862.

The roster of battles and casualties grew with such names as Brandy Station, Chancellorsville, Gettysburg, Vicksburg, Bristoe Station, Chickamauga, Mine Run, Knoxville, Chattanooga, Lookout Mountain, Missionary Ridge, and countless minor skirmishes. Lincoln continued to search for a general who could mold the Army of the Potomac into the instrument he envisioned. Ambrose Burnside and Joseph Hooker were discarded after disastrous battles. Following Gettysburg, President Lincoln felt he had found the general who would fight and win battles, and not involve himself in civilian or military politics. The general Lincoln now placed his trust in was the man who had turned back the second invasion of the North, Pennsylvanian George Gordon Meade. The officer corps of both armies lost irreplaceable men. The most recognizable casualty from either army was that of General Thomas Jonathan "Stonewall" Jackson following the battle of Chancellorsville.

The Confederate cruiser *C.S.S. Alabama* became the terror of the high seas in the Atlantic, capturing prizes and sinking Federal warships. Blockade runners still managed to evade the Federal Naval blockade, but many more ships were getting caught or sunk than before. The blockade was beginning to bite into the economy of the civilian population as many items became scarce. While there was high morale for such heroes as Lee and Jackson and matters military in Virginia, the economic situation provoked civilian unrest in what was called a bread riot in Richmond. The North was not immune to civilian strife over economic, military, and social policies either. Draft riots broke out in New York City and in several New England cities. Many casualties occurred among newly arrived immigrant laborers and the black population as rioters vented their feelings on those they considered responsible for the draft. The only hope of the Confederacy, now that the chance for European recognition had faded out, was to hang on long enough to make the Northern public weary of the high cost of war in material and human lives.

Christmas was relatively peaceful in contrast to the fury surrounding last year's holiday. The image of Santa Claus was invoked on both sides as serving those with the rightful cause. Many Southern parents would sadly tell their children that Santa Claus might not be able to run the Federal blockade and bring them presents, disguising the real reason of inflation and scarcity. At the beginning of the year, artist Thomas Nast portrayed Santa Claus in patriotic Union costume visiting and distributing gifts. Santa Claus had entered the realm of political propaganda to raise the morale of the troops and flagging civilian support for the war. Several more times during the war, artists would use the image of Santa Claus in centerfold drawings and other illustrations, more so in the North than the South. Writers for newspapers and chroniclers of the day would invoke Santa Claus and his Christmas sentiments for one cause or another.

Thomas Nast's Christmas number in *Harper's Weekly's* Christmas issue (December 26, 1863) was another sentimental illustration with a military motif called "The Christmas Furlough." The center panel shows a soldier being welcomed home by his wife in a warm embrace and kisses while friends and family in the background arrive to give Christmas greetings. One child is happily climbing Daddy's leg while another child that has not seen her father since shortly after her birth, shyly holds back, not quite sure what to think of this stranger she does not remember seeing. A table top tree and presents surrounding the base and a room festooned and garlanded is in the background. The left smaller panel titled "Eve" shows Santa Claus looking over the sleeping children in their crib, heavily laden with toys and other surprises for them. Below is a religious scene of the Nativity. The right smaller panel titled "Morning" shows the joy and excitement the children are showing upon finding the presents Santa Claus has left while relatives look on from a doorway. Below appears a scene of churchgoers arriving in the falling snow and calling out Christmas greetings. The very bottom of the centerfold is a scene of feasting at the Christmas table laden with the festive bounty.

A column titled "Merry Christmas" ran on the second page of the December 26 issue of *Harper's Weekly.*

"Ought it not be a merry Christmas? Even with all the sorrow that hangs, and will forever hang, over so many households; even while the war still rages; even while there are serious questions yet to be settled—ought it not to be, and is it not, a merry Christmas?

"How well Mr. Nast has seized the spirit of the great festival in the elaborate and beautiful picture which we publish this week! The central scene is the home of the soldier and his Christmas welcome from wife and darlings, for just that is central scene of our American holidays this year. It is the soldier who has saved us our homes and filled our holidays with joy. It is the soldier who is lifting the dark winter-cloud beyond which smiles the bright spring of national regeneration. It is the soldier who is securing the peace that will make the life of the children sleeping together in the crib, and over whom

Figure 4-2. *The Christmas Furlough* is the title of the centerfold in the December 26, 1863 issue of *Harper's Weekly*. Note how the artist covers all aspects of Christmas in the home. (Reproduced courtesy of The Picture Bank, Alexandria, VA.)

the dear old bear, Santa Claus, is bending, a long and happy holiday.

"Next year let us hope that the delicate, and thoughtful, and forcible pencil of our dear friend Nast may draw a picture of the National reunion, of the return of the prodigal who has been living on the husks and with harlots, the rebel soldier returning to his country and his fellow-citizens, the soldier who did not know that fighting the brave man whom we see in the picture of to-day, he was fighting his true friend, as well as honor and liberty. Peace on earth is the benediction. Blessed then the brave men upon the Rio Grande, in Louisiana, along the Mississippi, in the mountains of Chattanooga, in the Valley at Knoxville, upon the Potomac, and the Rappahannock, and the James River; among the North Carolina barrens and the South Carolina Islands, with the great army of sailors upon the rivers and the sea—to all, whether on sea or land, heroes of the good cause, honor and blessing; for their stout hands and hearts with the supporting sympathy and faith of the whole people, are the peacemakers of the nation."[1]

Santa Claus ran the blockade again this year in Augusta, Georgia, and brought Christmas joy to the household of Ella Clanton Thomas's children after she told her children the old elf couldn't make it. The Union Naval blockade, while still leaky in numerous spots, was still biting into the everyday lives of Southern civilians. Christmas was especially prone to inflated prices on goods, trinkets, fruits, and materials to make delectable sweets and other holiday goodies. As Christmas neared, many parents told their children not to expect a visit from Santa Claus, using the blockade (instead of the exorbitant prices and scarcity of materials) as an excuse for his not visiting. Many others exerted extraordinary skill and cunning to provide the barest essentials for continuing their children's holiday beliefs and faith.

On the last day of the year, Mrs. Thomas noted in her journal what she had planned in lieu of Santa Claus missing this year's appointed rounds. Her children's simple act of faith in Santa Claus caused her to dig a little deeper for a holiday offering.

"I have written so much that it is now after 9 o'clock and yet I have said nothing of Turner's and Mary Bell's party which we gave them last week in lieu of the Santa Claus presents. Mary Bell has been told that Santa Claus has not been able to run the blockade and has gone to war— Yet at a late hour when I went up stairs Thursday night of the party I found that with the trusting faith of childhood they had hung their little socks and stockings in case Santa Claus did come. I had given the subject no thought whatever but invoking Santa Claus['s] aid I was enabled when their little eyes were opened to enjoy their pleasure to find cake and money in their socks— Jeff was delighted— Mr Thomas bought Mary Bell at auction a saddle for which he gave $100. A most extravagant purchase. The same day he bought a hanging glass for $75. Cora gave Cora Lou two pairs of socks."[2]

Mary Boykin Chestnut in a gossip-filled diary entry on Christmas Day noted that despite the increasing dire straits the Confederacy faced, her Christmas table was still laden with the life of the land. A who's who of famous and known military officers graced the hospitality of the Chestnut South Carolina plantation. An interesting story was told by visiting General Simon Bolivar Buckner, the officer who surrendered Fort Donelson and its troops to former West Point classmate General U.S. Grant, after all his superior officers had fled. He told of seeing a humorous Yankee pictorial about the deceased Stonewall Jackson.

"General Buckner had seen a Yankee pictorial. Angels were sent down from [heaven to] bear up Stonewall Jackson's soul. They could not find it, flew back, sorrowing. When they got to the Golden Gates above, found Stonewall by a rapid flank movement had already cut a way in. . . . Somebody confessed they used half corn, half coffee as a beverage—but it was always popcorn, for while they roasted it the popcorn popped out.

"And now for our Christmas dinner. We invited two wounded homeless men who were too ill to come. Alex Haskell, however, who has lost an eye, and Hood came.

"We had for dinner oyster soup, soup a la reine. It has so many good things in it. Besides boiled mutton, ham, boned turkey, wild ducks, partridges, plum pudding. Sauterne, burgundy, sherry, and Madeira wine.

"There is life in the old land yet!

"Others dropped in after dinner, without arms, without legs. Von Borcke, who cannot speak because of a wound in his throat.

"Isabella said, 'We have all kinds now but a blind one.' Poor fellows, they laugh at wounds and yet can show many a scar.

"That lovely little Charlotte Wickham, Rooney Lee's wife—she is dying. Her husband is in a Yankee prison."[3]

Mrs. Mary Jones received a letter from her daughter in Atlanta regaling her with the activities of her children on Christmas Day.

"We spent Christmas with Aunt Eliza. A quiet, pleasant day: no one there except ourselves. We had agreed to dine together, so I carried up a ham and turkey. The children enjoyed hanging up their stockings, and Mamie said Christmas was a merry, happy day. Charlie carried a small bottle of cream to Aunt Eliza which he told her was to make 'sillybubble.' "[4]

Sallie Brock Putnam plotted the course Santa Claus would have to take to avoid the blockade to deliver his annual token acknowledgment of good behavior for the children of the South. Neither would he forget the soldiers in the field, but the Christmas boxes would be less bountiful than previous holidays. Putnam described the place church services filled in the Southern psyche during the holiday as the populace faced ever increasing shortages and vacant chairs around the table of family members serving in the army or those never to return. Taffy parties and starvation parties were all the rage in Richmond society with many homes hosting the events which were visited by friends and family. Knitting cliques for the knitting of socks and other articles of clothing destined for the soldiers in the field during the holidays were considered the height of patriotic duty, as was nursing at the hospitals scattered throughout Richmond.

Putnam vividly portrayed Richmond during the third Christmas of the war when she wrote in her wartime memoirs:

"Another annual revolution in the cycle of time brought us again to the Christmas season, the third since the bloody circle of war had been drawn around our hearts and homes. For days preceding the festival the anxious little ones, who had learned to share the cares and troubles of their elders, peered curiously into the countenances of mothers and fathers, for an intimation that good old Santa Klaus had not lost his bravery, and that despite the long continued storm of war, he would make his way through the fleet at Charleston or the blockading squadron at Wilmington, and from foreign countries, or perchance across the country from Baltimore, he would pick his way, flank the numerous pickets on the lines, and bring *something* to drop in their new stockings, knitted by mother herself. Sometimes the simple present that brought happiness to the child was purchased at the expense of some retrenchment in the table-fare for the week, or with the loss of some needed article of comfort in clothing. But the influence of childhood is magical. The children find their way to our hearts, and unloose the purse-strings when all other inducements fail.

"The Christmas-box for the soldier in the field was not forgotten; but it was less bountifully supplied than when the first Christmas dinner dispatched to him to be shared with his comrades in his soldier's tent. Santa Klaus once more generously disposed of socks and scarfs and visors, to the husbands, brothers, sons, and lovers in the army.

"In the Confederate Capital, the churches were always filled on this particular festival. On this day not the knee alone, but the heart was bowed, and the fervent prayers were offered that no more should the Christmas sun dawn on our land deluged in blood, but that when Christmas came next the sun of peace might shed its light on the hearts now breaking under the cruel oppression of remorseless war. The exercises at church were all that was left to remind us of Christmas of yore.

"Could the veil have been uplifted that hid the privacy of home, and the Christmas dinner of Richmond on this day have been exposed, we should have seen here and there, the fat turkey, the mince pie, the bowl of egg-nog and the other creature comforts, which ordinarily abound on the tables of Virginia on this occasion; but generally, (and particularly among those who were reduced to keeping-rooms) if from the accumulating expenses of the times, the turkey could be afforded it was accompanied simply with potatoes and corn-bread, and this was the dinner for Christmas on the tables of many, with whom all the luxuries of our own and foreign climes had been in every-day use. But this could all have been borne bravely, cheerfully, heroically—it is almost too trifling to notice, had not the vacant place recalled the memory of one or more, whose bones were bleaching somewhere on the field made red with the mingled blood of friend and foe. It was not the want of delicacies and luxuries that brought the tear to the eye of the mother, or heaved the father's bosom in a long-drawn sigh."[5]

Phoebe Yates Pember was the widowed matron of Chimborazo Hospital in Richmond from 1862 to the end of the war. A strong woman of conviction in a male dominated domain, she overcame the prejudices and pettiness of many surgeons who felt invaded by "one of them. . . ." Much beloved for her tireless exertions to make the hospital wards cleaner, more efficiently run places to restore the health of wounded and sick soldiers, Mrs. Pember also sought to stop the corruption and theft of supplies and furniture by the hospital staff throughout her tenure at Chimborazo. The soldiers loved her for the care and humane treatment she gave to the boys in her ward. In a letter written to her friend Mrs. Gilmer, Pember detailed the Christmas dinner prepared for the soldiers about Richmond and within the hospital ward. She also recounted the attempt at matchmaking by her host at a Christmas Eve party.

"It seemed to me I lived a week during the twenty-four hours which constituted Christmas. On the eve I was invited to Mrs. Randolph's and found all married people there, and more than I should have gone to meet had I known of it. The evening was not very agreeable, though Stephen was there, Mrs. Haxall was loud in her lamentations that two such *nice* people, who would make such a *nice*

match did not appear to appreciate each other. We did not get away till past midnight and by eight the next morning I was on my way to prepare for the important day. We made twenty-four gallons of Egg-Nogg inviting all in the whole Division to come and drink and gave to each a good sized cake. At two o'clock having roasted a dozen turkeys and seven gallons of oysters we shared them out and hoped that each man got his share. After all this was accomplished, I had the kitchen table carried into my little room, a personal turkey with all new accompaniaments set out and then sent for the poor outcast Marylanders to come and dine. Presided at the table of ten, caring for them, left them at five and dressed for a great dinner at Col. Skinner's, for with true Virginia hospitality they had not only invited me, but requested me to fill two vacant chairs by my side. I took Dr. Baylor and John Eager Howard, had dinner at seven, and went by invitation at ten to Dr. Gibson's to see the Christmas tree on which I found my Christmas gift pretty enough to be most acceptable and simple enough to preclude all feelings of obligation."[6]

Despite being surrounded by Christmas greens and a cedar Christmas tree, Richmond War Department clerk J. B. Jones was sadder and more burdened by inflation, disappointment and crime, than was his Christmas tree with decorations.

"No war news to-day. . . . It is a sad Christmas; cold, and threatening snow. My two youngest children, however, have decked the parlor with evergreens, crosses, stars, etc. They have a cedar Christmas-tree, but it is not burdened. Candy is held at $8 per pound. My two sons rose at 5 a.m. and repaired to the canal to meet their sister Anne, who has been teaching Latin and French in the country; but she was not among the passengers, and this has cast a shade of disappointment over the family.

"A few pistols and crackers are fired by the boys in the streets—and only a few. I am alone; all the rest being at church. It would not be safe to leave the house unoccupied. Robberies and murders are daily perpetrated.

"I shall have no turkey to-day, and do not covet one. It is no time for feasting."[7]

Cornelia Hancock, a young Pennsylvania Quaker woman, felt the patriotic and humane call to help care for the wounded from the Battle of Gettysburg. By Christmas, she was caring for Negro families at the Contraband Hospital in Washington, D.C., railing against the indifference and the scarcity of supplies sent them by the Philadelphia Freedman Relief Society. Hancock provided a Christmas of toys, food and a Christmas tree for the contrabands' holiday festivities.

"Willie's playthings have come for the children & some candy so I hope to make them feel Christmas—some. . . Christmas Day has passed. We had a Christmas tree for the children and gave every one in the hospital plum pudding for dinner. It was beautiful weather. Some contrabands entertained themselves fighting & generally seemed to have a good time."[8]

Comedic office seeker and satirist, writer Orpheus C. Kerr penned another skewed holiday missive to prick the country's humor during the war.

"Another Christmas finds our great strategic country in the toils of war, my boy, and the chiming of the bells is lost in the roar of ingenious artillery. Where blazes the yule log that misses not at least one manly form from its genial ring of quivering Christmas light; and where hangs the mistletoe bough beneath which at least one gentle, womanly heart beats not the quicker with fond thoughts of the lad whose first kiss upon her half reluctant lips was destined to burn in future there as her keepsake from a hero? Dear old Christmas! rich to memory in all the simple joys and fond, familiar sanctities of home, thou comest sadly upon me in my exile with the iron men of war, the waxen men of politics; and though I hail thee merry for thy cheery evergreens, God knows it is thy snow that presses nearest to my heart. But a truce to sentiment, my boy, when the most sentimental object I have seen for a week is the Conservative Kentucky Chap, whose imbibing method of celebrating the approach of Christmas invariably leads him into disquisitions upon the wrongs of the heroic White Man."[9]

Washington resident Elizabeth Blair Lee wrote to her husband Philip in the Navy from her parents' estate in Maryland, Silver Spring, about the bicycle she had bought her son and his idea who the "real" Santa Claus was.

"I got a velociped for Blair from me—He know Santa Claus 'is all story—' but Papa & Mama are the real Santa Claus Good night—forgive this scrawl

"I lost one pair of specs some days ago & broke my others today in the cold so have to go it blind tonight Still with fond faith in your unfailing indulgence—to your affecate Lizzie."[10]

Civil servant and political patronage appointee Benjamin Brown French spent Christmas day tasting and toasting the gifts he received from friends. After dinner French did what many modern day parent and Christmas reveler does after the holiday dinner, slip off into drowsy slumber.

"Last evening my good friend William Forsyth, brought a dozen bottles of old South side Madeira, as a present from Mrs. Forsyth to Mrs. French. We drank the health of the giver in it, at dinner, also our remembrance of Frank & his visitors. It is superb wine, such as would cost at least 5 dollars a bottle at any hotel. We enjoyed our Christmas dinner very much. After dinner the household scattered, and, I believed, slept—I did at any rate. . . .

"My Christmas presents the 4th Vol. of Pierre Irving's *Life of Washington,* by Mary Ellen—a Latin Dictionary by Willie Russell—and a gold toothpick by Ellen.

"I have given away 5 cents to a little apple girl yesterday, who asked for a Christmas gift! That is all. Now, while writing this, $50 from a Friend to me."[11]

In Greencastle, Pennsylvania, juvenile delinquency was a holiday problem encountered by newspaper editor McCrory. He complained about the town boys congregating in the doorway of the post office every evening, disrupting the townsfolk from conducting their business. One person complained that, "It usually requires the services of the constable to enforce order." Three days before Christmas the town newspaper,

Figure 4-3. *Frank Leslie's Illustrated Newspaper* came out with its own Christmas centerfold for 1863. Note that the Santa in the center panel bears no resemblance to Thomas Nast's creation. Published January 2, 1864, it gave equal coverage to activities at home and in the soldiers' camp.

The Pilot, reported the apprehension of a couple of boys charged with troublemaking.

"On last Friday morning one or two juveniles were arraigned before Squire Kauffman, on charges of making noise and otherwise disturbing the peace and quiet of the Post Office. The lads were very penitent and made to pay some costs, reprimanded, and sent to school."[12]

Greencastle put on its holiday face as the citizens went busily about preparing for the festive day's arrival.

"Christmas was coming and stores were advertising wares that would be suitable for the holidays. It was reported, 'The windows of the shopkeepers are already filled with toys and fancy goods.' Hostetter's grocery store, the only one of its kind in town, was ready to meet all cooking and baking needs of the season. Programs were planned by the various churches and fund raising activities of the Ladies Aid Society were scheduled, including four performances by the Philo Dramatic Association, a company of local young men, to be held in a hall in the A. L. Irwin store on East Baltimore Street. A special program was scheduled for Christmas morning in the lecture room of the German Reformed Church. It was also announced that singing school was being conducted in the lecture room of the Presbyterian Church. The local editor urged public support for this venture. R. A. McClure, the school's leader, was described as a gentleman of more than ordinary musical ability readying the singers for the carol season."[13]

Another incident making the rounds of the town that holiday, was the appearance of a "devil" intent on scaring bad children into renouncing their delinquent ways. The devilish impersonator walked about town on stilts to increase his size and frightful appearance. That backfired when some boys gave "the devil his due" by stoning him off the streets. No action was taken by the local constable for the lack of a victim coming forward to report the rock throwing incident. The "devil" of Greencastle was never seen again.

". . . Christmas came at its appointed time and the rituals and customs that had been a part of the community's style of living for generations were faithfully observed: fashioning evergreen decorations and wreaths for windows and doorways; searching for holly and mistletoe for indoor arrangements; finding and cutting the right cedar or pine and getting it into the house to be laced with home styled decorations; baking cookies, pies, and cakes; seeing to the gifts for the youngsters; preparing food ahead of time to be ready for the biggest meal of the year; attending the Christmas Eve services; lighting the windows' candles; caroling; and feasting for hours on that day of all days. All proceeded as usual."[14]

1st Lieutenant Thomas D. Houston of the 11th Virginia was incarcerated in Johnson's Island prison on his Christmas Day. Wounded and captured at Gettysburg, Houston recovered from his hip wound in Union hospitals. Fully recovered, Lieutenant Houston was sent to Johnson's Island where he spent the remainder of the war. Houston received from two female friends named Miss Lizzie and Miss Ella, letters and a box and barrel of goods containing the ingredients for which to make and eat merrily on Christmas Day. It was the reception of such boxes filled with food, clothing, and other articles of comfort that made the holidays bearable for soldiers locked away from families and homes. Exchanges and paroles were still being carried out, but on a slower basis as the number of captured soldiers grew daily until there existed the hindrance of a huge backlog of names and bureaucratic redtape. The cold confines of Johnson's Island were made a little warmer for Houston and his messmates by the receipt of Christmas boxes sent by "Houston's female friends," and detailed in his return letter thanking Lizzie and her friend for their kindness.

"The morning after acknowledging by mail the reception on the 25th of a Christmas box sent to myself and friends, I had the pleasure of receiving letters from you and Miss Ella. It is hoped the letter containing said acknowledgement has reached its destination. The barrel and box were received several days before, and I am at a loss to know how it is, my letter written immediately upon their reception has not reached you. Up to this time there has been no prohibition here to the reception and delivery of boxes.

"You, my dear friend and Miss Ella have certainly contributed much to the enjoyment of my mates and myself. Without your generous donations the days for merrymaking would have indeed been dull. As it is, we have gathered more than once around a table loaded with inviting luxuries. We have followed the pleasant but not always wise injunction,

‘Eat much! drink deep!
—Let—soundly sleep
The groans and sighs before thee!’

Thanks, thanks kind friends for the happiest days in prison. In future years, when the nine composing our mess shall be quietly settled in peaceful homes (some with and some without wives) more than one will have cause to remark with pleasure of the meals contributed by ‘Houston's female friends,’ and devoured by his male ones, in December 1863."[15]

Another resident of the Johnson's Island prison compound, was staff officer Major Henry Kyd Douglas, also wounded at Gettysburg and captured by Union soldiers in a battlefield hospital. Douglas's Christmas was also filled with Christmas boxes containing a multitude of perishables and clothing from friends along with a bitter "tasting" elixir.

"There came a carload of boxes for the prisoners about Christmas which, after reasonable inspection, they were allowed to receive. My box from home contained more cause for merriment and speculation as to its contents than satisfaction. It had received rough treatment on its way, and a bottle of catsup had broken and its contents very generally distributed through the box. Mince pie and fruit cake saturated with tomato catsup was about as palatable as ‘embalmed beef’ of the Cuban memory; but there were other things. Then, too, a friend had sent me in a package a bottle of old brandy. On Christmas morning I quietly called several comrades up to my bunk to taste of the precious fluid—of disappointment. The bottle had been opened outside, the brandy taken and replaced with water, adroitly recorked, and sent in. I hope the Yankee who played that practical joke lived to repent it and was shot before the war ended. But then there came from my same friend, Johnston of Baltimore, a box containing thirty pieces of clothing, for such disposition as I chose to make of them, and another box of hams, chickens, biscuits, and cigars for my own mess; and from Mrs. Mary T. Semmes—aunt of the ‘Alabama’ Semmes—another wholesale box of coffee, whiskey, sugar, cigars, gloves, soap, worsted night-caps, Tennyson's poems, a spinning top (from her grandson), etc. She duplicated it afterwards."[16]

Cuban born Lieutenant Colonel Frederic Cavada was captured at Gettysburg leading the 14th Pennsylvania. Writing in his diary, Cavada detailed life in Libby Prison, especially his Christmas experience for 1863.

"Christmas! at that name, what pleasant visions come thronging to the prisoner's mind, vision of hearth and home,—of mince pies, plum puddings, and bon-bons, of Christmas trees and child-laughter, and pretty little rosy mouths, sweeter for the sugar-plums, puckering into Christmas kisses! What prison-thoughts, that laugh at the rebel bars and bayonets, go traveling by swift air lines, afar off into cozy cottages among the northern snows, and over the wide prairies into western homes; north, south, east and west—over the whole land; fond thoughts, winged with love-lightning.

"The north wind comes reeling in fitful gushes through the iron bars, and jingles a sleigh-bell in the prisoner's ear, and puffs in his pale face with a breath suggestively odorous of egg-nog.

"Christmas day! a day which was made for smiles, not for sighs,—for laughter, not for tears,—for the hearth, not for the prison. The forms which I pass as I saunter up and down the low, gloomy rooms, are bowed in thoughts, and their cheeks are pale with surfeit of it; it seems very cruel, but the loving little arms that are felt twining about the neck,—the innocent laughing little faces that will peep out of the shadows, with sunbeams in their eyes,—the warm hands which grasp ours in spite of us,—all these must be thrust aside, and the welling teardrop in the eye must be brushed away, and . . . tut tut! what's in a uniform, after all, if the soldier cannot make his brain as thread-bare as its sleeve, nor his heart as hard as its buttons!

"There is a group in a dusky corner that I can see from here: some one is playing 'Home Sweet Home!' on a violin. It is a very dismal affair, this group: the faces are all sad,—no wonder, for the tune is telling them strange, wild things: there are whispering voices in its notes: I see that one by one the figures stroll away, and that they all seem to have discovered something of unusual interest to look at, out of the windows.

"I am invited out to-day to a Christmas dinner. Good! There is not much inducement left for phantasmal visitations, after a hearty meal. When I say I am invited *out*, I mean over there in the north-east corner of the room: I shaved my face, and combed my hair, this morning, for the occasion. I am promised a white china plate to eat from!

"When I arrive at the north-east corner, I enquire after my host, who is not present. I am informed that he is down in the kitchen, stewing the mutton(!) There he comes, in a violent perspiration, with a skillet in one hand and a tea-pot in the other.

"There are four of us,—the dinner is excellent,—I have never tasted a better, even at the *Maison Dorée*; the wine, not very choice, of course,—it is put down on the bill of fare as 'Eau de James, couleur de boue' [Cavada, having a little fun tongue in cheek, meant the water from the James River].

"It is true that the table is made from a box, that the table-cloth is a towel, and that I was requested to bring with me my own fork and spoon; but it is a decidedly *recherché* and ceremonious affair, notwithstanding; my host is polite and elegant to a fault.

"After dessert, having stepped over to my 'house' for my pipe, which I had forgotten in the excitement of making my toilet (an absence of mind probably due to my having combed my hair,) I return with unexpected celerity, and I find my host, and the two other guest, with their sleeves rolled up to the elbow, scouring the kettles, and washing the dishes!

"So Christmas-day passes away; there are many extra dinners gotten up, and numerous invitations to admired friends. Towards evening, the gloom has in a measure passed off from most of the faces; there is some laughing, and even cracking of jokes. A 'ball' has been advertised to take place in the lower east room as clear as day—a cloudy day, at least; there is a great deal of sport and merriment, after a while, and a great deal of bad dancing; toes are trampled upon with impunity—hats crushed—trowsers torn;—but the violinist scrapes away with supernatural tenacity, and he is the best-natured man in the room, for he is a 'fiddler' whom 'nobody pays.'

"At nine o'clock there is a loud cry of 'lights out!' from the sentries; the ball breaks up; blankets are spread on the floor; and the dancers, spectators, fiddler and all, are soon wrapped in the arms of the Libbyan Morpheus. Many strange visions are beheld; many pleasing dreams experienced; and many fond, familiar faces are photographed in the wondrous *camera obscura* which sleep makes of the dreamer's brain."[17]

John Ransom of the 9th Michigan Cavalry was spending his Christmas Eve and Day on Richmond's Belle Island in the middle of the James River. Commenting on how different his Christmas of the previous year was from the one at hand, would prove to be almost prescient. Ransom would be moved to the horrors of the uncompleted Andersonville in March of the next year. With a touch of wistfulness and the soul of an optimist, Ransom would jot in his diary on Christmas Eve; "Must hang up my stocking to-night for habit's sake if nothing else. I am enjoying splendid health, and prison life agrees with me. Wrote home to-day."

The following day, Ransom would scribble a narrative of the day's holiday activities and thoughts.

"Christmas.—One year ago to-day first went into camp at Coldwater, little dreaming what changes a year would bring around, but there are exchange rumors afloat and hope to see white folks again before many months. All ordered out to be squadded over again, which was quite a disappointment to our mess as we were making preparations for a grand dinner, gotten up by outside hands, Mustard, Myers, Hendryx and myself. However, we had our good things for supper instead of dinner, and it was a big thing, consisting of corn bread and butter, oysters, coffee, beef, crackers, cheese &c.; all we could possibly eat or do away with, and costing the snug little sum of $200 Confederate money, or $20 in greenbacks. Lay awake long before daylight listening to the bells. As they rang out Christmas good morning I imagined they were Jackson, Michigan, my old home, and from the spires of the old Presbyterian and Episcopal churches. Little do they think as they are saying their Merry Christmas and enjoying themselves so much, of the hunger and starving here. But there are better days coming."[18]

T he Union Armies across the Confederacy stood poised to resume in the spring where they had left off before going into winter quarters. In Tennessee, after breaking the sieges and driving back Confederate troops under Bragg at Chattanooga and Longstreet at Knoxville, Union morale ran high with the recent reverses even though supplies did not.

James W. Bartlett of the 35th Massachusetts took the time to explain to his wife about the recent siege of Knoxville and the driving off of the "Rebs" from the city. Bartlett's concluding lines from Blaine's Crossroads, Tennessee, were the loving Christmas sentiments of a man deeply missing his wife.

"This is the first time I have had that I could call my own for a long time. . . . I wish I had time to write all I desire dearest but I do not. You ask if absence conquers love. I do not find it so my dear but quite the reverse. All my thoughts are of you. I love you with the love of my boyhood and would sacrifice anything to make you happy. Your love has kept me whole and raised me to a higher elevation

of manhood than perhaps I should have reached without seeing all the temptations of this life and I thank God that he has given me a lovely wife and children. I suppose the children all got something in their stockings last night and had a great time this morning. God bless you and them is the sincere prayer of your loving husband—James."[19]

James Bartlett died of wounds in an Alexandria, Virginia, hospital six months later.

Another of Burnside's Ninth Corps soldiers writing home from Blaine's Crossroads was Fred Pettit of the "Roundheads" of the 100th Pennsylvania. After surviving the siege by the Confederates of Longstreet's Corps at Knoxville, Pettit and his comrades were threadbare in clothes and poorly shod. Morale amongst the troops was very high though the rations received were not as plentiful as last Christmas before Fredericksburg.

"I suppose that you are busy today eating your Christmas cakes, Christmas dinner, and all the other good things which old Christmas is supposed to bring. Well, I hope you will have a good time and enjoy this Christmas very much.

"Perhaps you would like to know how we are spending our Christmas in the army. Last night I was on picket and caught a bad cold and as you may suppose do not feel very funny. Last year I think I told you I had a mess of beans and pork for a Christmas dinner. This year I am not so fortunate. We have been furnished nothing but a small piece of boiled beef. But our sutler came up last night and we obtained a few crackers, a little cheese, and butter. But what do you think the price is? Crackers 50 cts. per lb., cheese 50 cts. per lb., and butter 80 cts. At these rates you can easily see what a dinner cost us.

"Perhaps you say we need not buy them. Well, standing picket all night and making your breakfast and dinner on a small piece of boiled beef without any bread does not go well when you have money in your pocket. For the last month we have had but one fourth to one half rations of bread stuff. Last winter we thought it hard to live on full rations. If matters continue this I fear I can-

Figure 4-4. "Snowy Morning—on Picket" is the title of this engraving from *Harper's* January 30, 1864 issue. Many soldiers in both armies spent long hours on picket duty. Bad weather and holidays were no exceptions. (K.R.)

not send you much more money. A soldier must live.

"My clothing is the worst I ever had at this time of the year. My toes stick through both of my shoes and everything else is about in the same condition.

"Perhaps you think we are discouraged and complaining. Not at all. Far from it. This army is now in far better spirits than the Army of the Potomac was at this time last year with plenty of rations and good clothing. We have beaten the enemy and feel confident of being able to do so still.

"We know that it is impossible to get supplies here fast enough for so large an army and therefore we do not complain.

"There is much talk of reenlisting again. I think a number of our regiment will reenlist. This shows perhaps our opinion of the war better than I can express."[20]

Fred Pettit would not live to see another Christmas. He died in a hospital from a wound received at the Battle of Cold Harbor in June the following year.

A third regiment transferred west as part of Burnside's Ninth Corps was the 2nd Michigan Infantry. Colonel Charles B. Haydon was making a journey to join the 2nd Michigan on Christmas Eve, after recovering from a wound received during the siege of Knoxville.

"The night was very cold but the day was beautiful. I sent out a foraging party which procured [original notation says seized] 30 bushels of corn & half ton of hay. We had an inspection. I corrected the rolls and examined the state of the rations. 'Tis the Night before Christmas'—not exactly the Christmas of civilization yet I have seen many worse days & nights than this. This delay has been very irksome to me. I begrudge every minute till I am with the regt. Inasmuch as I shall have no time to morrow I drank tonight the last bottle of wine I brought from home & wished Merry Christmas to everyone who deserves it."[21]

Haydon died the following March from a severe cold in a Cincinnati military hospital.

The Ninth Corps' 8th Michigan of Captain Ralph Ely was yet another regiment spending Christmas at Blaine's Crossroads. From the ashes of a few supplies rounded up rose a tasty and simple Christmas dinner of ingenuity from the 8th's cooks.

"This being Christmas, all feeling well and trying to get up something extra from Army rations for dinner. We had for headquarters mess a boiled pudding made of corn meal, unsifted, and cooks put in a cock and boiled with poor beef and it relished first rate."[22]

Abram Fulkerson of the 114th Illinois Regiment, left a succinct and economical diary entry for Christmas of holiday fatalities occurring at a ball and possible desertion at Camp Memphis.

"There was two men killed last nite at a ball. They were bayoneted by the guards for bad conduct. There was another shot to-day by one of the Reg. He would not stop when ordered. There was a man died in the hospital belonging to the Reg. His name was Wilson. The weather over cast like rain."[23]

Edwin Weller conducted a correspondence of friendship with Nettie Watkins of his hometown of Havana, New York, throughout the war. A member of the 107th New York Volunteers, Weller was on duty near Wartrace, Tennessee, on Christmas Eve. Weller could not decide if he would attend a Christmas party, though he dropped enough hints about the attendance of attractive members of the opposite sex.

"There is to be Christmas Party about two miles from here at a place called Bell Buckle tomorrow night. I have an invitation to attend but hardly know whether I shall go or not. There is a few very good looking ladies up there, and will be at the party I am told. I shall have a gay old time if I do go you can bet."[24]

The correspondence between Weller and his Nettie turned into something more meaningful and had a happy ending. Edwin Weller married Antionette (Nettie) Watkins five months after the war ended for Weller on November 15, 1865.

Lawrence Van Alstyne was a naive Union soldier saved from a financial disaster on Christmas Eve by a more worldly comrade seeing a scam in the making. This was Van Alstyne's second Christmas recorded in his diary spent in the South.

"As Tomorrow is Christmas we went out and made such purchases of good things as our purses would allow, and these we turned over to George and Henry for safe keeping and for cooking on the morrow. After that we went across the street to see what was in a tent that had lately been put up there. We found it a sort of show. There was a big snake in a show case filled with cheap looking jewelry, each piece having a number attached to it. Also, a dice cup and dice. For $1.00 one could throw once, and any number of spots that came up would entitle the thrower to the piece of jewelry with a corresponding number on it.

"Just as it had all been explained to us, a greenhorn-looking chap came in and, after the thing had been explained to him, said he was always unlucky at dice, but if one of us would throw for him he would risk a dollar just to see how the game worked. Gorton is such an accomodating fellow I expected he would offer to make a throw for him, but he said nothing, I took the cup and threw a seventeen. The proprietor said it was a very lucky number, and he would give the winner $12 in cash or the fine pin that had the seventeen on it. The fellow took the cash, like a sensible man. I thought there was a chance to make my fortune and was going to break the bank, when Gorton, who was wiser than I, took me to one side and told me not to be a fool; that the greenhorn was one of the gang, and that the money I won for him was already his own. Others had come by this time and I soon saw he was right, and I kept out. We watched the game for a while, and then went back to Camp Dudley and to bed.

"Christmas, and I forgot to hang up my stocking. After getting something to eat, we took stock of our eatables and of our pocket books, and found we could afford a few things we lacked. Gorton said he would invite his horse jockey friend, James Buchanan, not the ex-President, but a little bit of a man who rode the races for a living. So taking Tony with me I went up to a nearby market and bought some oysters and some steak. This with what we had on hand made up a feast such as we had often wished for in vain. Buchanan came, with his saddle in his coat pocket, for he was due at the track in the

afternoon. George and Henry outdid themselves in cooking, and we certainly had a feast. There was not much style about it, but it was satisfying. We had overestimated our capacity, and had enough left for the cooks and drummer boys. Buchanan went to the races, Gorton and I went to sleep, and so passed my second Christmas in Dixie."[25]

The Confederate Army under General Bragg had won a stunning victory over the Union Army commanded by General "Old Rosy" Rosecrans, in September. Despite so decisive a victory, the much despised Bragg managed to snatch defeat from the jaws of victory when he refused to let the Army of Tennessee follow the retreating Union army and destroy them in detail. Rosecrans and his army retreated to Chattanooga while the Confederate army lay siege from the surrounding mountains and tried to starve the Union army into submission. As at Vicksburg, rats, mules, and horses supplemented the decreasing rations of the cut Union supply lines.

Grant came to the rescue of the besieged Federal army with the improvised "cracker line" that kept the new inhabitants and longtime residents from starvation. Once enough materials and reinforcements arrived, the Union army unexpectedly attacked up the surrounding mountains where Bragg's army directed the long range siege. The swiftness of the attack left many Confederates prisoners, while those lucky enough to get away retreated back into Georgia and into winter quarters. The contrast of morale in the Confederate army was markedly low to that of their blue-clad foes. Support and confidence for the hated Confederate general, Braxton Bragg, while never high, was now at an all time low. Whiskey imbibed in camp mixed with the decline in morale was a disciplinary problem encountered at Dalton that Christmas. Surgeon John Farris of the 41st Tennessee complained that many officers joined guards and other soldiers in getting "beastly drunk." Officers who tried to restore some measure of order and discipline "were cursed and abused by drunken officers & privates alike. No regard was paid to any law or regulation."[26] A sergeant nonchalantly commented "Whiskey issued to the troops. Some of the boys got on a spree."[27]

John Jackman of Kentucky's Orphan Brigade, observed in his diary the availability of liquor and its effect on the regimental officers on Christmas Eve.

"Nothing going on of great interest. In the evening our Q.M. and Capt. G., owing to the proximity of 'Christmas-times,' and having taken on some 'pine-top,' were singing 'The Star-Spangled Banner,' with a vim." On Christmas Day, even the weather seemed to make a pronouncement of the situation facing the Army of Tennessee. "A cold, cloudy, disagreeable day. Went to Church in Dalton, in forenoon and to-night. Have just written a letter home, to send by flag of truce. Set in raining late at night. My Christmas dinner was bean-soup without bread. The boys are not seeing a great deal of fun—some 'tipsey.' "[28]

The chaplain of Quarles's Brigade brought to mind the true meaning of Christmas as a time of good will and charity towards the less fortunate, especially when it came to children. Reverend James H. M'Neilly also found out the true worth of a Confederate dollar, and tried a new substitute delicacy for the taste buds.

"Christmas came while we were at Dalton. The day was cold, rather bleak, but invigorating and each mess tried to have a dinner that would be a reminder of home. The beef that was issued to us for the day was of extra fine quality, and the captain of Company A had secured a fine turkey, which was cooked to a turn. I remember that I was that day like the proverbial jackass between the bundles of hay. I had received invitations to dine at several places, but three were especially attractive. First, in my own mess our roast of beef was large, juicy, and tender, and the gravy, rich, brown, and abundant, was ready to be absorbed by our fat biscuits. There were also potatoes and onions and for desert some sort of pie. Then I was asked to help on that turkey with 'fixin's,' and a cousin of mine, Captain McAdoo, of the artillery, had two ganders of uncertain age which he had tied to a stake in front of his tent and fed all day long for two weeks to get them fat. He was sure those ganders would make a dish fit to set before a king, and he wanted me to test their

tenderness or toughness, as the case might be. But finally my wavering appetite settled on the turkey after I had charged our own cook to save a piece of beef and some gravy for my supper. I don't think I have ever enjoyed a Christmas dinner more.

"All these festive enjoyments opended our hearts, and we wanted to give something for the poor. Now, there were a brood of children that infested our camp. They were children of a poor mountaineer, a shoe make, who was in the employ of the government. One of the luxuries we indulged in was peanuts, or, as the natives called them, goobers, and we frequently gave these children handfuls of the peanuts, hard-tack and parts of our rations. The little fellows had no shoes; and as they often came walking over ice or snow, their little feet aroused our pity, and we made them sit by our fire.

"Here, then, was our chance to do a real charity. We would give them enough money to buy them shoes—three pairs. We chipped in and raised about $100 in Confederate money (about $15 in real money). Before giving it to the oldest, a boy of thirteen years, I thought I would find out how he would spend it. So, after telling him how sorry we were that they were barefooted, I said: 'Now, suppose we were to give you and your little brother and sister a whole heap of money. I don't mean just one dollar or two, but fifty dollars or even a hundred. What would you do with it?' His eyes brightened, and, looking eagerly at a big sack in our cabin, he said: 'Why, we would just buy goobers with it, just as much as we could eat.' He never thought of shoes. So I bought a big bag of goobers, a bushel or more, costing $10 or $15, and gave it to them, and they enjoyed that Christmas Day as much as we did.

"While on the subject of Christmas cheer I will mention a toothsome delicacy which had a ready sale. It was ginger bread, or cakes. An enterprising squad had gone into the business of baking. They built an oven on a hill over against our camp and secured some baking pans about three feet square. They bought flour and bacon from the commissary, bought a lot of sorghum molasses in the country, and got the grease they needed by frying it out of the bacon. They had numerous customers, who bought and criticized freely; but as I had been paid $840, seven months' wages, all the Confederacy ever paid me, I concluded to invest some of my wealth in ginger cakes. I had a good many one-dollar Confederate bills. They were red-backed and about six inches by three in length and breadth. I remembered boyhood days when the old cake man came to town on court days with his basket of cakes, and five cents would buy a square eight or nine inches by six inches, and I suppose that one of my dollars, or at most two, would buy half of what the big baking pan contained. But when I handed him my dollar, saying, 'Give me the worth of that,' he just laid the bill on the big square of cake and cut out the size of it and gave it to me for my money. I was so surprised that I did not object, but took my little piece of cake and went away sorrowing that our currency had sunk so low as to be measured in terms of gingerbread.

"By the way, there was another delicacy which I bought, and I never saw another like it. A man came to camp selling sirup made from pumpkins. I had my canteen filled for one of those dollars, but I can't say I enjoyed the new-style sirup."[29]

Captain Richard Beard, wounded during the battle of Chickamauga, had recovered in La Grange, Georgia, until he thought himself fit to return to duty. When the Army of Tennessee went into winter quarters before Christmas at Dalton, Beard secured a furlough for twenty-five days and spent his Christmas in La Grange, a town he had grown fond of during his convalescence. While rooming in a boarding house of a Mr. Bohannon, Beard met two gentlemen from the 1st Tennessee Regiment and struck up a friendship. Captain Beard and one of the men decided to play a joke on the other friend at the expense of a "diseased" Christmas turkey, but they in turn became the joke's recipient.

"Soon after we were installed in our room, he (Bohannon) told us that he had a turkey for the Christmas dinner. This was delightful

news to us, and we looked forward with gratification to the coming Christmas. He frequently talked of his turkey, and it seemed to be the pride of his life. But on Christmas Eve, as I was sitting alone in our room, the old gentleman came in, looking sad and forlorn, and at last he said to me:

"'Captain Beard, I have bad news to tell you.'

"Surprised, I responded 'What is it, Brother Bohannon?'

"'The turkey died last night; he died of a sore throat.'

"'Well,' said I, 'that's bad, sure enough.'

"'Well,' said he, 'don't you think we can eat him anyhow?'

"'Well,' said I, 'I reckon so,' but I had no idea of eating any part of that turkey.

"The old gentleman passed out and soon Whitthorne came in, and I told him of the tragedy of the turkey. He was shocked, but game, and said: 'We'll not eat any of the turkey, but let's not tell Joe Percy anything about it, so, we'll have a joke on him.'

"Christmas Day came on and the Christmas feast was spread on the table. I thought to myself that I had never seen a finer looking turkey. There he lay in that dish, stuffed with truffles to the throat, swimming in rich gravy, and garlanded with sprigs of green parsley; I hated to turn that turkey down, but I had to do it.

"Brother Bohannon commenced carving. He whacked into the turkey, and put a large piece of the breast on his plate and handed it to me, saying: 'Captain Beard, have a piece of turkey?' 'No,' said I, 'Brother Bohannon, I have had too much Christmas, and I don't feel like eating any of it.' This rather stumped the old gentleman. The plate was passed to Whitthorne, and he declined. I don't recall his excuse, but this stumped the old gentleman more than ever. It then passed on to Joe Percy. 'O, yes,' said Joe, 'I'll take it. There is nothing that I enjoy more than a Christmas turkey.'

"The dinner came to an end, and we scattered. A short time after dinner, I was again in my room alone, and Brother Bohannon came in; he looked sad and woebegone. He sat down and said to me: 'Captain Beard, I can't understand why you didn't eat any part of the turkey at dinner?'

"'Well,' said I, 'the reason is that you told me the turkey had died with a sore throat, and I couldn't think of eating any part of a diseased turkey.'

"'O,' said Brother Bohannon 'didn't you know what I meant? I just meant that we had cut his head off.'

"This was a boomerang. I felt hacked. Whitthorne and I had lost the best part of the Christmas dinner on account of the facetious remark of Brother Bohannon; but we made up our loss to some extent by attacking the cold remnants of the turkey at supper.

"But Joe Percy had the joke on us."[30]

Confederate cavalryman E. Polk Johnson of the 1st Kentucky, Army of Tennessee, recalled his "Christmas medicine" and dinner at the Colonel's quarters in the army's winter camp at Tunnel Hill, Georgia.

"Christmas day at Tunnel Hill in 1863 was a brilliant wintry day. Snow lay upon the ground, and as the sun rose the mountains put on their tiaras of diamonds in honor of the occasion. When this had been attended to, the unprecedented happened: the Confederate States of America issued rations of whiskey to the 1st Kentucky Cavalry. In those days eighty-two of our counties had not gone 'dry,' and most of us took 'our medicine.' One of my comrades with a foresight unusual and commendable, looking far into the future which should sweep all to 'dryness' in every county, declined to partake of the unusual ration provided for him by a benevolent government, gave his share to me. I never did have luck in looking into the future or foretelling what was going to happen in Kentucky or elsewhere; consequently I took care of his share and my own also. Like the Scotch girl's baby, each share was 'such a little one' that no untoward results followed my combining and disposing of the two in one; but I have long since fallen into line with the ninety Kentucky counties and voted myself 'dry' also.

"The degenerate youth of to-day must have his perfumed bath in a steam-heated room. I had mine that Christmas day in a stream which murmured by the camp and had an icy margin. There was no steam heat to speak of.

"Once out of the bath, there was fresh 'linen' made of King Cotton's snowy product, and then, still more wonderful, a new gray uniform which through some happy dispensation to fate had come to me as a holiday gift, and fitted me perfectly. Once the new uniform was donned and the damp locks smoothed, it was time to go to the colonel's headquarters whither I had been bidden to dinner. Invitations to dinner with the colonel reminded one of angels' visits—they did not happen very often, and no one ever stayed away who had received one.

"Good old Tom Richards was our regimental bugler, the very best one in the army. He was my friend. We had drunk out of the same canteen when its contents were various—sometimes there was water in it. Tom had found a partridge net—something that few persons of to-day know anything about—and had gone out and captured an entire covey of partridges. There were no game wardens connected with the army at the time. The colonel and Thomas and the other headquarters people had these partridges for dinner and I was there as a guest."[31]

Picket duty lasting 48 hours called later that night for Johnson as he found out what the "feeling of the morning after" was like as he had a cold breakfast and dinner the next day. Fond remembrances of visions of partridges filled his head.

Private Jenkin Lloyd Jones spent Christmas in Bellefonte, Alabama, with the Sixth Wisconsin Battery on the march through the devastation the war had wrought on the county seat. The Confederate heartland was now vulnerable to invasion by Union troops since the entire Mississippi River was open to Union traffic moving at will after the fall of Vicksburg. Christmas was anything but "merry" for Jones and the other artillerymen.

"Christmas Night. Awoke, not to the chiming voices of happy children as they cried

'Wish you Merry Christmas,' but to the notes of the bugle calling us to be ready to move. Struck tents at 8 A.M. Roads much better than those we have passed. Marched fast most of the time, having to go much out of the way to avoid swamps or bluffs. Marched quietly along, absorbed in thinking of home, and what they are doing this Christmas Day. Came into camp late at night near the county seat of Jackson County. The buildings burned and gone to ruin. I was very tired and foot-sore. No crackers for supper, so we made up the Christmas supper on parched corn and coffee. Tooth ached badly, had but little sleep. During the night rained very heavy."[32]

In South Carolina, Corporal Henry Gooding was a member of the black troops of the 54th Massachusetts besieging Charleston. Earlier in the year the 54th had stormed the parapets of Fort Wagner at the entrance of Charleston Harbor on July 18, taking terrible losses in men and officers of nearly fifty percent casualties. One of those officers killed in the failed attack was the Massachusetts born Colonel Robert Gould Shaw, who would be buried by the Confederates in a mass grave with his men. Eventually Fort Wagner fell leading to the campaign to capture the city that fired the first shot of the war, Charleston. Gooding would write letters for publication in his hometown newspaper, the *New Bedford Mercury*, detailing the experiences of the 54th. It was from the front lines that Gooding described the Christmas present Charleston received from the Union troops laying siege to the city.

"Christmas has come and gone, but Charleston still holds her head high, as the leading city in the van of the rebellion. . . . But do, Mr. Secretary (Gideon Welles, Secretary of the Navy), let us have the 4th of July in Charleston, and we will not regret not having spent a merry Christmas therein so much.

"Yesterday (Christmas) morning, we gave the rebels in Charleston a Merry (or dismal) Christmas greeting, by throwing a few shell in among them. The shell thrown evidently set fire to some part of the city, as there was a grand illumination visible in a few minutes after the shell were thrown. The wind being then from the northwest and the

air very clear, the sound of the church bells could be distinctly heard at Fort Strong, but whether it was the regular ringing of Christmas bells by the Catholic and established churches, or merely the alarm bells on account of fire, is difficult to determine. From the hour (3 o'clock) it may have been both circumstances that occasioned the loud ringing of bells in the Palmetto City; one set of bells ringing to commemorate a glorious event, bringing joy and mirth to the rising generation, and reflection and thankfulness to those of mature age,—and the other, to warn the guilty conspirators of the avenging flame thrown in their midst, ready to leave them houseless, unless they make efforts to extinguish it.

". . . Christmas was rather a dull day with us, the 54th. But the 3d U.S. had a stirring time—eating and drinking. Apple dumplings, equalling a young mortar shell in weight, with rye whiskey sauce, was the principal item on the bill of fare. So far as my observation went, apple dumplings formed the first and last course, but the boys enjoyed them not withstanding the seeming lack of talent in the pastry cooks. The dinner to the boys shows a warm attachment between the shoulder straps and the rank and file, for the expense was borne by the officers."[33]

From the relatively secure backwater of the war at Pine Bluff, Arkansas, Captain Thomas Nichols Stevens wrote to his wife of fond wishes to be at home. Because reality intervened, Stevens advised both himself and his wife to make the best of the situation each was in.

" 'A Merry Christmas' to you my Carrie, and to our little darlings—to bright-eyed Lulu and baby Mary. O, that I could be with you today to visit with you through this pleasant holiday—& the next seven. Would it not be a pleasant Christmas?

"For me it would, and I'm sure 'twould be for you. But we cannot be together today, so we will each think of the other and thus spend the day as happily as we may. Did you ask what I had good for dinner? I had stewed potatoes, bread and coffee. I think that was all. The bacon which was cooked with the potatoes I couldn't eat. Somehow I can't swallow it & feel comfortable. Beef we couldn't get. It is getting scarce here. We had a couple of chickens yesterday, but we never keep good victuals, for fear we won't get a chance to eat them. Procrastination is a terrible thief you remember, and I wouldn't wonder if he steals eatables sometimes. At any rate we won't trust him.

"There was a dance in town last night at which the beauty of Pine Bluff & Uncle Sam's blue-coated chivalry were well represented, it is said. I didn't attend, so I have to take hearsay for it.

"Today I am at work a part of the time, and loafing about Camp the rest. No more mail yet. We have no news here. Everything is about as dull as can be, except work—

plenty of that. We have to drill 2 1/2 hours every forenoon, beside our other work.

"I hope, dearest wife, that by the next Christmas I may be at home, to leave you no more.

"I am sorry I could send you nothing for the holidays, but there is nothing to be had here."[34]

On the battleground that Virginia continued to be, the dividing line separating the two armies during Christmas of 1863 was the Rappahannock and Rapidan Rivers again. The repulse of General Meade's Army of the Potomac against the Confederate fortifications and breastworks of Mine Run drifted into a static stalemate that brought that campaign to a close, and both armies went into winter quarters."

Figure 4-5. Union and Confederate pickets toasting each other from across the river on Christmas Day. Despite strict regulations against fraternizing with the enemy, many twists of Rebel tobacco were traded for Yankee coffee during lulls in the fighting. (K.R.)

Captain Henry Chambers of the 49th North Carolina stationed at the important rail center of Weldon in his home state, seemingly kept getting a little closer to home each Christmas. The day was proclaimed to be duty-free as the men opened packages from home and the old Virginia custom still created a bang on Christmas Day.

"In accordance with an order from regimental Head Quarters read on parade yesterday evening, there was no duty required of the men today and no roll call after reveille. There was some drinking in those companies where boxes had been received from home and a great many cartridges were wasted in Christmas guns. This is the third Christmas for me in the army, one at Manassas Junction, one at Fredericksburg and the third at Weldon, a considerable distance nearer home each time. May the next find us all at home enjoying peace, prosperity and independence."[35]

The 16th Mississippi was camped in the snow covered town of Gordonsville, an important supply depot and railroad center for the Army of Virginia in central Virginia. Franklin Lafayette Riley wrote wistfully in his diary about the memory of home a Christmas dinner served by the ladies of Gordonsville inspired.

"Snow, Wed. Thurs. and Fri., cold but clear. There are a number of soldiers from the Commissary Department in Gordonsville. The town is not large, but it contains 2 hospitals, numbers of freight cars and store houses, piles of supplies, some not so well covered. The 16th Miss. was in Gordonsville a year and a half ago. To-day (Christmas) I walked to the Presbyterian Church to hear Rev. Daniel Ewing, who is also post chaplain. Service enjoyable. After church, the ladies gave us an excellent Christmas meal: 3 kinds of meat, hot bread, butter, potatoes, vegetables, pies, cakes. . . . I haven't had a meal like this in over a year, when I was home. How I wish I could be there to-night!"[36]

Captain William J. Seymour of the 1st Louisiana Brigade of the famed Louisiana Tigers, nearly went without an eggnog to celebrate Christmas while camped near Raccoon Ford on the Rappahannock River.

"On this Christmas Eve [1863] our Head Quarters were in an old dilapidated negro cabin belonging to and near the residence of Mr. Eliason—a quarter mile from Raccoon Ford. The Commander of the Brigade, Col. Monaghan of the 6th [La. Regt.], had gone over to Division Head Quarters to assist Gen. Hays, who had temporarily succeeded to Gen. Early in command of the Division, in duly observing the memorable Eve that preceeded the anniversary of the natal day of our Savior—leaving Major New, our Inspector Genl., and myself 'at home' to bewail our less fortunate lot. The night was excessively cold and we passed the evening in toasting our toes before a roaring fire—talking of home & the dear ones there in anything but a joyous strain, now and then by way of parenthesis, stopping to anathematize a sable son of Africa whom we sent to Lynchburg after a demijohn of whiskey; but who, much to our annoyance, had not yet made his appearance. We had made up our mind to go egg-nogless to bed, when—about 11 0'clock—the welcome sound of horses hoofs on the crisp snow outside attracted our attention; out we rushed & there we found the tardy 'Mose' with his well filled demijohn. The eggs were quickly beaten—the sugar stirred in and then the whiskey added, and we had one of the most delicious noggs that ever mortal man quaffed. Taking a couple of glasses apiece, we retired merrily to bed—to forget the hardships of a soldier's life, and dream of a joyful reunion with the dear absent ones far away in the Southland."[37]

Courier Theodore Stanford Garnett of General J.E.B. Stuart's staff recounted his Christmas serenading some local ladies with a band that included the camp banjo player, Sam Sweeney, who would be dead a mere two weeks later.

"Christmas came and found us all in low spirits at the prospect of a dull time. At night we would often get together our Amateur Glee-Club with old Sam Sweeney as leader of the band, Bob, his cousin, the left violinist, Pegram with his flute, and occasionally Major McClellan with his fine guitar, and your humble servant with the triangle and all

Figure 4-6. Relieved from picket duty, this squad of men can return to the warmth of their winter huts and perhaps find some leftover Christmas dinner or a late arriving box from home. (K.R.)

assembling in the General's tent, go through with a mixed program of songs, jokes, back stepping and fun-making generally until the general, tiring of our performances, would rise up on his buffalo-robe and say, 'Well, Good evening to you all, gentlemen,' and in five minutes thereafter the camp would be hushed in sleep.

"On Xmas night, in 1863, a serenading party left camp to go into the Court House, and give the ladies some music. How well I remember Sam Sweeney's banjo that night!,—almost the last time he ever played it, poor fellow,—for in less than two weeks from that night he was in his grave. Von Borcke in his memoirs of the 'Confederate War' has, unintentionally I am sure, done Sam an injustice,—or in other words he has mistaken Sam for his cousin Bob. Both of them were excellent musicians, but Sam Sweeney was the world-renowned banjo-player, while Bob Sweeney's instrument was the violin. They were both 'good fellows,'—and richly deserve the praise which Capt. John Esten Cooke has bestowed upon their personal and artistic merits. They were both with us that night serenading;—stopping at one house to awake, as we thought, the fair sleepers with our dulcet strains, we found that they had not retired, and as soon as they discovered who we were, the door was thrown open and all hands invited to enter. We accepted, and found in the parlor an egg-nogg party going on. It was at once proposed to clear the floor for a dance, and in a few minutes our partners were selected, the music struck up, and we chased the golden hours with flying feet until the dawn of the day reminded us of our camp behind the hills, towards which with unwilling steps, we wound our way, first having escorted our ladies to their respective homes, thus realizing the sentiment of the old Sailor's song—

" 'We'll dance all night, till broad day light
    And go home with the girls in the
        morning.' "[38]

As if by omen with the death of Sam Sweeney, 1863's holiday would be the last Christmas for the fun-loving J.E.B. Stuart as he would fall mortally wounded five months later at the Battle of Yellow Tavern.

Philip H. Powers of the Army of Northern Virginia's Cavalry Corps, wrote to his wife from headquarters about his distinct lack of any Christmas spirit, and empathy for his wife attending to four children alone. Homesickness pervades his letter like a gloomy day that gets darker until he makes a solemn vow not to celebrate Christmas until reunited at home with his family.

"As Christmas will be pretty well over before you receive this, I need hardly wish you a Merry holiday. There is no holiday you will say for a poor woman with four children, a body full of ailments and pain and a husband in the rebel army. Tis true—I have not in fact wished you much merriment, but as I have had none of the social enjoyment and pleasures usual at this season and my mind has been much with you I have indeed wished and prayed that you might be comfortable and happy with our Richmond friends during the season, and have longed incessantly to be with you. . . . Christmas Day, I had promised myself, or rather my friends, a bowl of egg nogg—but the spirits did not arrive—and consequently I passed a quiet and sober day in my tent reading the 'Woman In White'—which I finished. . . . And this morning I made the egg nogg—but have not been very well, and did not enjoy it—and today I hardly left my tent.

"I do not care to celebrate Christmas until I can do so with my children—and my wife—when will that holiday come?. . . I hope the children enjoyed themselves yesterday—I thought of them when I first awaked, and of their stockings—Fortunate for them they were in Richmond where something could be had from Santa Claus."[39]

Captain Robert Emory Park of the 12th Alabama Regiment spent Christmas at Orange Courthouse where he engaged his black cooks in building a dirt chimney for his tent. He desired that the 12th be transferred to Alabama so he could do recruitment duty to fill the depleted ranks of his regiment. Pack did not like the cold climate of Virginia in winter. Stating that "Christmas Eve in the army bears no resemblance to preparations at home for Christmas festivities," Pack recounted what was not on his holiday menu for dinner on Christmas Day.

> "Ate hearty dinner, minus the home turkey and cranberries and oysters, egg nogg and fruit cake, and then wrote to my mother and sisters. Ordered on fatigue duty tomorrow at 8 1/2 o'clock. Sorry, because the men are busy completing their log cabins."[40]

Artillery private Henry Robinson Berkeley noted in his diary about the quality of beef served for his battery's Christmas dinner and the drawing of lots for the one lucky soul who won to consume it.

> "Camp very quiet. Our dinner consisted of some soldier bread and black rice and a piece of salted beef about two inches square. The beef not being worth dividing, we cast lots for it. John Lewis Berkeley won and ate it. The rest of us, five in number, ate our rice and bread. The Hardy boys and George Bray got a little merry about dark. A little apple-jack had gotten into camp."[41]

Samuel Pickens of the 15th Alabama had "all my Xmas on Xmas Eve" because he was engaged in preparing his winter quarters for inhabiting. On Christmas Eve after chinking and planking his house with other members of his mess, he was invited to his major's quarters to dine.

> "He had an elegant dinner—baked turkey, ham & cabbage & potatoes, genuine coffee & sugar &c. wh[ich] we enjoyed exceedingly & did ample justice to. To-night Col. P sent for me to drink eggnog with him & had very pleasant time indeed. I helped beat it & we succeeded in making it first rate. As theres nothing I like better of course I enjoyed it. . . . Returned to grd. & found all handy wrapped in arms of Morpheus."[42]

Mrs. Lee, afflicted with arthritis and bound to a wheelchair, hoped the General would spend Christmas Day with her and their family. He was in Richmond conferring with President Davis and he could stay, it would be the first Christmas Mary Lee had spent with her husband since 1859. But General Lee returned to his headquarters camp, deliberately sacrificing and subduing his desire to spend the holiday with his family in order to set an example of obedience to duty for the soldiers under his command. It would not be a happy Christmas for the Lee family as their son Rooney was in a Northern prison and Rooney's wife Charlotte was dying. General Lee's letter to his wife conveyed the heartbreak and loneliness he felt on Christmas Day.

> "I am filled with sadness dear Mary at the intelligence conveyed in your letter of last evening. I have been oppressed with sorrowful forebodings since parting with Charlotte. She seemed to me stricken with a prostration I could not understand. Dear child she promised to be better the next morning & I wrote to her in a cheerful & hopeful mood which I could not feel. That you may know my sorrow in all its breadth & depth, as far as I know my own heart, I feel for her all the love I bear Fitzhugh [Rooney]. That is very great. I pray she may be spared to us. Yet God's will be done. The blow so grievous to us is intended I believe in mercy to her. She was so devoted to Fitzhugh. Seemed bound up in him, that apparently she thought of & cared for nothing else. They seemed so united, that I loved them as one person. I would go down tomorrow, but from your letter have no hope of finding her alive, or of being able to do anything for her. I feel that all will be done for her that human power can, & oh I pray that our Merciful Father will yet spare her, or gently take her to Himself! Telegraph me if I can yet reach there in time.

> "I received today the two boxes you sent. Distributed the socks & am much obliged for the turkey."[43]

In the Union camps during the Christmas holidays, the change in sutlers was an improvement for John Haley's stomach of the 17th Maine and the victuals received for a mere whistled tune. The "Merry Christmas" of the holiday held little regards for Haley this Christmas.

> "'Merry Christmas' has no significance to me. I had no work to do, so the time was passed answering letters. This condition of repose is the reward of being on guard at the sutler's. This post is a very desirable one, as the clerk and yours truly are on most friendly terms, so I fare well. We have signals by

which we know when the time comes for a 'wave offering.' The subscriber whistles Penny Royal tunes and is promptly rewarded by seeing a hand thrust through the aperture in the tent, loaded with eatables. This man Furlong is from Massachusetts and not of the same breed as the sutler, who is a Baltimore Dutchman and too mean to feed a flea."[44]

Charles Barber of the 104th New York had food on his mind as he recalled the holiday he left behind two years before while on picket duty along the Rapidan River.

"We have been on short rations again my Christmas days rations was only three crackers two oz of meat and coffee with salt in it instead of sugar I thought of the happy Christmas I had at home two years ago with my family and the good hearty victuals and the good supper we had at Joe Coopers. it is two years this morning at two o clock that I left home the last time taking that old bed quilt which has long since been destroyed by the incidents of war. time especially in war time brings round rapid changes 8 or 9 months more I hope will bring me safe home again and the months are speeding by fast as the untireing wheels of time can roll on."[45]

Officer Elisha Hunt Rhodes of the 2nd Rhode Island Volunteer Infantry took a Christmas Day ride on his new horse about the environs of Camp Sedgwick.

"This is Christmas day and the third one I have passed in the Army. I have enjoyed a good long ride on my new horse Kate. I traded Old Abe for her and think I have one of the finest horses in the Army. She is a beauty and very fast, both running and trotting. I gave a dinner to a party of officers, and we tried to celebrate Christmas in a becoming manner."[46]

Color Sergeant Peter Welsh of the Irish 28th Massachusetts spent Christmas near Stevensburg, Virginia, and described his winter quarters to his wife. Christmas was dull for Welsh as he complained that even the sutlers were barren of anything good for Christmas.

"I am not in need of any clothing we get stockings from the government cheaper then you could buy them at home 32 cents a pair the thing i am most defeciant of is gloves i have none i bought a pair of boots i also had gloves but lost them in the fall campaign My dear wife we have got our winter quarters built we are pretty comfortable considering where we are we have small houses built four men in each house the roof covered with four pieces of shelter tents they are dry and warm I hope you spent Christmas pleasent i spent it very dull there was nothing to be got here even the sutlers were unable to get up anything for Christmas. . . . My dear wife i must now conclude by wishing heave[n']s choisest blessings on you."[47]

One sergeant from the 16th Maine Regiment came up with a novel approach to get a Christmas furlough by using a biblical passage from Deuteronomy 20:7. "And what man is there, that have betrothed a wife, and hath not taken her? Let him go and return unto his house, lest he die in battle and another man take her." A sympathetic officer approved the request and the sergeant spent the Christmas holidays at home hopefully in the arms of his wife.[48]

From the office of the Provost Marshal at Harper's Ferry, clerk Charles H. Moulton of the 34th Massachusetts, wrote to his mother of his wish to peek upon the family gathered for the holiday.

"This week comes Christmas—two such occasions that I have been restrained from the opportunity of hanging up my stockings. But, nevertheless, I am glad to hear that I am so well remembered at home, that a plate is placed on the table on all these occasions of feasting. I think we shall indulge in a turkey dinner on Christmas, at the expense of our kind landlady. We of the P.M. staff were made the recipients of an oyster supper a few evenings by one of the restaurant proprietors in return for the patronage we had bestowed upon them.

". . . O, for a silent peek in upon that jovial family circle."[49]

Charles Francis Adams, Jr. found himself back in Warrenton foraging for the materials to build the winter quarters in which he spent Christmas. Similar to his last Christmas, Adams took up architectural pursuits again as described

Figure 4-7. The 40th Massachusetts Infantry spent its third Christmas of the war in camp at Miner's Hill, Virginia. (USAMHI)

in a letter sent to his father at his diplomatic post in England.

"This evening finds me in reality in winter quarters. To-night for the first time this year I feel comfortable in my new house, the admiration of all who see it, with a fire-place, candles, chairs and table. I must describe it even if I am verbose, for not even Mrs. John D. Bates, on moving into No. 1 Boston, experienced half the satisfaction I feel in this offspring of my undeveloped architectural talent. It cost me twelve dollars in money. I bought half of a roof of a building from which the soldiers had stripped the sides. This was divided at the ridge-pole and the two sides constitute the two sides of my house, six feet high by fourteen long, the front and rear logged up, with an open fire-place in the rear, covered with an old hospital tent fly, and with a floor of boards—warm, roomy and convenient, two beds, three chairs and a table, and every thing snug. Don't talk to me of comfort! Bah! Everything is relative. I have more real, positive, healthy comfort here than I ever did in my cushioned and carpeted room at home!"[50]

Adams was snug as a bug in a Christmas stocking.

Alfred Bellard, formerly of the 5th New Jersey, was now a member of the Veteran Reserve Corps. The Veteran Reserves were units of soldiers that were recovering from wounds or sickness but able to do light duty in rear areas of the war. The distinctive uniform was a light blue jacket and trousers. Initially called the Invalid

Corps, the name was changed after front-line soldiers jokingly named it the "Inspected and Condemned Corps" for the initials stamped on worn-out equipment by the Quartermaster. Bellard spent Christmas Day on duty patrolling the streets of Washington, D.C., inspecting intoxicated soldiers for passes.

"On Christmas Day the noise in Washington reminded one of the 4th of July in the North, with firing of guns and the small boy with his firecrackers. We had a double patrol out on that day, as there were so many drunken soldiers in the city without passes, that they needed looking after."[51]

Confederate raider *C.S.S. Alabama* under the command of Admiral Raphael Semmes, hunting for Federal prizes in the Pacific, spent Christmas Day incognito sailing under a French flag. Boarding officer George Townley Fullam was busy disembarking prisoners on dry land and boarding other ships to discover their nationalities.

"Christmas Day. Sent all prisoners on shore this morning, having anchored off Malacca last night. Returned on board at 9.45. 10 a.m. Hove up and stood on course. Chased a bark which on boarding I found to be the *Gallant Neill* of and to Madras from Singapore. Hoisted the French colours to many ships during the day. P.M. Spliced main brace and drank to sweethearts and wives. 5.45 p.m. Came to in 25 fthms. Several vessels anchored around us. 7 p.m. I boarded a ship ahead of us and found her to be the *Puget* of Marseilles, Singapore to Madras. Calm with steady rain."[52]

This would be the last Christmas the *Alabama* would be hunting the oceans for Federal ships. She was sunk off the coast of Cherbourg, France, on June 19, 1864, by the *U.S.S. Kearsarge* after a duel at sea.

Once again for the third Christmas of the war, as the Army of Tennessee settled into winter camp at Dalton, the clothing account book of Co. C was opened by the mysterious scribe of the 4th Kentucky, and he penned his annual Christmas inscription.

"Dec 25th 1863. Yes, old Brick, another Christmas has come and gone, and we are still combatting with the Vandal horde; Are likely to be doing that same this time next Christmas. What a pity."[53]

HARPER'S WEEKLY.
A JOURNAL OF CIVILIZATION.

Vol. VIII.—No. 418.]   NEW YORK, SATURDAY, DECEMBER 31, 1864.   [SINGLE COPIES TEN CENTS.
[$4.00 PER YEAR IN ADVANCE.

Entered according to Act of Congress, in the Year 1864, by Harper & Brothers, in the Clerk's Office of the District Court for the Southern District of New York.

Figure 5-1. Cover page to *Harper's* 1864 Christmas issue captures the timeless excitement of the day in its title "Christmas Morning." (K.R.)

5

CHRISTMAS OF TRIUMPH, CHRISTMAS OF DESPAIR

he fourth year of the war was grinding to a close. In all geographical departments the floundering Confederate armies were gasping for existence. Military reverses were constricting and shrinking the South's area to maneuver. In effect, the Confederacy's will to fight was ebbing away.

On Christmas Day in Tennessee and Alabama, Hood's Army of Tennessee was running for its life with the Union army of Thomas and Schofield in dogged pursuit. Only the determined resistance of Generals S. D. Lee and Nathan Bedford Forrest's troops kept the Confederate army from complete destruction. Many were too busy marching and skirmishing to note the passing of the day. The killing and dying would not cease for the observance of the holiday.

At Petersburg and Richmond, Lee's dwindling army sat huddled behind ever-extending entrenchments. Desertions were reaching alarming proportions as those that lost hope headed homeward after receiving written exhortations of needy families. Grant and his generals pondered ways to get around the flanks of Lee's entrenchments, or at least stretch the thinning Confederate line still further to the breaking point. So close were the lines that many Union soldiers could hear the church bells of Richmond peal on Christmas Day and wryly noted the similarity of positions to that of the 1862 Peninsula Campaign.

Many Union and Confederate soldiers alike were hoping this would be the last Christmas of the war. While some partook in festive celebrations of the day, others wrote somber reflections of their experiences and feelings in letters home or in diaries. Some Union soldiers would optimistically scribble about impending victory upon hearing the news of Sherman's capture of Savannah. But it would still be a difficult row to hoe, fraught with many trials and tribulations before the Confederacy rolled over and breathed its last.

President Lincoln received the best Christmas present of his presidency on Christmas Eve, when he was handed Sherman's telegram dated December 22, 1864.

"To his Excellency, President Lincoln: I beg leave to present you as a Christmas gift the City of Savannah, 150 guns and plenty of ammunition; also about twenty-five thousand bales of cotton. W. T. Sherman Major-General."

It had been a trying year for Lincoln as his political fortunes had looked very bleak. On all military fronts the war seemed to stagnate as newspapers published the mounting casualty lists and the public tired of the human cost of the war. A negotiated peace with the Confederate government had started to look good to some sections of the war-weary public. General McClellan had based his political platform on just such a negotiated settlement for the up-coming presidential election. It was not until Sherman's army took possession of Atlanta on September 2 that the fortunes of war seemed to begin smiling on Lincoln's administration again.

Through the end of September and into October, Confederate reverses helped solidify Lincoln's once sure defeat into a winning mandate at the polls with fifty-five percent of the popular vote. The ticket of Lincoln and Andrew Johnson received 212 electoral votes to McClellan and George H. Pendleton of Ohio's 21 votes. Balloting in the military where McClellan had once been a popular general, showed him losing to Lincoln by almost four to one.

Several days after the election, General McClellan resigned from the Army and declared his disappointment with the election's outcome.

The Confederate armies continued to experience defeat at the battles of Franklin and Nashville, in the Shenandoah Valley, and with the capture of Atlanta. The Union occupation of Savannah renewed the desire for victory in the North.

President Lincoln, as he had the previous three Christmas Eves, sat down with his Secretary of the Navy, Gideon Welles, to affix his signature to a batch of pardons and death sentence commutations. Welles, with his long white beard and wig, had more than a passing resemblance to Santa Claus. While he considered the President's granting of pardons as a sign of weakness, Welles nonetheless aided the President, by going over Secretary of War Edwin Stanton's head to bring them to Lincoln's attention.

On this Christmas Eve, Secretary Welles had his own favor to ask the Chief Executive. Mrs. Welles had a young lady friend who had come to Washington from Virginia to nurse her sick mother at the beginning of the war. The mother had since died and left the young woman stranded for several years in the Northern capital. Now she desired to return South to marry a "rebel whelp" as Welles described the situation. The problem was she was unrepentant in her Southern sympathies and refused to sign an oath of allegiance. Because she had been in the North for four years, she felt the need to get home to marry her fellow, reasoning her youth was fast slipping away from her. Lincoln asked how old she was and Welles answered "about twenty-three."

The Navy Secretary requested the President read the young lady's statement which he had brought with him, cautioning the President that it was intemperate in its tone. Lincoln declined by saying it may prejudice his decision, but he wanted to know more about her. That was when Gideon Welles dropped his bombshell. She was sitting right outside the door!

Welles stated the young woman had requested to be there in case the President might wish to question her. Abraham Lincoln was curious to see what she looked like, so he conspired with the man he called "Father Neptune" behind his back. Welles was to ask her a few more questions out in the hallway, "accidentally" leaving the door ajar. The Secretary was then to go off on a short errand, leaving the President a minute to get a good look at the matrimonial-bound rebel.

Welles did as he was bid, asking several questions of the young lady, then excusing himself to go off on a pseudo errand for a minute or two. Through the open door, the ardent Virginian and the President of the United States sat looking at one another. Seated at the Cabinet table, Abraham Lincoln looked sadly at the woman who was supposed to be his enemy, a Confederate sympathizer who refused to take a loyalty oath so she might receive a pass to return home. The people on both sides of the contested issues were locked in a killing war, but he had no hate for her or her fellow rebellious statesmen. Lincoln glanced away from her and pondered the irony of the moment. When he looked back at her, she was smiling at him. "Her thin, forlorn face was transformed." For a fleeting moment he thought of going over to speak to her. Putting on his best stern, Presidential expression, he watched as Secretary Welles returned down the hallway. The young lady softly spoke a few words to Welles before the Cabinet member entered the room and closed the door behind him.

What did the President think of this request, asked Welles? In reply, the President said she should be allowed to return home. With that, he picked up his pen and scrawled out a pass allowing her through the lines. He dated it "Christmas Day, December 25, 1864," and signed his name to the paper. "That makes it a Christmas present," he noted and gave the document to Secretary Welles.

Welles expressed his gratitude and repeated what the woman had spoken to him. "She said you weren't at all like the monster you had been pictured. She said you reminded her of her father. And she wished you a very merry Christmas." When asked if he had told the young lady the President would sign the pass, Welles replied affirmatively that he had had no doubt of it from the very beginning. After wishing President Lincoln many very merry Christmases now and in the future, the Secretary took his leave. The young lady's name was Laura Jones. It was Abraham Lincoln's last Christmas.[1]

Christmas was very much in the newspapers all across the country. The Christmas Eve edition of *Harper's Weekly* ran the story of "Santa Claus's Wish Council," a moral tale wrapped in Santa Claus's indignation with avarice, wanton waste, and man's disregard for his fellow man. James Gordon Bennett's Christmas Eve edition of the *New York Herald* printed "Santa Claus Visits The New York Herald Office" to complain to the editor of the paper on his enforced boycott of the innocent children in the South because of the Union blockade. In the same issue was the healthful benefits of "Skating At Christmas Time."

It was not until the December 31 issue of *Harper's Weekly* that the Christmas cover and centerfold appeared. The front cover was adorned with the picture "Christmas Morning" showing mother and father peering around the bedroom door at the wild joy taking place amongst the children opening and playing with their Christmas presents.

The editorial titled "Christmas" would rejoice that final victory could be seen on the horizon at last. Stating that the country desired only peace, it went on to declare that it would continue to prosecute the war to achieve that aim over its prodigal states.

"It is a merry Christmas although the cloud of war yet rests upon the land. It is merry because the great gale of victory parts the cloud and gives glimpses of the heaven of peace beyond. It is merry because every man feels now that the people are able to subdue the rebellion; and the merriest of all because they have just declared that they will do it, and show from the Mississippi to the sea that they are doing it. . . .

"To-day, then, under the Christmas evergreen, the country asks only for peace, and breathes only goodwill to all men. Despite the sharp war, its bountiful feast is spread. It stands, as Mr. Nast represents in the large picture in today's Number, holding the door open to welcome the rebellious children back to the family banquet. It does not forget one of their crimes. It remembers the enormity of their attempt. It will take good care that the root of bitterness is destroyed forever, and that the peace of the household shall be henceforth secure. But it asks what it can command. It says now, as it has said from the beginning, 'Submit to the laws made by all for the common welfare, and there will be no more war.'

"Nor does that country for a moment forget the sad and solitary hearts and hearths upon which the light of the holy season shines. It is a grief too deep for anger, and it requires that such sorrow as this Christmas sun beholds shall be made impossible hereafter. The rest from their labors, the young and brave who have made this country better worth living in. The hearts that are broken with those completed lives time will soothe, but can never wholly heal. Yet never did the seed sown more surely grow and flower and crown the happy harvest-home than those precious lives. In a deeper national faith, in a purer national purpose, in soberer, simpler, nobler individual lives the harvest of that heroism shall be seen.

"'Come home—come home, then,' says the mother. 'While you refuse you shall be scourged with fire. I have no anger. Your crime grew because I suffered it to grow. I have no anger, for in the heart's-blood of my darlings my sin is washed away. I ask for peace, I breathe only good-will. But Peace you have learned that I mean to have!'"[2]

The editorial set up Thomas Nast's annual Christmas number, a holiday political propaganda drawing titled "The Union Christmas Dinner." The center showed President Lincoln welcoming President Davis, General Lee, and other Confederate generals and politicians to the table of States. Under Lincoln's feet his message "The door has been for a full year open to all" is all but hidden. The empty chairs of the Southern states noted by the initials on the backs of the chairs. On the wall behind the bounty-laden table are the names and faces of the heroes of the Union along with the aims and ideals of the war swathed in holiday greens. The four corners of the drawing have three illustrated conditions for surrender and a biblical allusion for the return of the prodigal states. A fifth illustration at the center bottom shows the folks at home toasting a blessing to "our soldiers and sailors." Santa Claus in his sleigh with reindeer on rooftop appears in silhouette behind the word Christmas in the title. On either side of the title is a city skyline with a prominent church steeple and a winter army camp with a sentry standing guard and several soldiers gathered around a campfire.

General William Tecumseh Sherman rode unnoticed into the city of Savannah with his staff on the morning of December 22. Around nine o'clock he stood atop the roof of the Savannah custom house, surveying the city he had once been posted to as a young officer in the army, but now served as its martial conqueror. Sherman's first concern was the garrison and occupation of the city. Later in the morning a wealthy cotton broker offered Sherman the use of his home as his headquarters instead of the Pulaski Hotel. It was there that one of the first visitors he received was U. S. Treasury agent A. G. Browne.

Browne tried to claim all captured contraband in the name of the government, but Sherman refused his request as his army needed food and supplies. Any surplus would be turned over to the Treasury, and all cotton would be placed under guard. A. G. Browne was known to be "a shrewd, clever Yankee." Browne did make a suggestion that would earn him Sherman's permanent gratitude: the suggestion that Sherman should send the city of Savannah as a Christmas gift to Lincoln by telegram. Realizing the adroitness of such an idea, Sherman wrote out his message. The President received the communique on Christmas Eve.

Christmas Day in Savannah was rainy. The troops were turned out in the rain to hear Sherman's order of congratulations read and then dismissed to cook and eat their Christmas

Figure 5-2. Thomas Nast used the holiday season as a backdrop for his politically charged centerfold entitled *The Union Christmas Dinner* which graphically stated his views toward peace with the Confederacy. Issued December 31, 1864. (K.R.)

Figure 5-3. Christmas dinner hosted by General Sherman in Savannah after he captured the city and presented it to President Lincoln as a Christmas present. (K.R.)

dinners between rainstorms. Sherman hosted his own festive holiday dinner for twenty people, complete with silver and china provided by his host Charles Green. Wine was provided by grateful merchants and several turkeys foraged by an officer on Sherman's staff. Sherman's holiday would receive a sad emotional blow around Christmas. When the mail caught up with the swift moving army at Savannah, Sherman was given a newspaper article by a friend that announced the death of his youngest son Charles, whom he had never seen.

A member of Independent Pennsylvania Battery E of the 20th Corps, artilleryman John Anderson, wrote to his father of Sherman's Christmas gift.

"Dear Father, The Loyal Men of the North have had as a Christmas Gift from Sherman, the City of Savannah and a beautiful gift it is,

the most beautiful city I ever have been in . . . Lincoln is a sore blow for the South. . . ."[3]

Another soldier, officer Adin Underwood of the 33rd Massachusetts Infantry, would recall Christmas in Savannah and Sherman's promise to the regiment's band. It turned out to be not quite the honor that the regimental band was expecting.

"Before Christmas Day, came the news to Sherman's Armies here, that the other part of his Army of the Cumberland under Thomas, had defeated Hood at Nashville. The troops were nearly wild with joy, as was the whole country. Savannah and Nashville were the two great victories that made the campaign complete.

"Thanksgiving Day, the thirty-third [regiment] was in the capitol of Georgia, Christmas, now in its great commercial city, Savannah; at least its band was there, that day. Sherman had promised the band of the regiment that it should be the first band to play in the city after its capture, and Christmas Day, according to the promise, it was playing 'John Brown,' 'Yankee Doodle,' 'The Star Spangled Banner,' 'Dixie,' in Pulaski Square, to an over-joyed crowd of darkies of all ages, sizes and colors, swarming to hear the 'Linkum Band'; singing, shouting, crying and dancing for joy, that 'De day ob de lord hab come.' They swarmed in to the number of thousands, and there was such a mass that Sherman reluctantly, had to order the square cleared, finally. Some of the members of the regiment went into the city Christmas Day to celebrate the victory on their own account, were rather misunderstood and not appreciated by the provost-guard, and were ignominiously quartered in the guard house. . . ."[4]

Many company messes cooked and ate their Christmas dinners between rainstorms, some eating the bounty of fresh oysters from the nearby sea, others ate a fare that at best was bland. Fife Major William Humphrey of the 101st Illinois wrote home admonishing the folks about what had become the staple of his regiment's diet.

"While you were eating your good dinner we soldiers would have been glad to have the crumbs that fell from your table. I will tell you what our meals were this day: Breakfast, rice and beef. Dinner, rice. Supper, beef and rice. Rice is our favorite dish now."[5]

Fellow comrade in arms with the 123rd New York Infantry, Rice C. Bull, jotted in his diary about the abundantly supplied Christmas dinners he envisioned the soldiers in other Union armies to be enjoying compared to his meager holiday menu.

"The people of the North had hardly ceased their rejoicing over the real Christmas present our Army had made them in the Capture of Savannah, before General Sherman began preparations for the final chapter of the campaign, the March through the Carolinas. After we reached Savannah, and before we had been put on full rations, he secured and was having placed in wagons supplies for the next movement.

"The men of our Army had a lean and hungry Christmas in Savannah. While the Armies nearer home in Virginia and Tennessee were having turkey dinners, furnished and forwarded them by the people of the North, we at Savannah, were so far away we could not be reached. We had boiled rice, Georgia fresh beef that was left from those driven along the way with us on the march through the state, and coffee."[6]

The Confederate army of General Hardee was encamped upon the banks of the Savannah River following the evacuation of the city a few days earlier. Johnny Green of the Orphan Brigade's 4th Kentucky Infantry, wrote of his wish for Christmas after helping to evacuate the army from Savannah. He received a rare windfall this Christmas Day.

"Peace on Earth, Good will to men should prevail. We certainly would preserve the peace if they would go home & let us alone. . . .

"Our commisary sends word for each Orderly Sergeant to come to his wagon & he will issue one piece of soap to each man. This is indeed good news. Since the Skirmish began at Stockbridge Nov 15th we have not had a chance to wash any more than our faces occasionall & never our feet or bodies until now. We have never had our clothes off & no clean clothes until now. The quartermaster brought clothes out from Savannah to issue to us; they would otherwise have been burned up in Savannah.

"I got my piece of Soap & took a bath in the Savannah River. Lathered well & then soused in good & took a swim. It was pretty cold too. I donned my new clothes, cotton under clothes & grey Jeanes Jacket & trousers, & washed as best I could my old clothes, dried them & put them in my feed sack. As there was no cooking utensil in the regiment except a coffee pot or two I had to do my laundry work in cold water & you can gess [sic] it was poor."[7]

John S. Jackman, also with the Orphan Brigade, described the prospects for his Christmas dinner in the rain. He also lamented, as did many other veteran soldiers of both sides, about the fourth Christmas he had spent in the army.

"For breakfast had fresh pork, biscuit, baked sweet-potatoes etc.— Cool disagreeable morning—at noon cold rain commenced falling. Bad prospect for a Christmas dinner— can't cook in the rain. Slept all evening. Rain pouring down. Has been a most gloomy day—being the fourth birth day spent in the army. At night, sat up late chatting around a smoky fire built under a shed out of the rain. 'Dr.' Davis, seeing his 'christmas.' "[8]

Union and Confederate soldiers had fought with great ferocity in the heat of battle, but so too could they show extreme acts of kindness towards each other. The much quoted biblical phrase "Peace on Earth, Goodwill towards men" summed up the holiday charity ninety Michigan men and their captain demonstrated towards the civilians living outside Savannah. On Christmas Day the Union soldiers loaded several wagons with food and other perishable supplies and distributed their gifts about the ravaged Georgia countryside. The destitute Southerners thanked the jolly Union "Santa Clauses" who had tied tree branches to the heads of the mule teams to "resemble" reindeer.[9]

In other parts of the rapidly shrinking Confederacy, Christmas was a busy time for troops on both sides of the conflict. Remnants of Confederate troops from Hood's army were retreating swiftly to get to a safe haven following the Army of the Tennessee's disastrous defeat before Nashville. The Union commands of Generals Thomas and Schofield were rapidly following after the retreating, but still dangerous, columns of Confederate troops. Attempts by the Union army to cut off and gobble up the fleeing rebels was met by stiff resistance from cavalry of General Nathan Bedford Forrest's command and General S. D. Lee's collected troops.

One of those trying to prevent capture by traveling out of reach of the pursuing Union troops, was the wounded Captain Samuel T. Foster of the 24th Texas Cavalry (Dismounted) of Granbury's Texas Brigade. Part of the recently killed General Patrick Cleburne's famed Division, Foster sustained a leg wound, but refused to be left behind with the hundreds of other wounded Confederates the doctors would not move.

Catching up with his regiment after finagling passage on an ambulance, Foster bought a horse and equipment for $800.00, considering the deal cheap. Relating the events of Christmas Eve and Day in his diary, Foster showed considerable bitterness for Hood's generalship and wishing for the peaceful assignment of 1862.

". . . Some of my men go out in the country and get some Whiskey, and we have a Jolly Christmas night. Have some good bread to eat. . . . Leave camp at day light this morning. It is raining slowly, very dark and gloomy— Had a drink of whiskey this morning to remind us of olden times, but it was not furnish[ed] by Genl Hood. We bought it with our own money.

"This is Christmas 1864. Where were we last Christmas. If we choose to go back to Arkansas Post 1862 we will find ourselves there comfortably situated in our winter quarters. If we had counted noses then, and again today the missing would outnumber the present.

"Then we were anxious to get into a fight with the Yanks; and even feared that the war would end and we never get to see one. Now we have seen too many of them, as is evidenced by our number present today—Then we were called feathered bed soldiers—now we are war veterans; but Yankee bullets will kill one as quick as the other. Then Hood was in command of the Brigade in Va. Now he is in command of the remnant of the Army of Tenn. after having butchered 10,000 of them around Atlanta Ga. and as many more in Tenn. at Franklin and Nashville, where he betrayed his whole Army—He might command a Brigade—and even a division but command the Army, he is not the man.

"Genl Joe Johnson has more military sense in one day than Hood ever did or ever will have. . . .

"But after all, this is Christmas and (as the Irishman would say) 'a wee drop' makes an old soldier forget his troubles and hardships for the present, make merry as much as is our power to do. Everyone seems to know that today is Christmas, and so to make the best of it."[10]

An officer of the 59th Illinois in the pursuing Union army, Lieutenant William McAdams, detailed his Christmas holiday in a New Year's Day letter to his wife describing the dire state of the collapsing Confederacy.

"A Merry Christmas and a Happy New Year to you and little Willie. The year just past has been an eventful one. Many battles have been fought and very many boys have been killed and many others wounded and maimed and many hearts have been made to mourn. . . .

"The Rebel cause has certainly suffered greatly of late. Their cause is a desperate one and they will employ desperate means before they will give up the struggle. There is strong talk about their arming the negroes to fight for their cause.

"General Lee wants more men. General Hood wants more men. They now only have one army that amounts to anything and that is at Richmond. Grant and Sherman certainly take Richmond and the day is ours.

"We were marching on Christmas Day and did not have a very agreeable time but today we are in camp & have good comfortable quarters and we had a good New Years dinner. We had roast turkey, fresh ham, warm biscuits, good coffee, condensed milk, one large can of preserved cherries, fresh peaches, two cans and one can of fresh cherries. Fresh raspberries, fresh butter and other things too tedious to mention and we have had an agreeable time. Our corps followed the rebels from this place toward Florence and I learn today that our corps is now marching for Huntsville, Ala."[11]

Another Union regiment, the 45th Ohio regiment of Major General David Stanley's 4th Corp, was marching on Christmas Day as noted in the diary of David Humphrey Blair of Co. D.

"Christmas and we marched very rapidly. The cavalry had gone rather far ahead and were turned upon by some organized rebel infantry that had escaped thus far and so we were needed for support. We marched rapidly, rations had been consumed and no more at hand. All were hungry, almost starving. Rain and sleet drenched our shoulders, knapsacks very heavy. Mud very deep and heavy. All were wet and muddy and we had a memorable time in general on that Christmas of 1864. . . ."[12]

Somewhere on the road in Tennessee in pursuit of his regiment, the 95th Illinois, the diary entry of a soldier with the presidential name of John Quincy Adams related his scanty Christmas diet.

"Weather cloudy and a little rain. Today is Christmas. Our presents are somewhat limited. For breakfast we had hardtack and coffee. Henry Freeman and myself cross the river in pursuit of the regiment and found them at 9 AM a distance of three miles out. They foraged meat, provisions and c [coffee]. . . . Our dinner consisted of hardtack and meat and supper, hardtack and roast pig. . . ."[13]

An artillery private with the 6th Wisconsin Light Battery, Jenkin Lloyd Jones, and his battery were left behind within the fortifications of Fort Gillem guarding Nashville. The battery was hoping to join Sherman's army when it marched north after the beginning of the new year. Exhilarated with the news from all fronts, especially in front of Nashville, Jones spent time recording his meditations and thoughts on church and the state of affairs in his realm. On Christmas Eve, optimism breathed through his diary jottings.

"A pleasant night on guard though rather cold. Thawed but little during the day. My health still continues very good. Camp all hilarity over the good news from all quarters. It gives new hopes of the coming dawn. Father Abraham has called for 300,000 more troops. This is right, says the soldier. It shows no faltering or weakness of resolution on our part, while the Confederacy's brightest lights are wringing their hands in anguish and despondency. But it makes me sad that it once more threatens to deprive my loved parents of the solace and comfort. I pray God that my dear brothers be spared to stay with them in their old age.

"It is Christmas Eve, and I am all alone. Dan and Milt have gone to town. Griff is on guard. Nobody to interrupt my quiet meditations, and I can but think of the many happy hearts that now beat in my Northern home.

It is in the striking contrast with our situation here, where time glides by so idly and it seems at times uselessly. I can hardly realize that it is really Christmas time, so associated is the winter with snow and frozen ears and good times to me. It is hard to recognize it in this mud and rain with bare, frozen ground for days. But it is not always to be thus. I am happy in anticipation of hard-tack and salt junk for to-morrow's dinner as many that count on roast turkey and 'fixings.' And still many at home are not happy. I can fancy the heavy cloud that hangs over their hearts as they are anxiously awaiting the return of us from the field. Yes, they think of us morn, noon, and eve. May we be true to their memory and return with clear conscience, unsullied by the vices in camp."

On Christmas Day, theology and melodies danced in Jones' head.

"A warm day, misty and muddy. All is quiet. Health very good. 8 A.M. had our regular Sunday morning inspection, after which Griff and I attended church. Were there in time for Sabbath school, went in and listened to the sweet melody 'There is a Happy Land,' and 'Homeward Bound,' which sounded very sweetly to my ear. Read the 2nd chapter of Matthew in concert, then went above to listen to a sermon from the 13th and 14th verses of the same chapter. The Calvinistic dogmas preached stronger than I ever listened to from an American pulpit. Did not like it at all.

"Returned to feast on Irish potatoes, Uncle Sam's Christmas dinner. Mail received. Brought us news of a dinner having been started us from home At night Griff and I attempted to while away the remaining hours by sundry attempts at singing, but we retired early, and the third Christmas in the army was gone."[14]

Private W. H. Bird was home in Alabama on a thirty day furlough from the Army of Northern Virginia. Just before Christmas, local girls and friends cajoled him into extending his leave without authorization from the 13th Alabama through the end of the holidays. He did not need too much arm twisting to be convinced into staying.

"Well, time continued on and my furlough about to expire, and Christmas closing in on us every day. I had to start back in two days before my paper was out so I could get transportation on it; and we had another rousing social gathering the night before I was to start, and there were three or four boys that had got furloughs, and all commenced to begging me to stay until after Christmas, it being the 20th of December, and having such a nice time and the girls looking so neat, and all of them begging so hard for me to stay, that I began to think right smart about staying and risk the consequences. I was pretty sure that my Captain, B. A. Bowen, wouldn't care, as the army had gone into winter quarters, [at Petersburg.] So I made up my mind to stay at home until after Christmas. Well, we had a fine time of course, with plenty to eat, and with girls day and night; and on the last night of 1864 we had a nice social and I bid farewell to the girls as they would start for Home."[15]

Farther west in the Officer's Hospital in Little Rock, Arkansas, Lieutenant Thomas Nichols Stevens of the 28th Wisconsin, Co. C, wrote to his wife on Christmas Eve. Convalescing from an illness, Stevens wistfully wrote of his wish to be home sharing the preparations and tidings of the day.

"To-day & to-night you are as busy as you can be, I suppose, with your Christmas Tree and other holiday arrangements for the children, but not too busy, I know, to think of me and wish I could be with you to see and help, as I am wishing I could be, even for a day. . . . Here I have done but little but sit about and read all day, and can do nothing else this evening except sit & think of my own wife and our little ones, and all our friends at home, and wish them a Merry Christmas. To-morrow we are having a Christmas dinner at our hospital—don't know as it will be anything extra, and don't care, so long as my loved ones cannot share it with me. I have thought I would hang up my stocking tonight, for I feel almost certain I should get something in it—say a dose of pills or a quinine powder! I'll think of it and make up my mind before bedtime. . . ."

On Christmas Day, Stevens wrote another letter to his wife relating the hospital's yuletide dinner and his blue feelings that evening, no doubt caused by the dreary weather and absence from home.

"Merry Christmas, dearest! and a right Merry one may it be to you all at home. Here it is anything else, almost. It is a dull, dreary, gloomy, solemn, drizzly Sunday compelling one to have the blues whether he will or no. I'm glad I'm not to spend another in the army.

"We have had enough to eat here at the hospital, and that which is good enough. Shall I tell you what we had for dinner? The doctor got up a good one in honor of the day. We had roast pig, chicken, mashed potatoes, raw onions, cold slaw, boiled cabbage, kraut, parsnips, Jelly Apple-pie, mince pie (both kinds horrible) coffee, & bread and butter. Wasn't that good enough?. . . . I hope you are not having as dreary a day at home. How I want to be with you to-day—but it's no use wishing that. Shall be there a year from now,—that's one comfort. . . ."[16]

Fighting on Christmas Day occurred along the North Carolina coast as a bombardment of Fort Fisher involving the concerted plans of the Union Army and Navy got under way for a second day. At 2 o'clock a Federal landing party began an assault on the sand fort guarding the entrance to the Cape Fear River. A non-commissioned officer in the 3rd New York Infantry, Edward King Wightman wrote to his brother describing the bombardment, landing, and impromptu Christmas dinner on board the transport *Weybosset*.

"At sunrise on Christmas morning, everything was quiet. The sky was cloudy but the sea tranquil and disturbed only by a gentle swell. There was no wind blowing, and the beach was only three miles distant. Everything seemed to favor our enterprise, and the troops, who had been eighteen days embarked (long enough to visit Europe and return), were eager to land. . . .

"Early in the forenoon our artillery opened . . . I can imagine nothing like the bellowing of our fifteen inch guns. The belching of a volcano with accompanying explosions may suggest a corresponding idea. The din was deafening. Above the fort the countless flash[es] and puffs of smoke from bursting shells spoke for the accuracy of our guns while occasionally columns of sand were heaved high in the air suggested that possibly the casements were not safe and cozy after all . . . By two o'clock the batteries on the bar had been silenced, our consort of gunboats had worked in and taken positions near the shore, and five hundred men, Brg. Gen. Curtis commanding our little brigade, were making for the beach in yawl boats, arranged in line of battle. We watched anxiously. Before they touched shore, the men were actually deploying at skirmishing and advancing at a double quick ere they reached dry land. A rousing cheer—a stenatorian Christmas cheer—went up from the whole fleet.

"Forward the first line ran with their heels toward us and their front to the enemy while, more rapidly than I can write, a solid line of battle formed close behind and followed on. A moment later a white flag fluttered from the sand hill, and one hundred fifty 'gray backs' surrendered themselves and a piece of field artillery. Jack Knowles and I, seated on the pilot house, shook hands on the strength of it. 'Now for our Christmas dinner,' said my worthy comrade cheerily, 'I guess we can afford to feast on sour bacon and hard tack in honor of that performance,' and so we did, watching lynx-eyed the moving panorama on shore, pointing out probable points of attack with our forks, calling attention to the gallant charges by gestering [sic] eloquently with crackers, and making all sort of odd noises by trying to chuckle while masticating."[17]

The attack failed as General Butler recalled his troops, and by dusk, 700 men were stranded as the heavy tidal surf pounded and broke up boats sent to retrieve the troops still on the shore. Two days later they were rescued. On January 15 of the New Year, Wightman was killed leading his regiment across the parapets of Fort Fisher as the "Gibraltar of the Confederacy" finally fell into Federal hands.

Prison experiences of 1864 were ones of despair, especially so for those confined to the hells of Andersonville or frigid Johnson's Island and Point Lookout. One lucky prisoner who managed to live through the confines of Andersonville before escaping from a moving train while being transferred to another prison camp near Charleston, was John Ransom of the 9th Michigan Cavalry.

Ransom was beginning his second year of captivity, having spent the last Christmas on Belle Island in Richmond before being shipped to Andersonville in March. On the run for the second time since escaping, Ransom ran into the 80th Ohio marching to Savannah. On Christmas Day Ransom received his Christmas gift, an unexpected reunion with his former cavalry regiment.

"Christmas day and didn't hang my stocking. No matter, it wouldn't have held anything. Last Christmas we spent on Belle Island, little thinking long imprisonment awaiting us. Us escaped men are to ride in a forage wagon. The army is getting ready to move. Are now twenty-four miles from Savannah and the rebels falling back as we press ahead. NIGHT.—At about nine o'clock this morning as we sat in the forage wagon top of some corn riding in state, I saw some cavalry coming from the front. Soon recognized Col. Acker at the head of the 9th Michigan Cavalry. Jumped out the wagon and began dancing and yelling in the middle of the road and in front of the troop. Col. Acker said: 'Get out the road you—lunatic!' Soon made myself known and was like one arisen from the dead. Major Brockway said: 'Ransom, you want to start for home. We don't know you, you are dead. No such man as Ransom on the rolls for ten months.' All remembered me and are rejoiced to see me back again. Lieut. Col. Way, Surgeon, Adjutant, Sergeant-Major, all shake hands with me. My company 'A' was in the rear of the column, and I stood by the road as they moved along, hailing those I recognized. In every case had to tell them who I was and then would go up and shake hands with them at the risk of getting stepped on by the horses. Pretty soon Co. 'A' appeared, and wasn't they surprised to see me. The whole company were raised in Jackson, Mich., my home, and I had been regarded as dead for nearly a year. Could hardly believe it was myself that appeared to them."[18]

Another Union soldier who was not so lucky, was Michael Dougherty of the 13th Pennsylvania Cavalry. Incarcerated on Christmas Day in Andersonville, Dougherty commented in the diary he kept about the privation he faced that day, and wished friends at home an enjoyable day.

"Christmas Day Thinking of our friends at home enjoying themselves and how we are situated here No rations of any kind Little our friends at home think of us in this situation God grant them health to enjoy this holiday and may they enjoy themselves well and live long to enjoy many more This is my sincere wishes to my poor mother and sisters I hope I shall see them soon."[19]

Confederate officer Captain Robert Park of the 12th Alabama Infantry, spent his Christmas as a prisoner of war in the chilly confines of Point Lookout at the junction of the Potomac River and Chesapeake Bay. In a mouth-watering diary entry, Park reminisced about the feast and holiday fellowship happening at home.

"Christmas Day— How keenly and vividly home recollections come to my mind to-day! I see the huge baked turkey, the fat barbecued pig, delicious oysters, pound and fruit cakes, numerous goblets of egg-nog and syllabub, etc., etc., on my beloved mother's hospitable table. My brothers and sisters are sitting around it as of yore, and my dear fond mother, with warmest love and pride beaming from her still handsome blue eyes, now somewhat dimmed by approaching age, sits at one end bountifully helping each plate to share of the welcooked eatables before her. How happy I would be if I were with them! I can repeat the words of the familiar song—

'Do they miss me at home, do they miss me? 'Twould be an assurance most dear

To know that some loved one was saying
To-day I wish he were here.'

Those touching words, too, of 'Home Sweet Home' flash before my memory, and I cannot restrain the tears that rush to my eyes. Over three months have passed since I have heard from home and mother. What changes may have occurred since my capture, the 19th of September! [3rd Winchester] Two of my brothers are members of the First Georgia Reserves, now guarding the 30,000 Yankee prisoners at Andersonville—one is a major, and the other, a youth of sixteen years, is one of Capt. Wirz's sergeants. These two no doubt absent from the annual home reunion. Others may be too. I hope and feel that my brothers are civil and kind to the Yankees they are guarding. They are too brave to act otherwise. My poor prison dinner was instead contrast with my Christmas dinners at home. It consisted of beef soup, a small piece of pickled beef, some rice and a slice of loaf bread. Lastly, to our astonishment, about three mouthsful each of bread pudding, not very sweet, were handed us."[20]

From another of the many notorious and squalid Northern prison camps to rival those run by the South, Private William W. Downer of the 6th Virginia Cavalry posted his own dream of home in his diary.

"This is Christmas Eve and how lonely I feel. The thought of home and my dear wife makes me feel as if I had not a friend on earth, but, nevertheless I feel there is one who is able willing and ever ready to help us in time of need. In him I place my trust and ask for help and he alone. Oh that I could have enjoyed the presence and the children as I expected on this particular occasion. Tonite as usual my little children will hang up their socks for old Chris to put something in them; but they have no Pa Pa at home to fill them but; I hope their Ma Ma will fill them as we usually do. I feel like tonight my wife has offered up her prayer to God for my preservation and safe return to her and my little children. God grant that the time may speedily arrive when I shall be with the family again oh that I could say in the language of our Savior, not my will but thine be done. Oh God."

On Christmas Day, Downer recorded the reverie he enjoyed until reality awoke him with the dawn.

"Today is Christmas day and a most beautiful day it is. My thoughts are still on home. Last night I had the most pleasant dream and felt truly happy until I was awakened and realized nothing but a dream. I had been exchanged and reached home in safety. It was breakfast and my wife had prepared a large loaf of bread for breakfast. It was on the table smoking and a large pint of butter setting in the middle of the table. I was seated to the table and, oh; how I enjoyed it. I really thought the best I had eaten. My wife sitting at the head of the table looking upon me with delight not eating a mouthful.

"Willie and Towles sitting on my left calling on Pa for something about every moment and my little baby sitting on the floor, when I awakened and, oh; what disappointment when I raised up in my bed and realized nothing more than a dream.

"I thank God although I am sepperated [sic] from home and all that is near and dear to me I have my health and strength. This morning I have a nice cup of coffee for breakfast given me by Ferdinand Beasley being quite an addition to my breakfast. I am expecting to receive a box of clothes, tobacco and some money from cousin Tap Goodloe Baltimore City which will be a great relief to me. I hope it may come during the Christmas holiday. I have only received one letter from home as yet Dec. 25th 1864."[21]

Along the siege lines outside Richmond and Petersburg, the Union Army of the Potomac and Confederate Army of Northern Virginia remained relatively static and quiet as troops bedded down in winter quarters. A routine of dodging sharpshooters' bullets, mud, military punishment, and pervasive boredom was the common soldiers' lot.

Daniel Chisholm of the 116th Pennsylvania, one of the regiments composing the Irish Brigade, was eyewitness to a particularly grisly Christmas Day example of military justice meted out.

Figure 5-4. Weighing out rations in a winter camp. Note the horse on the left has his own accommodations and blanket. (K.R.)

"To day our Division was ordered out to see a man of the 5th New Hampshire Regt shot. He was shot at 12 O'Clock, the time they always shoot or hang them."[22]

Another Union witness to punishment for the less serious crime of bounty jumping, Orrel Brown of the 16th Maine, commented in his diary on the physical effect on one of the accused.

"On guard, pleasant day, rainy night, had a nice dinner, received two Christmas presents from ladies in town, Dr. Mintezer hung two bounty jumpers by their thumbs this PM. One of them unable to speak or stand when he was taken down."[23]

Across the way behind the Confederate entrenchments, slowly dying hope, want and despair was manifesting itself in the diaries and letters of Lee's troops. From his journal covering December 23 through Christmas Day, 16th Mississippi Infantry member Franklin Lafayette Riley, reported the news of Savannah's fall and lack of materials to celebrate the holiday. The prime ingredient for eggnog would go sorely lacking this year for Riley.

"Sherman has taken Savannah and is marching on Charleston. Hoke's Division has left to defend Wilmington. Rumor has it that we will relieve Wilcox's men Jan. 1 and that we will exchange quarters.

"Yester-day we were told that the merchants and ladies of Richmond will give us a New Year's feast. Good! We have something to look forward to. Not much celebrating this Christmas, possibly because Christmas falls on Sun. More likely, liquor is scarce because we lack money. It's been almost two months since we were paid. Usual picket firing to-day. Otherwise we have had a quiet Christmas."[24]

Fifth Alabama Regiment's Samuel Pickens noted the scant rations endured in the trenches between Richmond and Petersburg, on his fourth Christmas in the army.

"Christmas Day & quite a preety one. Very cold in the morning, but moderated towards evening. All quiet along the lines. At home this is a season of festivity, but with us poor rebels in the army it is almost exnecessitate a fast day. Rations are more scant than usual. For breakfast we had one or 2 'hard tacks,' a scrap of bacon & a cup of coffee. For dinner had to wait to draw rations & had a good hearty meal about dark of biscuit, beef, sugar & coffee & rice."[25]

General Gordon at his headquarters near the Petersburg front, received a rare and pleasant surprise from his wife during a Christmas that was "facetiously" merry.

"Christmas came while we were fighting famine within and Grant without our lines. The Southern people from their earliest history had observed Christmas as the great holiday season of the year. It was the time of times, the longed-for period of universal and innocent but boundless jollification among young and old. In towns and on plantations, purse-strings were loosened and restraints relaxed—so relaxed that even the fun-loving negro slaves were permitted to take some liberties with their masters, to perpetrate practical jokes upon them, and before daylight to storm 'de white folks' houses with their merry calls: 'Christmas gift, master!' 'Christmas gift, everybody!' The holiday, however, on Hatcher's Run, near Petersburg, was joyless enough for the most misanthropic. The one worn-out railroad running to the far South could not bring us half enough necessary supplies; and even if it could have transported Christmas boxes of good things, the people at home were too depleted to send them . . . The brave fellows at the front, however, knew that their friends at home would send them the last pound of sugar in the pantry, and the last turkey or chicken from the barnyard. So they facetiously wished each other

'Merry Christmas!' as they dined on their wretched fare. There was no complaining, no repining, for they knew their exhausted country was doing all it could for them.

"At my headquarters on that Christmas day there was unusual merrymaking. Mrs. Gordon, on leaving home four years before, had placed in her little army-trunk a small package of excellent coffee, and had used it only on very special occasions—'to celebrate,' as she said, 'our victories in the first years, and sustain us in defeat at the last.' When I asked her, on the morning of December 25, 1864, what we could do for a Christmas celebration, she replied, 'I can give you some of that coffee which I brought from home.' She could scarcely have made an announcement more grateful to a hungry Confederate. Coffee—genuine coffee! The aroma of it filled my official family with epicurean enthusiasm before a cup was passed from the boiling pot. If every man of us was not intoxicated by the indulgence after long and enforced abstinence, the hilarity of the party was misleading."[26]

News of Sherman's capture of Savannah also reached the frontline troops of the Union army as quickly as their Confederate counterparts on Christmas Day or the day after. Captain J. P. Beach of the 4th New Jersey Volunteers, recorded the news received by his regiment at Petersburg, and the abundant amount of liquor available in contrast to the rebels across no man's land.

"December 24, Changed quarters to-day on account of their taking the first regiment men out of each company with which they have been serving and forming them into a seperate battalion. Plenty of rum around tonight, it being Christmas Eve. December 26, At 8:30 A.M. An order came around stating that Sherman had captured Savannah and 180 pieces of artillery and 25,000 bales of cotton. Usual amount of firing."[27]

A trooper in the 4th Pennsylvania Cavalry before Richmond, Albert H. Artman, wrote in his diary about the boredom and lack of activities in camp. The day after was a complete reversal as the news of Savannah's capture swept the camps

Figure 5-5. To ease the boredom many soldiers kept diaries. Of Christmas Day in the Army of the Potomac one cavalryman wrote "Nothing of importance going on." (K.R.)

and was marked by a celebration of artillery firing salutes.

"I spent Christmas in camp. Nothing of importance going on. The day very cold. Tuesday December 26, 1864—In camp a salute of 100 guns fired in honor of the fall of Savannah."[28]

Officer Elisha Hunt Rhodes of the 2nd Rhode Island Infantry made notice of the inattention the religious aspect of Christmas received. Serenaded repeatedly by collections of officers and a band from other regiments, Rhodes' tent was the entertainment place to be on Christmas Eve. He wondered, as did many soldiers this holiday, whether this would be the last Christmas spent in the service.

"This is the birthday of our Saviour, but we have paid very little attention to it in a religious way. Last night a party of officers from the 49th Penn. Vols. came to my quarters and gave me some fine music. Just as they left a party of officers from the 37th Mass. Vols. came and gave me a serenade. I invited them in and entertained them the best that I could. About midnight Company 'F' (a new Company) arrived in command of Capt. John A. Jeffreys. This gives me six full Companies, and I now have one of the largest Regiments in the Brigade. About two o'clock this morning I turned in for sleep. This morning it being Sunday as well as Christmas we held our usual inspection, and then I took a ride and dined with some friends. It does not seem much like Sunday or Christmas, for the men are hauling logs to build huts. This is a work of necessity, for the quarters we have been using are not warm enough. This is my fourth Christmas in the Army. I wonder if it will be my last."[29]

An artillerist with the 4th Regiment New York Artillery, H. E. Sears, wrote home to his sister plagued with an outbreak of boils and a toothache. Just before Christmas, he was also

Figure 5-6. Colonel Elisha Hunt Rhodes wrote of men building log huts on Christmas Day near Petersburg, Virginia. Once the walls were erected, tent canvas was used to cover the roof. (USAMHI)

one of eight thousand witnesses to the execution of five men. The band played a funeral dirge as the condemned men marched behind, then they were blindfolded, made to kneel down, and shot.

> "One had to be shot four times before he dide [died] It seams rather hard as well as brutal but what a sad deth [death] as well as a disgraceful deth to be taken out of this world in strong health They were buried without any coffins but put into the grave just as they were shot."

Of Christmas Eve, Sears told his sister of the caroling and music in camp before Richmond.

> "But today is Sunday and a very plesent day Now it is Christmas to but I doe not feal [feel] very Merry yet The band played very pretty pieces of music most all night I could hear them and a company of singers went

about singing Christmas Eve songs I have been to day to see another doctor about my face and he gave something to quiet my nerves. I ment [meant] to have finish this letter yesterday but I could not as I wish you Merry Christmas and while I am trying to write you I suppose that you ar at Church I would like to have attended Church today but I could not for I feal so bad."[30]

Out at City Point, the Union Army's sprawling supply depot, hospital, and headquarters complex at the confluence of the James and Appomatox Rivers, practicing Quaker and nurse Cornelia Hancock spent Christmas cooking and serving the boys in blue.

> "Christmas is over. We had it to perfection here, a splendid dinner for 1400 men; just think of it, cooking a sumptuous dinner of turkeys, pies, etc. for that number. Is it not

Figure 5-7. Hospital dining hall at City Point, Virginia, where army nurse Cornelia Hancock helped serve Christmas dinner to 1400 men. In a letter she wrote "The hall was decorated tastefully with evergreens and was really pretty as a picture." (USAMHI)

appalling? Miss Hart had charge of the dinner and, of course, it was a success. She is so smart. I had moved into my new kitchen and gave her full sway there. It was handy to where the dinner was set in the Government kitchen where 400 can be seated at once. The hall was decorated tastefully with evergreens and was really pretty as a picture. It was photographed, I believe."[31]

Lonely and despondent on Christmas Eve, newspaper correspondent Sylvanus Cadwallader of the *New York Herald* searched out another homesick soul with whom to share commiseration of the holiday in the army for another year.

"On Christmas eve, 1864, I was restless, discontented and homesick. On going to my tent about ten o'clock p.m., I sat for an hour brooding over the pleasures of past anniversaries, and the gloominess of the present. Filling my pockets with cigars I walked to the Adjutant's tent, where a light was still burning, and found Col. Bowers stretched out in a large camp-chair in front of a fire, and wearing a subdued, downcast countenance. To my inquiries as to what was the matter, he replied that he had been thinking of his mother, his home, and the difference between his present surroundings, and those of happier times.

"We chatted but a few minutes when Gen. Rawlins entered and wanted to know if we had not heard the bugle blow 'tap' and 'lights out,' and whether he should be obliged to put us under arrest for such flagrant violation of army regulations? We turned the tables on him by inquiring why he was wandering about camp at that time of night? He made his excuses similar to those of Col. Bowers. Within five minutes we heard the tread of some one else approaching, and Gen. Grant walked in. We all greeted him with a burst of laughter, and requested honest confession. He went over the same string of sentimental expressions. But conversation soon took a wide and pleasant range, and we talked for more than an hour about everything uppermost in our minds, excepting war; and until all my cigars had been consumed.

"Asking us to keep our seats a few minutes, Grant went to his tent and returned with an unopened box of large, excellent cigars which some one had just sent him from New York. We smoked one or two, each, from this box, when it was agreed that we ought to be in bed. The General insisted on our taking one more smoke before breaking up. Instead of lighting mine I put it in my pocket, and I said I would smoke it the next Christmas Eve in memory of that one. I had to take another, however, and smoke then."[32]

One Confederate officer did make it to church in Richmond. Captain Henry A. Chambers of the 49th North Carolina, wrote a stunning descriptive commentary in his diary of a day and part of an evening spent attending services at the holiday festooned St. Paul's Episcopal Church and Washington Street Presbyterian Church.

"This morning my mess, thanks for supplies from home, had 'eggnog' followed by an excellent breakfast. After this, Lieutenant Krider and I went to church in the city. At eleven o'clock we went to St. Paul's (High Church Episcopal) Church and heard a most excellent discourse from its talented rector, Dr. Platt. The Church which is Gothic in its architecture, was beautifully decorated with evergreens. Five festoons of cedar hung from the five ornaments in the center of the church to the bannisters of the gallery on each side. A great wreath was festooned around the walls of the church below and another around the bannisters of the gallery above. The pulpit was wreathed with evergreens and a cross wreathed with them stood behind the pulpit. On the cross was another and smaller cross of gilt and on the bannisters in front of the choir was the word 'Emmanuel' in large gilt letters. The church was crowded and many were outside and could not get seats at all."

At 3:15 in the afternoon, Captain Chambers and his companion visited the Washington Street Presbyterian Church to hear his favorite clergyman preach. Lieutenant Krider then journeyed back to the trenches while Chambers stayed on for evening services again at St. Paul's.

"The church presented a magnificent spectacle. The gorgeous evergreen decorations, the Gothic architecture, the brilliant gaslight, the large assemblage of finely dressed ladies and officers, the splendid robes of the officiating clergymen, the exquisite singing and chanting of the choir, the solemn responses of the congregation, the deep, stirring peals of the large organ, all combined made one of the most impressive scenes I ever witnessed. After the sermon was over, I returned to the trenches. And thus, I spent Christmas, the fourth since I have been in the war. I spent as I never spent a Christmas before, attending divine services in a city. I had fondly hoped to spend this day at my beloved home, but have been disappointed. Would that I could but feel the hope that before another Christmas Day comes, I and all the soldiers would be at our homes, free from the hated foe, our independence secured and our Confederacy on the high road to prosperity."[33]

Over in the Shenandoah Valley, General Jubal Early's dwindling army began to bed down in winter quarters. It had been a devastating fall from mid-summer's campaign zenith deep into enemy territory when Washington nearly panicked as Early's Confederates appeared before the fortifications of the city. A day's delay in the march, doing battle on the banks of the Monocacy near Frederick, and the timely arrival of troops from Grant's Army of the Potomac into the fortifications ringing Washington, put an end to the Confederacy's third invasion of the North. Defeats at Winchester, Fisher's Hill, and Cedar Creek, by the Union army under General Phil Sheridan's command, left the Confederates in the Valley gasping at the sudden reversal of fortunes.

The destruction of the Army of Northern Virginia's food supply began in earnest as Sheridan's troops applied Sherman's tenets of warfare of fire and ransack up the Valley turnpike. Christmas in the Valley would be cold, bleak, and full of despair to both the army and civilian inhabitants.

Artillery private Henry Robinson Berkeley of Kirkpatrick's Battery, had seen hard action and death from the Wilderness campaign through Early's victorious foray into Maryland, and tragic defeats and destruction during the autumn. Remarking in his diary, kept since the early days of 1861, Berkeley saw the face of the future and it was not hopeful.

> "Christmas Day. The fourth Christmas since I have been in the army. Not so dry and hard a one as the last; but the future looks dark, gloomy, bloody, and hopeless. I heard Mr. Gilmer, our chaplain, preach a very good sermon in the morning and [heard] a Methodist minister that night."[34]

Religious conviction was about all many soldiers had that dark Christmas of 1864. Berkeley was captured the following March at Waynesboro and sent to Fort Delaware until June when he signed the oath of allegiance and went home.

Cornelia Peake McDonald who had survived the rapacious Yankees two years before after literally saving her Christmas dinner from the hands of a trooper in Winchester, faced a bleak Christmas brightened only through the charity of neighbors and friends. McDonald's husband had died at the beginning of the month in Richmond, while she had been en route to nurse him. She was left with seven children to care for that Christmas, resisting relatives insistence that she distribute her children into the care of family members.

> "The days slowly dragged on and Christmas came. Our friends took care that we should not be entirely without pleasures and comforts; so one sent a turkey, another cakes and oysters, and all something, the best they could get. Of course that could not last, people could not give always, nor did I wish them to do so. I knew that I must make an effort of some kind to provide for the family, what it was to be I knew not. I had three hundred dollars in Confederate money,

worth fifteen in silver or paper of the Federal Government. How I tried to make it last, so that I would not have to go out among strangers to try to earn money when I only wanted to hide myself and my sorrow from the light of day."[35]

In Harper's Ferry, the Catholic priest of the 14th Louisiana, Reverend James B. Sheeran, scribbled in his journal the number of masses celebrated on Christmas Day while recovering from an illness caught as a prisoner of war in Fort McHenry.

> "Sunday, Christmas Day, Say my first Mass at 8. Hear some confessions. Say my second Mass at 9 1/2 and my third at 10. Then returned to my room. There were no Vespers. The doctor had made ample preparations for Christmas so we spent an agreeable afternoon."[36]

The combative priest detested Yankees, derisively calling them "Lincoln's Bandits" and trying to convert Union prisoners to the Confederate point of view when he had a captive audience. In a fine twist of irony, Father Sheeran was pastor of a Catholic church in Morristown, New Jersey, years after the end of hostilities.

Henry Kyd Douglas, a prisoner of war the previous Christmas, was exchanged in March from Point Lookout. A member of Jubal Early's staff, Douglas was able to find gaiety, entertainments, and other social pleasures at Christmas time in the ravaged Valley.

> "On Christmas Day I went to dine at the most hospitable mansion of Mrs. Gilliam. There I found General W. H. F. [Rooney] Lee, General R. D. Johnston—a dinner party of eight gentlemen and five ladies, and a most agreeable one. I remained all night and helped to make a jolly bowl of eggnog before breakfast the next morning. . . . Winter was upon us and for a time the war drums ceased to throb. . . . Social pleasures were abundant and, while the tenure of life was so uncertain, entertainments, dances, marriages were plentiful. The sound of parlor music and of 'dancers dancing in tune' might be heard within cannon shot of the enemy. To go into a parlor for a call or for a waltz with sword and spurs, while orderlies outside held horses

ready to mount at the first alarm was no unusual thing. To spend half the night in the saddle that the other half might be spent in social revelry was not strange enough to cause comment."[37]

A study of contrast existed between the civilian worlds of New York, Frederick, and Washington in the North, and Richmond and other cities in the South. The mix of military good news and Christmas exuberance made the neighborhoods of Washington resemble Independence Day. John M. Bell, a civilian employee in the Navy Department, wrote to a friend in the 1st Mass. Light Battery about the explosive nature of his Christmas night.

"I will suppose I am with you and wish you a 'Merry Christmas' and not only one but many. In advance I will wish you a Happy New Year and trust that it will find you blessed with a grand share of Life's prosperity and continual success in your present pursuits & business.

"To day is Christmas—all night long (and it continues) there has been a continual blaze of fire crackers and reports of pistols and guns which sound as most like the skirmishing at the front. This noise keeps the dogs in the neighborhood howling away with perfection and the great discord is really quite amusing. The day seems more like the 4th of July at home than anything I can think of."[38]

A good many of the patrons about the streets that night were inebriated celebrants according to the admonishing tone of Bell's observations to his friend.

The diary notations of John B. Jones in Richmond was remarkable in its similarity as he

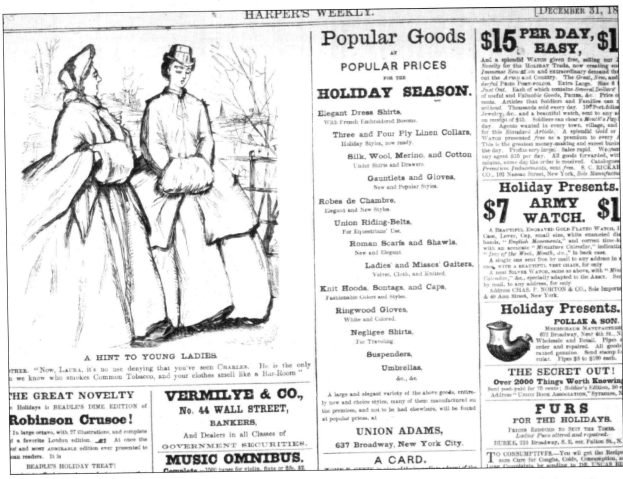

Figure 5-8. While the South faced its bleakest winter of the war, Northern merchants advertised their gift suggestions in newspapers and *Harper's Weekly*. (K.R.)

spent a day of leisure with his family from the stress of bad news at the War Department.

"Clear and pleasant—white frost. All Quiet below. It is believed on the street that Savannah has been evacuated, some days ago. I have not yet seen any official admission of the fact.

"We have quite a merry Christmas in the family; and a compact that no unpleasant word shall be uttered, and no SCRAMBLE for anything. The family were baking cakes and pies until late last night, and to-day we shall have FULL rations. I have found enough celery in the garden for dinner.

"Last night and this morning the boys have been firing Christmas guns incessantly—no doubt pilfering from their fathers' cartridge-boxes. There is much jollity and some drunkenness in the streets, not withstanding the enemy's pickets are within an hour's march of the city.

"A large number of the croaking inhabitants censure the President for our many misfortunes, and openly declare in favor of Lee as Dictator. Another month, and he may be unfortunate or unpopular. His son, Gen. Custis Lee, has mortally offended the clerks by putting them in the trenches yesterday, and some of them may desert."[39]

In New York City, society lady, friend to "Copperheads," and wife to a judge, Maria Lydig Daly wrote of Christmas dinner seated next to the hero of Mobile Bay. Further recounting her Christmas night at the theater, Daly gushed over the performance of the leading actor

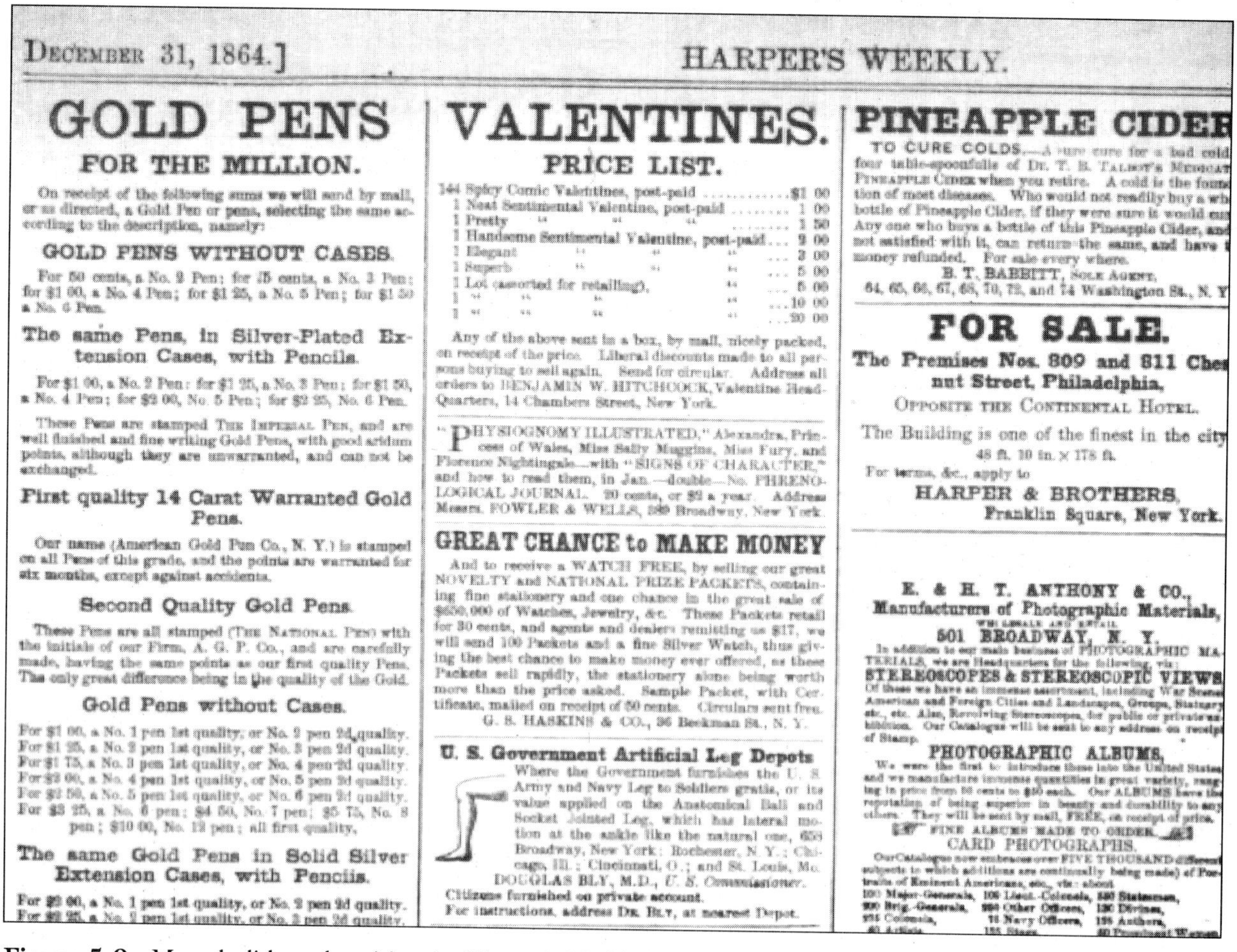
DECEMBER 31, 1864.] HARPER'S WEEKLY.

GOLD PENS
FOR THE MILLION.

On receipt of the following sums we will send by mail, or as directed, a Gold Pen or pens, selecting the same according to the description, namely:

GOLD PENS WITHOUT CASES.

For 50 cents, a No. 2 Pen; for 75 cents, a No. 3 Pen; for $1 00, a No. 4 Pen; for $1 25, a No. 5 Pen; for $1 50 a No. 6 Pen.

The same Pens, in Silver-Plated Extension Cases, with Pencils.

For $1 00, a No. 2 Pen; for $1 25, a No. 3 Pen; for $1 50, a No. 4 Pen; for $2 00, No. 5 Pen; for $2 25, No. 6 Pen.

These Pens are stamped THE IMPERIAL PEN, and are well finished and fine writing Gold Pens, with good iridium points, although they are unwarranted, and can not be exchanged.

First quality 14 Carat Warranted Gold Pens.

Our name (American Gold Pen Co., N. Y.) is stamped on all Pens of this grade, and the points are warranted for six months, except against accidents.

Second Quality Gold Pens.

These Pens are all stamped (THE NATIONAL PEN) with the initials of our Firm, A. G. P. Co., and are carefully made, having the same points as our first quality Pens. The only great difference being in the quality of the Gold.

Gold Pens without Cases.

For $1 00, a No. 1 pen 1st quality, or No. 2 pen 2d quality.
For $1 25, a No. 2 pen 1st quality, or No. 3 pen 2d quality.
For $1 75, a No. 3 pen 1st quality, or No. 4 pen 2d quality.
For $2 00, a No. 4 pen 1st quality, or No. 5 pen 2d quality.
For $2 50, a No. 5 pen 1st quality, or No. 6 pen 2d quality.
For $3 25, a No. 6 pen; $4 50, No. 7 pen; $5 75, No. 8 pen; $10 00, No. 12 pen; all first quality.

The same Gold Pens in Solid Silver Extension Cases, with Pencils.

For $2 00, a No. 1 pen 1st quality, or No. 2 pen 2d quality.
For $2 25, a No. 2 pen 1st quality, or No. 3 pen 2d quality.

VALENTINES.
PRICE LIST.

144 Spicy Comic Valentines, post-paid	$1 00
1 Neat Sentimental Valentine, post-paid	1 00
1 Pretty " " "	1 50
1 Handsome Sentimental Valentine, post-paid	2 00
1 Elegant " " "	3 00
1 Superb " " "	5 00
1 Lot (assorted for retailing), "	5 00
1 " " " "	10 00
1 " " " "	20 00

Any of the above sent in a box, by mail, nicely packed, on receipt of the price. Liberal discounts made to all persons buying to sell again. Send for circular. Address all orders to BENJAMIN W. HITCHCOCK, Valentine Head-Quarters, 14 Chambers Street, New York.

"PHYSIOGNOMY ILLUSTRATED," Alexandra, Princess of Wales, Miss Sally Muggins, Miss Fury, and Florence Nightingale—with "SIGNS OF CHARACTER," and how to read them, in Jan.—double—No. PHRENOLOGICAL JOURNAL. 20 cents, or $2 a year. Address Messrs. FOWLER & WELLS, 389 Broadway, New York.

GREAT CHANCE to MAKE MONEY

And to receive a WATCH FREE, by selling our great NOVELTY and NATIONAL PRIZE PACKETS, containing fine stationery and one chance in the great sale of $650,000 of Watches, Jewelry, &c. These Packets retail for 30 cents, and agents and dealers remitting us $17, we will send 100 Packets and a fine Silver Watch, thus giving the best chance to make money ever offered, as these Packets sell rapidly, the stationery alone being worth more than the price asked. Sample Packet, with Certificate, mailed on receipt of 50 cents. Circulars sent free.
G. S. HASKINS & CO., 36 Beekman St., N. Y.

U. S. Government Artificial Leg Depots

Where the Government furnishes the U. S. Army and Navy Leg to Soldiers gratis, or its value applied on the Anatomical Ball and Socket Jointed Leg, which has lateral motion at the ankle like the natural one, 658 Broadway, New York; Rochester, N. Y.; Chicago, Ill.; Cincinnati, O.; and St. Louis, Mo.
DOUGLAS BLY, M.D., *U. S. Commissioner.*
Citizens furnished on private account.
For instructions, address DR. BLY, at nearest Depot.

PINEAPPLE CIDER

TO CURE COLDS.—A sure cure for a bad cold four table-spoonfuls of DR. T. B. TALBOT'S MEDICATED PINEAPPLE CIDER when you retire. A cold is the foundation of most diseases. Who would not readily buy a whole bottle of Pineapple Cider, if they were sure it would cure. Any one who buys a bottle of this Pineapple Cider, and not satisfied with it, can return the same, and have the money refunded. For sale every where.
B. T. BABBITT, SOLE AGENT,
64, 65, 66, 67, 68, 70, 72, and 74 Washington St., N. Y.

FOR SALE.

The Premises Nos. 809 and 811 Chestnut Street, Philadelphia,
OPPOSITE THE CONTINENTAL HOTEL.
The Building is one of the finest in the city
48 ft. 10 in. × 178 ft.
For terms, &c., apply to
HARPER & BROTHERS,
Franklin Square, New York.

E. & H. T. ANTHONY & CO.,
Manufacturers of Photographic Materials,
WHOLESALE AND RETAIL
501 BROADWAY, N. Y.

In addition to our main business of PHOTOGRAPHIC MATERIALS, we are Headquarters for the following, viz.:

STEREOSCOPES & STEREOSCOPIC VIEWS

Of these we have an immense assortment, including War Scenes, American and Foreign Cities and Landscapes, Groups, Statuary, etc., etc. Also, Revolving Stereoscopes, for public or private exhibition. Our Catalogue will be sent to any address on receipt of Stamp.

PHOTOGRAPHIC ALBUMS.

We were the first to introduce these into the United States, and we manufacture immense quantities in great variety, ranging in price from 50 cents to $50 each. Our ALBUMS have the reputation of being superior in beauty and durability to any others. They will be sent by mail, FREE, on receipt of price.

FINE ALBUMS MADE TO ORDER.

CARD PHOTOGRAPHS.

Our Catalogue now embraces over FIVE THOUSAND different subjects (to which additions are continually being made) of Portraits of Eminent Americans, etc., viz.: about

100 Major-Generals, 100 Lieut.-Colonels, 550 Statesmen,
200 Brig.-Generals, 250 Other Officers, 130 Divines,
275 Colonels, 75 Navy Officers, 125 Authors,

Figure 5-9. More holiday advertising in *Harper's Weekly*. This New Year's Eve edition for 1864 contained an ad for Valentine's Day cards! (K.R.)

of the era; chillingly presaging the actor's soon-to-be-infamous actor brother four short months in the future.

"Spent a pleasant Christmas in Laight Street. No one of the Suydams except James, who is a passive member of society, present. Hannah dined with us, so it was strictly a family party. We did not give or receive handsome presents. In truth, the times do not admit it.

"Tonight, we are going to see Booth in 'Hamlet.' The scenery is very beautiful and characteristic of the Polonius and Orphelia. [It is] very good, and Booth, everyone admits, is as great a Hamlet as ever died upon the stage. The scenery and architecture are old Gothic. It looks like an old Scandinavian stronghold, and the effects of moonlight are admirable in the scenes with the ghost and grave diggers' scene.

"Dined yesterday at Mrs. Charles Gould's, where we met the Admiral and Mrs. Farragut. I was seated between the Admiral and Dr. [Isaac] Cummings and had a good talk with the hero. He is a simple, direct man, says what he thinks, with little polish but much originality, no doubt often expresses ideas as he thinks out new methods of attack when excited by the occasion."[40]

Like another Lee, Elizabeth Blair Lee momentarily let her guard down on Christmas Eve and expressed pent-up bitterness over the many long absences endured during her marriage to her husband S. Philip Lee, commander of the Navy's Atlantic Blockading Squadron.

"This is the fifth lonesome Christmas—& when I add to it, all the 'good time' which Old Billy told me I wasted—it counts up a long list of wasted years which I regret more & more bitterly as my sands grow fewer—."

On the day after Christmas, while wintering in the Blair house directly across from the White House, Elizabeth talked of the toys that had belonged to her son that were taken from the Blair estate "Silver Spring" by the rebels of Early's army that summer.

"We had a quiet pleasant Christmas—Blair wishes every day was Christmas—he is an exuberantly happy chap The toys are very welcome to him in the stormy days of winter

for the Rebs carried off his store of toys which Becky & Bernie had hoarded from his birth but they may now be gladdening some little ones in Virginia—I have felt disappointed all this Christmas time—for I had put it in to my heart for a year nearly that you would be here & I never felt so let down & anxious & thus it is we nurse up our fancies but disappointments will come up with more intense realizations on some days more than others—I see this in Mother of late years—she avoids much ado about any anniversary I now look to the end of the War as that is talked of as a thing soon to come—but it must come soon—."[41]

Jacob Engelbrecht reported his Christmas spent in the U.S. Hospital No. 1 at the Hessian Barracks in Frederick, Maryland.

"Christmas this year came on Sunday—at the U. State Hospital [Barracks] in sick & wounded had a real Christmas dinner plenty of Turkies Geese & Chicken &c—all the Barracks were Rigged out with evergreens Flags &c—all in first rate style all persons (loyal) were admitted—I was there the first day—the dinner was the Second day at night the Soldiers had a Exhibition & fun & also another Dinner &c —."[42]

In Augusta, Georgia, Ella Gertrude Clanton Thomas was trying to decide what changes wrought by the war this Christmas were going to mean to her world. Writing about the status of her servants and other emotions experienced during Christmas, Thomas helped a mother less fortunate than herself while seeing the similarities that the next Christmas might hold.

"America has gone down to see her mother and Fanny—Patsey has gone to see some of Bob's family up town—all them trying to pass 'a Merry Christmas.' I have just written a ticket for Daniel to go to a party at Dr. Ed Eve's While writing the idea occurs to me, Shall we have any servants to write tickets for when another Christmas comes around?. . . . To use a phrase which is quite popular when a place is captured I expect Augusta 'to go up,' namely 'up the spout.' Can any better proof be given the effect of revolutions than

Figure 5-10. The January 2, 1865 issue of *Harper's Weekly* contained a centerfold entitled "New Year's Day" in which Thomas Nast compared the prosperous North with the devastated South. (K.R.)

the fact that I should announce such an expectation with military slang.

"Yesterday was Christmas Day. Both that and today have been dull, gloomy and cloudy days. In the morning Mr Thomas Turner and Mary Bell and I went to the Episcopalian Church, St Paul's. It was dressed very handsomely—Over the altar the words 'Glory to God in the Highest' were hung, the letters as fresh and evergreen as the sentiment should be in every heart. This was the subject of Mr Clark's text—The music was grand and inspiring. To my taste there is something especially appropriate in the Episcopalian service for Christmas day. It is fitting that the commemoration of our Saviour's birth should be attended with great solemnity. The tones of St Paul's organ as played upon by Mr Illsey thrilled me with such intensity of feeling that it would have been a relief to have bent my head over and in feminine parlance 'taken a good cry.' I like the Episcopalian Church, the organ the imposing ritual, everything better than I do the preaching— Mr Clark's voice is quite suggestive of sleep and I am now so prosaically sleepy that I can write no more. . . .

"A refugee lady who lives in a car out at the depot, by the name Kirksey was to see me a few days since. Alluding to the difference between this Christmas and last she added while tears coursed their way down her cheek, 'Oh Mrs Thomas my husband was such a good man. Every Christmas he filled the children's stockings with something for Santa Claus presents.' Her husband was a conductor on the Georgia R Road was taken prisoner and is now at Camp Chase. The idea occurred to me that next Christmas I might be unable to provide my children with Christmas gifts and I placed five dollars in Mary Bell's hand and told her to give it to the lady to buy some apples for her children. I also gave her some potatoes and meat."[43]

Sallie Brock Putnam reminisced about the sad festivities of Christmas in Richmond, but carrying on the holiday with forced cheerfulness.

"We were now in the midst of winter—the cheerless season to which we looked forward with dread. It was the fourth year of the war. The festivities of Christmas were rendered mournful by the fall of Savannah, and the demolition of hopes which had trusted in that city, as a stronghold which could not be taken. With saddened mien we turned our steps toward the sanctuaries of God. On this occasion our praise and thanksgiving were blended with fasting and prayer, with deep humiliation and earnest contrition.

"We left the temples of the Most High, and wended our way back, many of us, not to the luxurious homes, where once the festival was gladdened by the reunion of loved ones, but to humble, contracted lodgings which were all that remained to us, to call 'home.' Instead of the sumptuous banquet, around which we were wont to gather, we sat down to the poverty-stricken board. We counted again the vacant chairs, and glazed with eyes blinded by tears, upon sombre living woe, that indicated whither borne our domestic idols.

"With brave attempt at cheerfulness, we decked our dwellings with evergreen, cedar, arbor-vitae, and holly, and here and there, under the magical influence of the kind old patron saint of the holiday, the Christmas tree once more reared its cheery head, laden with a precious and incongruous burden of bonbons and simple toys."[44]

Refugees flooding into Richmond to avoid the depredations of Union soldiers and stay with relatives was a common occurrence throughout the war. Alice West Allen remembered when she was eleven years old during Christmas of 1864, and she and her siblings were sent by her fearful parents to stay with relatives. As was the case with many children, the danger for them was a big adventure.

"The last Christmas of the war my parents thought our home would soon be in the enemy's lines [Sheridan's ransacking of the Valley], so they decided to send us to Richmond until the danger was over. We were wild with delight at the thought of going to the big city. . . .

"We were delighted when we got to Richmond. The next morning our aunt took us out shopping; and as each of us had one hundred dollars to spend, we thought we could give presents to all at home. We soon found that toys and candy were as costly as food. A dear friend of my mother's found that we were to spend Christmas in the city, so she invited us to a Christmas tree given to President Davis' children. The tree was a lovely holly laden with homemade candles and dolls made out of hickory nuts and Canton flannel; then there were cotton and Canton flannel rabbits, dog and cats, and numerous other presents all homemade, as was everything on the supper table—homemade coffee, tea, sugar, and everything. I have never seen anything that looked so pretty to me. Probably some of it was due to Maggie and Jeff Davis, our President's children. Maggie Davis had the honor of presenting the gifts, and I fell in love with her when I saw her worshipped by all. She and her brother were full of fun and mischief, and we played hide and seek all over the house; they the leaders in every game. Mrs. Davis called me to her side and said: 'Your dress, I see, is very much like Maggie's. You are both happy in wearing dresses made from your mothers' wedding gowns.' I think she just wanted to make me feel good."[45]

Near the Christmas season of 1896, Mrs. Varina Howell Davis wrote for publication her memories of Christmas in the Confederate "White House" during the last year of the war. Faced with a scarcity of materials and foodstuffs, Mrs. Davis made a truly memorable Christmas for her own children and many orphans of Richmond despite severe hardship.

"Christmas was ushered in under the thickest clouds; everyone felt the cataclysm which impended, but the rosy, expectant faces of our little children were a constant reminder that self-sacrifice must be the personal offering of each mother of the family. How to satisfy the children that nothing better could be done than the little makeshifts attainable in the Confederacy was the problem of the older members of the household. There were no currants, raisins or other ingredients to fill the old Virginia recipe for mince pie, and the

children considered that at least a slice of the much-coveted dainty was their right . . . Apple trees grew and bore in spite of the war's alarms, so the foundation of the mixture was assured. The many exquisite housekeepers in Richmond had preserved all the fruits attainable and these were substituted for the time-honored raisins and currants. The brandy required for seasoning at one hundred dollars a bottle was forthcoming, the cider was obtained, the suet at a dollar a pound was ordered—and the eggs and liquor to be procured, without which Christmas would be a failure to the Negroes.

"Rice, flour, molasses and tiny pieces of meat, most of these sent to the President's wife anonymously to be dispersed to the poor, had all been weighed and issued, and the playtime of the family began, but like a clap of thunder out of a clear sky came the information that the orphans at the Episcopalian Home had been promised a Christmas tree and the toys, candy and cakes must be provided, as well as one pretty prize for the most orderly girl among the orphans. The kind-hearted confectioner was interviewed by our committee of managers, and he promised a certain amount of his simpler kinds of candy, which he sold easily at a dollar and a half a pound, but he drew the line at cornucopias to hold it, and sugared fruits to hang on the tree, and all the other vestiges of Christmas creations which had been on his hands for years. The ladies dispersed in anxious squads of toy-hunters, and each one turned over the store of her children's treasures for a contribution to the orphans' tree. My little ones rushed over the great house looking for their treasures—eyeless dolls, three-legged horses, tops with the upper peg broken off, rubber tops, monkeys with the squeak gone silent and all the ruck of children's toys that gather in a nursery closet.

"But the tug of war was how to get something to decorate the orphans' tree. Our man servant, Robert Brown, was much interested and offered to make the prize toy. He contemplated a 'sure enough house, with four rooms.' His part in the domestic service was delegated to another and he gave himself over in silence and solitude to the labors and pains of an architect.

"My sister painted mantel shelves, door panels, pictures and frames, for the walls and finished with black grates in which there blazed a roaring fire, which was pronounced marvelously realistic. We all made furniture of twigs, and paste-board, and my mother made pillows, mattresses, sheets and pillow cases for the little bedrooms.

"Christmas Eve a number of young people were invited to come and string apples and popcorn for the tree; a neighbor very deft in domestic arts had tiny candle molds made and furnished all the candles for the tree. However, the puzzle and triumph of all was the construction of a large number of cornucopias. At last some one suggested a conical block of wood, about which the drawing could be wound and pasted. In a little shop a number of small, highly colored pictures cut out and ready to apply were unearthed, and our confectioner friend, Mr. Pizzini, consented to give 'all the love verses the young people wanted to roll with candy.'

"About twenty young men and girls gathered around small tables in one of the drawing-rooms of the mansion and the cornucopias were begun. The men wrapped the squares of candy, first reading the 'sentiments' printed upon them, such as 'Roses are red, violets are blue, sugar's sweet and so are you,' 'If you love me as I love you, no knife can cut our love in two.' The fresh young faces, wreathed in smiles, nodded attention to the readings, while with their deft hands glued the cornucopias and pasted on the pictures. Where were the silk tops to come from? Trunks of old things were turned out and snippings of silk and even woolen bright colors were found to close the tops, and some of the young people twisted sewing silk into cords with which to draw the bags up. The beauty of these homemade things astonished us all, for they looked quite 'custom-made,' but when the 'sure-enough house' was revealed the young people clapped their approbation while Robert . . . bowed his thanks for our approval.

"Then the coveted eggnog was passed around in tiny glass cups and pronounced good. Crisp homemade ginger snaps and snowy lady cake completed the refreshments of Christmas Eve. The children, allowed to sit up and be noisy in their own way as an indulgence, took a sip of the eggnog out of my cup and the eldest boy confided to his father: 'Now I just know this is Christmas'. . . .

"At last quiet settled on the household and the older members began to stuff stockings with molasses candy, red apples, an orange, small whips plaited by the family with high-colored crackers, worsted reins knitted at home, paper dolls, teetotums made of large horn buttons and a match which could spin indefinitely, balls of worsted rags wound hard and covered with old kid gloves, a pair of pretty woolen gloves for each, either cut out of cloth and embroidered on the back or knitted by some deft hand out of homespun wool. For the President there was a pair of chamois-skin riding gauntlets exquisitely embroidered on the back with his monogram in red and white silk, made, as the giver wrote, under the guns of fortress Monroe late at night for fear of discovery. There was a hemstitched linen handkerchief, with a little sketch in indeliable ink in one corner; the children had written him little letters, their grandmother having held their hands, the burthen of which composition was how they loved their dear father. . . .

"A bowl of eggnog was sent to the servants, and a part of everything they coveted of the dainties.

"On Christmas morning the children awoke early and came in to see their toys. They were followed by the Negro women, who one after another 'caught' us by wishing us merry Christmas before we could say it to them, which gave them a right to a gift. Of course, there was a present for every one, small though it might be, and one who had been born and brought up at our plantation was vocal in her admiration of a gay handkerchief. As she left the room she ejaculated: 'Lord knows Mistress knows our insides—she just got the very thing I wanted.'

"For me there were six cakes of delicious soap, made from the grease of ham boiled for a family in Farmville, a skein of exquisitely fine gray linen thread spun at home, pincushion of plain brown cotton material made by some poor woman and stuffed with wool from her pet sheep, and a little baby hat plaited by the orphans and presented by the industrious little pair who sewed the straw together. Another present was a fine, delicate little baby frock without an inch of lace or embroidery upon it, but the delicate fabric was set with fairy stitches by the dear invalid neighbor who made it, and it was very precious in my eyes. There was also a few of Swinburne's best songs bound in wall-paper and a chamois needlebook left for me by young Mr. P., now succeeded to his title in England. It was a Brobdingnagian thimble—'for my own finger, you know,' said the handsome, cheerful fellow.

"After breakfast, at which all the family, great and small, were present, came the walk to St. Paul's Church. We did not use our carriage on Christmas or, if possible to avoid it, on Sunday. The saintly Dr. Minnegerode preached a sermon on Christian love, the introit was sung by a beautiful young woman and the angels might have joyfully listened.

"Our chef did wonders with the turkey and roast beef, and drove the children quite out of their propriety by a spun-sugar hen, life-size, on a nest of blanc-mange eggs. The mince pie and plum pudding made them feel, as one of the gentlemen laughingly remarked, 'as if their jackets were buttoned.'. . . They waited with great impatience for the crowning amusement of the day, 'the children's tree.'

"All throughout the afternoon first one little head and then another popped in a door to ask: 'Isn't it 8 o'clock yet?' burning with impatience to see the tree.

"When at last we reached the basement of St. Paul's Church the tree burst upon their view like the realization of Aladdin's subterranean orchard, and they were awed by the grandeur.

"The orphans sat mute with astonishment until the opening hymn and prayer and the last Amen had been said, and they at a signal warily and slowly gathered around the tree to receive from a lovely young girl their allotted present.

"The President became so enthusiastic that he undertook to help in the distribution, but worked such wild confusion giving everything asked for into outstretched hands, that we called a halt, so he contented himself with unwinding one or two tots from a network of strung popcorn in which they had become entangled and taking off all the apples he could when unobserved, and presenting them to the smaller children. . . .

"We went home to find that General Lee had called in our absence and many other people. General Lee had left word that he had received a barrel of sweet potatoes for us, which had been sent to him by mistake until he had taken his share (a dishful) and given the rest to the soldiers. We wished it had been much more for them and him.

"The night closed with a 'starvation' party, where there were no refreshments, at a neighboring house. The rooms lighted as well as practicable, some one willing to play music on the piano and plenty of young men and girls comprised the entertainment. . . . The officers, who rode into town with their long cavalry boots pulled well over their knees, but were splashed up to their waist, put up their horses and rushed to the places where their dress uniform suits had been left for safekeeping. They soon emerged, however, in full toggery and entered into the pleasures of the dance with bright-eyed girls. . . .

"O, in the interchange of the courtesies and charities of life, to which we could not add its comforts and pleasures, passed. . . . Christmas in the Confederate mansion."[46]

On this fourth sad Christmas of the war, the mysterious phantom scribe's annual holiday jottings failed to appear in the clothing account book of Co. C, 4th Kentucky Infantry. Somewhere during the year's violent clashes across Georgia's battle scarred land, the unknown penman fell as a casualty of the war. Another unknown soldier would rejoice in the festivities of Christmas no more.

Figure 5-11. Savannah, Georgia, General Sherman's Christmas present to Abraham Lincoln in 1864.

Figure 6-1. *Harper's Weekly* for December 30, 1865, contained its first non-military cover page since the war began. (K.R.)

6

Peace of Reunion, Goodwill Towards Former Foes

The war ended and the Nation mourned. The Nation was re-united after the shock of President Abraham Lincoln's assassination in April. All hostilities had ceased by Christmas, the first after five years of harsh and devastating war. Many soldiers were mustered out of the service. Many more did not return home, having found their last sleep in an unmarked grave on the numerous battlefields where war's hard hand touched them. This Christmas there would be 623,026 vacant chairs beside the hearth.

Four conspirators, including Mary Surratt, were hung in July while lesser players in the assassination were imprisoned for lengthy jail terms or died in jail. During the fall and into the winter leading into Christmas, the nation went about the business of healing itself. Andersonville Prison commandant Captain Henry Wirz, was hanged in November after being found guilty of cruel and inhumane treatment of Union prisoners. No Union prison commandant was ever tried on similar charges. To the victors went the spoils of righteousness. The Thirteenth Amendment to the United States Constitution abolishing the institution of slavery was ratified by the majority of twenty-seven states, including South

Carolina, Alabama, North Carolina, and Georgia, in November and December. On December 18, 1865, the Thirteenth Amendment of the United States Constitution became law. All eyes would look westward as the Nation sought to fulfill its manifest destiny. Many people had nothing to return to in devastated areas traversed by war. Others hungering to see new places, moved west to settle in new homes and seek new riches.

Plenty began to abound in Southern areas long starved by the Union blockade in Richmond and other cities farther south. The wealth of the Nation went on display in Northern shop windows, store shelves and city markets. In New York City, the Washington Market had for the holidays, oysters from the East and York Rivers, salmon from rivers in the upper state, Catawba wines, game fowl of all varieties, venison, beef, mutton, poultry, pork, and lamb for Christmas feasts. Christmas tree sellers now sold the established and popular holiday tradition, and were competing for space at Washington Market to sell their green wares. Wreaths and other ornamental and fragrant greens were also sold. Christmas trees became a growing market from the one vendor of trees in 1851. Toys and other items appealing to shoppers for gifts were advertised in newspapers and showcased in store windows. Christmas had entered the commercial realm.

The Christmas cover of *Harper's Weekly* had a religious illustration of the Christ Child, a decidedly un-military cover of the Prince of Peace. Thomas Nast's annual holiday centerfold had Santa Claus as the main focus, with domestic scenes of the family enjoying a Christmas dance with the children and telling of Christmas ghost stories before the decorated blazing Yuletide hearth with the listeners hanging in rapt suspense. To the left and right of Santa Claus's image, were the pictures of a young boy with his Christmas gift of a bugle while dressed in a child's military uniform and little girl holding her new doll. Underneath Santa Claus was the message he pointed to, "Merry Christmas to All" while in the background were all sorts of winter amusements from ice skating to young boys battling with snow balls behind snowy entrenchments. Holiday scenes graced the upper corners of church and home amid the falling snow.

Brightly lit windows at dusk reminded one of the inner warmth provided by both, as carolers and churchgoers traveled by. But it was the final illustration of the Christmas number stretched across the bottom of the page that reminded the viewer of the recent war. Upon a stage were the victorious military leaders of the Union with the heads of the beaten Confederate generals at the feet of "Ulysses the Giant Killer." Jefferson Davis and some of his minions were portrayed as clowns and buffoons while the new President, Andrew Johnson, conducted the theatrical proceedings from the orchestra pit. The holiday drawing was a sharp propaganda poke at the beaten South. Inside a drawing by Sol Eytinge showed the joys of family members and a servant as each person showed other relatives what they had received as the children played with their Christmas gifts. The moral Christmas tales of "The Toy Seller" and "The Lessons of Santa Claus" included in the issue contained virtuous messages about the meaning of the holiday.

On the editorial page of *Harper's Weekly* December 30, 1865 Christmas edition, the editors opened the issue with an editorial entitled "Merry Christmas."

"The Christmas greeting of this year will be more exciting than for many a year past. For if all the clouds that lowered upon our house are not in the deep bosom of the ocean buried, the sun has fully pierced them, and the genial light of peace makes such a festival as has long been unknown to us.

"It is just one year since the final crash of the rebellion began in the fall of Savannah. The triumphant march of Sherman was the overture to the rapid drama of the Spring, and between the snows of last year and of this one one of the largest armies of the world has melted back into the mass of the people without the least trouble or danger to the public tranquility. This is but one of the innumerable points in which the peculiar quality of the American system is apparent.

"As the old year closes upon happy faces and merry homes the prospect of the new is not such as to threaten the duration of that condition which makes the people hopeful and gay. Every American trusts the public

Figure 6-2. *Selling Christmas Greens—A Scene in Richmond, Virginia* by W. L. Sheppard. From New York to Richmond, tree vendors became a regular part of the American Christmas. (K.R.)

sagacity and heroism as he never did before. If he does not clearly see the issue of many grave questions, he has learned by ample and inspiring experience that they will not necessarily be wrongly settled because the settlement is for the present hidden. If we are prouder than ever before, it is legitimate pride. If we are more confident, it is justifiable faith. For if ever there were a true movement of the people it was the late war, and if ever a people moved steadily and nobly forward it was this people who did so.

"For the heroic dead, the flower of our youth which the fierce war withered, there will be a forever renewed tenderness of private remembrance and of public respect with every Christmas season. In our festive garlands we shall twine a leaf of rue, and in the glistening evergreen of holly and ivy see more than the sturdy plants. For the living who returned from the bitter field there will be always at every season a Christmas welcome in all faithful hearts. And for those who so long maintained the fight against the Union and liberty there will always be mingled feelings as the old domestic and religious feast returns. Yet among those feelings hate and vindictiveness have no share. The festival commemorates the birth of Him who died for all men, and thereby proclaimed and sealed their common humanity.

"And if the Christmas light could show the late enemies of the United States that peace is born only of good will to men, we should all gladly join hands from sea to sea and raise our voice in one vast millennial chorus, the jubilant thunder of which would break all political, social, moral, and mental chains in the world, 'Glory to God in the highest, peace on earth, good will to men!' "[1]

In Augusta, Georgia, the sting and bitter humiliation of the recently concluded war still lingered in the diary of Ella Gertrude Clanton Thomas. She worried about the effect new found freedom would have on former slaves while she revealed the doubt she felt about the institution.

"Another Christmas has come and gone and another year has passed. I could bow my head and weep, oh so bitterly, did I permit my mind to follow its impulse & think of the bright hopes that have been dashed to the earth, the sad condition of our beloved country, but God disposes of all things and it is too late. I do not know what to think. Sometimes I am inclined to look upon our defeat as a Providential thing and then I grow sceptical and almost doubt whether Providence had anything to do with the matter. Slavery had its evil and great ones and for some years I have doubted whether Slavery was right and now I sometimes feel glad that they have been freed and yet I think that it came too suddenly upon them. As it is we live in troublous times. Lawless acts are being committed every day and the papers are filled with the robberies which are constantly taking place."[2]

Benjamin Brown French reminisced about skating on Christmases past and the winter when the energy of youth permitted a marathon of skating from morning to night.

"There is only one thing that, in my old age, I envy the young people in their enjoyment of, and that is skaiting. I remember my supreme pleasure when in my younger manhood I could buckle on my skaits and sweep away over the polished surface of some miles square of ice, feeling like 'a bird let loose.' From morning till night have I skaited, and from dusk till past midnight, many's a time and oft, with more real pleasure than I can now express. In those days ladies did not skait; now they do, which must be a still stronger inducement for the young men to engage in that delightful pastime. If I had a good opportunity, I would once more put on a pair of skaits and try for a broken head or a rush forward! I fear my old ankles would hardly endure the strain that 195 pounds of *incorporation* would require of them!

"We are all enjoying ourselves I hope, during these days of holly and mistletoe. We ought to do so as there is no shadow of the present over us. We have a comfortable house, good food and plenty of it, and all the means of comfort and happiness, and if we are not comfortable and happy we ought to be whipped! . . ."[3]

Figure 6-3. Nast's centerfold entitled *Merry Christmas to All* concentrated on the joys of reunited families, but contained one last jab at the beaten South with its reference to "Ulysses The Giant Killer." (K.R.)

In New York City, Mrs. Maria Lydig Daly spent Christmas Eve readying a Christmas dinner for the children of deceased fathers who had been soldiers in the war. On Christmas Day, Daly and her husband who was a judge, attended the dinner with several dignitaries, and a Christmas program put on by the fatherless children.

"Been all day at the Union Home and School, busy getting a dinner for the soldier's children on Christmas. Invited Major General Barlow and Parke, Mr. Townsend Harris, Judge Brady, etc. . . . Had a most satisfactory and delightful morning. Went to eight o'clock mass, saw the sun just rising above the buildings and the park as I crossed Waverly Place, the sky as bright and clear as spring. I thought of the words of the old carol, 'Royal day that chasest gloom.' I went to St. Joseph's, where the congregation was mostly poor people; I like to go to church with the poor, particularly on Christmas.

"Then home to breakfast, then sent off my presents and prepared for going to the soldier's children. General Parke and Mr. Harris came in good time and we met General [Prosper M.] Wetmore at the Home. The Judge addressed the children, giving an account of Christmas—a little sermon in fact. The children hymns, a hymn on the nativity, and some patriotic songs, hurrahs, and gave three cheers for General Parke. They had a capital dinner prepared for them and we all came home very much touched by what we had seen. Poor little fatherless children! It was very delightful to see them all so happy.

"Went to Laight Street to dinner, hoping for a pleasant family reunion. Found Kate and the Judge not coming, Hannah sick, and Uncle Lydig installed, Father having asked him. It showed plainly that Father has more consideration for him than for us. We shall dine there no more on Christmas! I will be patriotic and Christian and dine another Christmas with the poor by preference. I think we would be greater favorites if we were less esteemed outside the family, so that all the wounds we receive, all the dishonor, is from our own familiar friends, the members of our own household. Whilst my husband is with me and loves me, I am independent of the whole world. Should I be so unfortunate as to outlive him, it will be of little consequence who else may be left, either of the family or of friends."[4]

Floride Clemson of South Carolina, commented on the gifts she received for Christmas and made for presentation to others in her household. Clemson was from the South and because of the scarcity of hard cash, resorted to making her presents from available materials.

"Yesterday (Monday, Xmas) was a dull, warm, cloudy day, but towards evening it cleared. I received no gifts except some mint candy from Mother, & a couple of tame squirrells from the Pickins. I made eight little photograph frames out of pine burrs, acorns, beechnuts, & beans, two for the Pickins, two for the Cornishes, two for the Frosts, & two for Ella Lorton. I also made a couple of serpentine braid trimmings, three feather dusters, & gave a comb to Mother & and a cravat to Father. I went to church in the morning (which I helped dress on Saturday) making six pine cedar wreaths for it. The evening I spent at Mr. Elliotts, had a pleasant evening, & a nice game of snap draggon, & some pictures of the East to look at & enjoy. I must confess I felt pretty homesick though, thinking of the pleasant Merry Xmas times I used to spend with Lizzie Robinson & the Woods. I will never have such happy days again I fear."[5]

It was a poem titled *By the Christmas Hearth* published in the Christmas edition of *Harper's Weekly* that best summed up the first Christmas of the post-war country. The first peaceful Christmas in five long ravaged years of war. Now that the countless battlefields had gone silent; where tens of thousands of men raised the battle cry amidst the din of small arms and deeper roar of cannons, the cries of the horribly wounded men and beast in the maelstrom of carnage, or the last silent expulsions of breath by the dying, all that would now fade into the tortured dreams of the survivors, until the memories were softened by time, and years later the veterans would recall only the glory of war.

Figure 6-4. In 1866 Thomas Nast designed a centerfold totally dedicated to Santa Claus. In it he included the first known drawing of Santa's workshop. His most notable achievement was to place the home of Santa Claus at the North Pole so that no country could ever claim him as its own. (K.R.)

To-day at the home beside the hearth,
    Warm with the ruddy embers' glow,
We keep our Christmas, so unlike
    The Christmas of a year ago,
When in the camp at earliest dawn
    The grimy-throated cannon woke
Our slumbers, and with in the East
    The golden light of morning broke.

Ah! Then the smoke of battle hung
    Its sulphorous cloud our land above,
And bitter feud and hatred filled
    Brave hearts that should have warmed
        with Love;
But now at home beside the hearth
    We keep the day with song and cheer,
While from each spire the Christmas bells
    Ring out with voices sweet and clear.

Bring holly, rich with berries red,
    And bring the sacred mistletoe;
Fill high each glass, and let hearts
    With kindliest feelings flow;
So sweet it seems at home once more
    To sit with those we hold most dear,
And keep absence once again
    To keep the Merry Christmas here.

Christmas and its holiday accoutrements only gained greater popularity in the years following the war from its rooted foundation of all the customs and traditions that were set just prior to the Civil War. Businessmen found ways of appealing to consumers to purchase goods, not only items for presents, but also decorations and sentiments for celebrating Christmas. Decorations were still homemade, but now were becoming commercially mass produced and available in quantity. German glass ornaments were being imported as German peasants blew glass decorations in a myriad of different shapes and forms. Enterprising entrepreneurs sought to fulfill the demands for ornaments, candle and taper holders, tinsel and decorative garlands, and tree stands (invented in 1867). An 1869 issue of *Harper's Bazaar* told of all the different ornaments available for tree decorations, including the "snow-clad veteran, Santa Claus, his bag emptied of its treasures with which he has adorned the tree: globes, fruits and flowers of colored glass,

bright tin reflectors, and innumerable grotesque figures suspended by a rubber string. Other figures included clowns with cap and bells, funny little men concealing their faces behind funnier masks, as they spring up and down; Bismark leaping upon Napoleon's shoulders, exaggerated seraphim with flapping wings, and strange-looking old women with heads larger than their bodies."[6] Ornaments of historical figures such as George Washington and others adorned Christmas trees alongside storybook figures.

Though the Christmas card arrived in the United States in 1851, German-born printer Louis Prang of Roxbury, Massachusetts, was the first to mass produce Christmas greeting cards in America. Most of the first cards Prang produced were of floral designs, seashells, butterflies, insects, and later more seasonal covers of the Virgin Mother and Christ Child and Santa Claus were included. Printed on high quality paper, his later cards were manufactured with silk fringes, tassels and heavy gold gilt edges. Refusing to turn out cards on inferior paper or sacrifice his high standards of quality, cards printed on cheaper stock paper from Europe and the U.S. drove printer Louis Prang from the Christmas card portion of his business.

In 1867, Charles Dickens arrived in the United States for his second tour of America. His first trip to America in 1842 had started out triumphantly until he became ill. It ended disastrously as he loathed the rough and tumble nature of the Americans and their provincialism. The press and lack of copyright laws did not endear him to the Americans, whom he attacked for pirating and printing his novels in newspapers. Upon returning home to England, Dickens wrote of his travels in *American Notes* in which he skewered many of the foibles and characterizations he made about Americans and their institutions. He later followed that up with a vindictive rendering of *America* in his comic novel *Martin Chuzzlewit*.

Needing money for his large family and strained marital situation, Dickens embarked on his second and last tour of America. The tour was a triumph financially as Dickens's readings were well attended from tour beginning to end. Programs consisted of him reading passages from his famous and much loved novels and short sto-

Figure 6-5. Many illustrations during this first Christmas of peace contained subtle reminders of the recent war. This drawing entitled *Christmas Presents* shows a sword and cap over the mantle and a young man with an "empty sleeve"—an often used symbol for the returning veteran. (K.R.)

ries. Much requested by audiences, Dickens read repeatedly from *A Christmas Carol* from city to city. While in Boston during the Christmas holidays, Dickens stayed with James and Kate Fields at their home. James T. Fields was partners with William D. Ticknor in the publishing firm Ticknor & Fields which published many of America's foremost literary talents like Nathaniel Hawthorn and a long list of others.

In a diary kept by Kate Fields, she ascribed the place Dickens deserved in the rebirth Christmas had in the hands of the Victorians. Dickens joined several other guests for a holiday dinner at the Fields' house.

> "We are again at home in our dear little nook by the Charles, and tonight the lover of Christmas comes to have dinner with us. . . . At night came Mr. Dickens and Mr. Dolby, Mr. Lowell and Mabel, Mr. and Mrs. Dorr, to dinner. It was really a beautiful Christmas festival, as we intended it should be for the love of this new apostle of Christmas."[7]

On Christmas Eve, Dickens gave a reading of *A Christmas Carol* in Boston that brought about the conversion of a New England manufacturer named Fairbanks who was in the audience that night. The novella's message had a profound effect on his "puritan antipathy" towards Christmas that night.

> "Among the multitude that surged out of the building came a Mr and Mrs Fairbanks (the former was the head of a large-scale factory), who had journeyed from Johnsburg, Vermont, for the occasion. Returning to their apartments in Boston, Mrs Fairbanks observed that her husband was particularly silent and absorbed in thought, while his face bore an expression of unusual seriousness. She ventured some remark which he did not appear to notice. Later, as he continued to gaze into the fire, she inquired the cause of his reverie, to which he replied: 'I feel that after listening to Mr Dickens's reading of *A Christmas Carol* tonight I should break the custom we have hitherto observed of opening the works on Christmas Day.'
>
> "Upon the morrow they were closed. The following year a further custom was established, when not only the works closed on Christmas Day, but each and every factory (worker) had received the gift of a turkey."[8]

Sarah Josepha Hale was the editor of *Godey's Lady's Book,* and the person responsible for requesting her illustrator to "Americanize" the illustration of the Royal Family's Christmas tree. Hale was also the woman who campaigned relentlessly and finally badgered President Lincoln to declare the fourth Thursday of November as the official National holiday of Thanksgiving. In 1868, Sarah Josepha Hale wrote in her book, *Manners,* about the growing popularity of the tradition of the Christmas tree and the meaning of the holiday tree to the home festivities and children.

> "Christmas is the bright household festival that comes to gladden old winter, bring joy to life, good cheer, family gatherings, and tokens of love. To children especially it is the happy epoch, to be joyfully anticipated and joyfully remembered. Merry Christmas! The words are full of happy meanings to warm every heart. Even when gloom darkens the minds of the elder members of a family, when sorrow or adversity has checked their pleasures, there is ever a little reserve of Christmas merry-making for the young folks. 'We must not, on this day, throw a gloom over the children,' is every parent's thought.
>
> "And so the Christmas-tree rises in its glad greeness, laden with its glittering presents, and bright with the tapers that display its rich fruits. And the stockings are hung up for Kris Krinkel, and filled with such wonderful treasures as fairy lore never exceeded in the fancy of the little ones, who pull out the toys and presents of the season. Wise and good mothers take this time of Christmas joy to teach the little hearts, made happy by home cherishing, to remember the poor and desolate, and that it is more blessed to give than to receive....

CHRISTMAS-TREES

> "We are glad to notice that every year the German custom of making Christmas-trees for children is becoming more common amongst us. Few things give greater delight to the little

Figure 6-6. *The Illustrated London News* issued this scene of children gazing at the Christmas Tree in 1865. During the post-war years it was "Americanized" and often reappeared in newspapers throughout the country. (K.R.)

ones, or link happier recollections with the season and the home. As an easy manner of constructing them may not be known to all our readers, we insert a sketch of the German mode, written by an American lady.

"Before giving the description of this wonderful tree, I would say a few words of warning to those who decorate it with their loving gifts, which make sweetness and perfect its beauty. Do not load its green boughs with the *sugar candies now 'made to sell.'* You can adorn your Christmas-tree with healthful gifts of Nature—apples, pears, grapes, nuts, and other fruits that the little ones love. You can add lumps of real sugar, white and clean as crystal, if sweets are indispensable; and there are sugar candies honestly prepared from good sugar, and made beautiful without coloring. But pray do not allow your children to eat *'white earth'* colored with *carlot!*

HOW THE TREE WAS MADE

"The first winter German servants were in my house, as Christmas drew near, Augusta came to me one day, with her countenance glowing with enthusiasm, making her usual little curtsey, said, 'Will the mistress please have a Christmas-tree?'

"I cannot give her pretty broken English. 'A Christmas-tree, Augusta? I do not know how to arrange one.'

"'Mine bruder will do dat.'

"The brother was a carpenter; so I consented to the proposal, and invited a party of children for Christmas Eve. The day before Christmas, the 'bruder,' Gottlieb, appeared, looking as though he had come from the wood of Dunsinane, with a tree upon his back, a beautiful spruce, seven feet high. This was to be set up in the back parlor; but how was it to stand upright?

"The carpenter had brought for that purpose a board or plank, a *foot square and an inch and a half thick:* a moulding, merely for ornament, was on the edge of the board. In the middle of this square, which was prettily covered with moss, was a round hole, into which the trunk of the tree, cut for the purpose, was tightly fixed. To my surprise, it stood firm and steady, balancing itself, the board not even nailed to the floor.

"Small wax-candles, red, green, yellow, and white, were then fastened to the tree in little rims of tin, that had clasps to attach them to the branches, in such order as not to endanger the boughs above them, and cause a general conflagration. Then, small glass balls, gilt and colored, were hung on by strings, looking like ripe and beautiful fruit. The most valuable fruits, however, the Christmas gifts, were then suspended from the branches, excepting books and boxes too heavy for that purpose: they were deposited on the nursery carpet, at the foot of the tree.

"To children, Christmas is a peculiar delight: they never tire with its repetition. The Christmas-tree is, in their eyes the perfection of beauty,—the wonderful show they have been looking forward to for weeks, every day of which is counted. What happiness it gives them! The elderly people feel young in witnessing their joy. Yes, Christmas is for children and the childlike."[9]

A prodigious amount of literature was published on the subject of Christmas and Santa Claus during the latter half of the nineteenth century. Many soldiers and civilians who wrote their reminiscences of the Civil War from the softened distance of the post-war years, shared their Christmas experiences with their readers. Magazines and journals such as *Confederate Veteran, The Southern Historical Society Papers,* and *Century Magazine* were collection points for these wartime stories. Regimental histories published by unit historians (many reproduced in the preceding chapters) and state historical society publications were also rich veins for mining holiday tales. The former First Lady of the Confederacy, Varina Howell Davis, recounted her Christmas of 1864 in a New York newspaper article. Others from the rank of general all the way down to the privates of both armies published their remembrances in newspaper articles and papers submitted to veteran organizations such as the Grand Army of the Republic, the Military Order of the Loyal Legions of the United States and similar Confederate veteran counterpart organizations.

In 1887, Wilbur Hinman, a former officer in the Union army, published his fictitious novel *Corporal Si Klegg and His "Pard."* Hinman wrote of the misadventures of raw Union recruit Si Klegg and his foray into army life with his pard Shorty. A disguised memoir made up into a comic novel, Hinman imparted valuable information on the life of an infantryman. In one chapter Hinman wrote of the childlike Si Klegg's anticipation of a Christmas box from Santa Claus as he hung up a stocking from his tent pole to be filled. On Christmas Day, Klegg gets his box only to find empty disappointment and a note from a quartermaster's helper saying thanks for the goodies. Many real soldiers during the war had similar experiences.

"The day before Christmas the brigade to which Si's regiment belonged was ordered out on a reconnaissance. It was a rainy day. The brigade went charging over the fields and tearing through the woods and thickets, sometimes on the double-quick, trying to catch a squad of rebel cavalry, and then creeping up to gather in some of the enemy's pickets. Late in the evening the brigade returned to camp. Si thought he had never been so tired before in his life. All day his drooping spirits had been cheered by the hope of finding his box when he got back. But it had not come, and he was inconsolable.

" 'Ef I was you I wouldn't open yer box 'fore Christmas mornin',' said Shorty, as he and Si stood around the fire, getting supper. 'And what d'ye think now about Pete Jison's turkey 'n' mince pie?'

"Si didn't say anything. His grief was too deep for utterance. He didn't care whether the spangled banner had any stars left at all or not. Wet, weary, footsore and thoroughly disgusted, he went to bed and soon asleep, dreaming of Christmas at home, and mother, and Annabel, and turkey-stuffing, and plum-pudding.

" 'Hello, Si, wake up here! Merry Christmas to ye!'

"It was Shorty, routing out Si, soon after daylight. As soon as Si opened his eyes he saw his stocking full of something or other, pinned to the tent just above his head. He jumped to his feet with as much eagerness as when, in his juvenile days, he used to find candy apples and jumping jacks sticking out of his well filled hose.

"The average army stocking was wonderfully made. A new one, after being worn a couple of days, looked more like a nose-bag for a mule than anything else.

"Si soon found how the boys had conspired against him. They all knew about the box which he had so anxiously expected, and which none of them believed he would get. So, after he went to sleep that night, they slyly pulled off his stockings—for Si slept with them on, as did nine-tenths of the soldiers—filled them with wormy hardtack, bacon-rinds, beef-bones, sticks, and bits of old harness, pouring in beans and rice to fill up the chinks, and pinned them to the tent above him.

"The greatest mistake a soldier ever made was to lose his temper on account of a harmless joke. Si was wise enough to take it good-naturedly as he emptied the 'nose-bags' and drew them on his feet.

"It was a raw December morning, with a keen, nipping air. As Si skirmished around for his breakfast he realized that all his festive anticipations of a few days before were doomed to utter and irremediable disappointment.

" 'It's tough, fer Christmas, ain't it, Shorty?' said Si, as he gnawed his hardtack.

"If his box would only come he might yet be happy, so to speak; but hope had given way to despair.

"It was more than four weeks after that time, when the debris of the battle had been cleared away, that Si's Christmas box found its way to the front. Its contents, what was left of them, were in a condition to make angels weep. The teamsters had pried it open and rioted upon the savory dainties that loving hearts and hands had prepared for Si. A small section of Annabel's cake was left, and the ravagers, with a refinement of cruelty, had written on the paper wrapped around it:

" 'This is bully cake. Try it!'

"Almost everything in the box had been eaten, and what remained was a hopeless ruin. Rough handling, that would have done credit to a railroad baggage-master, had broken bottles of pickles and jars of fruit, and the liquids had thoroughly baptized the edibles that the mule drivers had spared. It was a sorry mess, and Si's heart ached as he gazed upon the wreck.

"The forenoon of Christmas day was dull enough. The boys were let off from drill and spent the time chiefly in writing letters and chasing the pensive *pediculus* [lice]."[10]

Other books written after the war and dealing with Christmas or Christmas scenes were a pair written by Louisa May Alcott titled *Hospital Christmas* and *Little Women*. Thomas Hardy recounted Christmas and the annual holiday pageant play of St. George and the Dragon in *Return Of The Native*, while Frank A. Burr told of *Christmas In Libby Prison*. American printings of Charles Dickens's *A Christmas Carol, The Pickwick Papers, Sketches By Boz,* and his collection of *Christmas Stories* were published both before the war and in numerous editions towards the end of the century. All the listed titles have memorable Christmas scenes that are often quoted at Christmas today. Five chapters from Washington Irving's *Sketchbook Of Geoffrey Grayon, Gentleman* were published in 1875 in a book devoted entirely to Irving's five vignettes of Christmas celebrations in England titled *Old Christmas,* and paired with illustrations by Randolph Caldecott. Another book written by a Civil War veteran in 1903 for children was Thomas Nelson Page's wartime tale of *A Captured Santa Claus.*

In the 1890's a number of magazines were started with Christmas or Santa Claus as the focus. *St. Nicholas Magazine* was probably the most famous and was published for a number of years well into this century, thrilling children with stories about the patron saint and his adventures, always with a message or moral. The bachelor Santa Claus gained a mate in 1899 when Katharine Lee Bates created Mrs. Claus to share Santa Claus's life at the North Pole and provide him comfort from his long and grueling journey once a year.

Thanks to the loving care and reviving of the customs and traditions of the winter holiday and its patron saint by Victorians on both sides of the Atlantic, Christmas and Santa Claus arrived in the twentieth century ready to adapt to the small changes that would occur in this modern age. But that is another tale for another time. Santa Claus, who would become uniquely American from the many ethnic components in his background, would go forth into the world as an American counterpart, accepted and loved by many countries and citizens of the world.

But I heard him exclaim,
Ere he drove out of sight,

"HAPPY CHRISTMAS TO ALL & TO ALL A GOOD NIGHT!"

ENDNOTES

CHAPTER 1

1. Clement C. Moore, *The Night Before Christmas*, (Dover Publications: 1971), pp. 24-25.

2. Cooke, ed., *A Celebration of Christmas*, (G. P. Putnam Sons: 1980) p. 62.

3. Jill Wolf, *A Victorian Christmas—Yuletide Family Traditions*, (Antioch Publishing Company: 1991), p. 11.

4. Clement A. Miles, *Christmas Customs and Traditions—Their History and Significance*, (Dover Publications, Inc.: 1976), p. 265.

5. Ibid, p. 266.

6. Daniel Foley, *The Christmas Tree*, (Chilton Company: 1960), p. 77.

7. *Dansville Advertiser*, (Dansville, New York: December 1862).

8. Cooke, p. 63.

9. Foley, p. 80.

10. *The Complete Works of Charles Dickens Containing The Complete Christmas Books and Stories*, (Walter J. Black Co.), Part II, "A Christmas Tree," pp. 3-4.

11. Black and Black, ed., *The Complete Works of Washington Irving, A History of Old New York*, (Twayne Publishers: 1984), Chapter IX, p. 87.

12. Tim Hallinan, *A Christmas Carol Christmas Book*, (Rudolph de Harak & Associates, Inc.: 1984, IBM), p. 66.

13. Ibid, p. 72.

14. Charles Dickens, *The Pickwick Papers*, (The American News Company) p. 194.

15. Ibid, pp. 195-196.

16. *Santa Claus Magazine*, December, 1991, Dan Weeks, "Love and Joy Come to You."

17. Moore, p. 26.

18. Harnett T. Kane, *The Southern Christmas Book* (David McKay Company: 1958), p. 13.

19. Ibid, p. 18.

20. Ibid, p. 15.

21. Ibid, p. 16.

22. Ibid, p. 17.

23. Ibid, p. 17-18.

24. Virginia's observance of Old Christmas or Twelfth Night was ended in 1759.

25. Catherine Clinton, *Plantation Mistress*, (Pantheon Books: 1982), pp. 177-178.

26. Kenneth M. Stampp, *The Peculiar Institution— Slavery in the Antebellum South*, (Random House: 1956), p. 169.

    Also of interest, see Frederick Law Olmstead's *The Cotton Kingdom*.

27. Ibid, p. 365.

28. Ibid, p. 170.

29. Ibid, p. 169.

30. Nan Custis Lee DeButts, ed., *Growing Up in the 1850's—The Journal of Agnes Lee*, (University of North Carolina Press: 1984), p. 4.

31. Kane, p. 49.

32. *The Collected Works of Charles Dickens Containing the Complete Christmas Books and Stories* (Walter J. Black Co.) Part I, "A Christmas Carol," p. 9.

33. Kane, p. 193.

34. Daniel E. Sutherland, *The Expansion of Everyday Life 1860-1876*, (Harper & Row, Publishers: 1989), pp. 260-261.

35. E. B. Long with Barbara Long, *The Civil War Day By Day—An Almanac 1861-1865*, (Doubleday & Company: 1971), p. 15.

36. Cole and McDonough, edd., *Witness to the Young Republic—A Yankee's Journal, 1828-1870*, (University Press of New England: 1989), p. 337.

37. Quynn, ed., *Diary of Jack Engelbrecht, Volume III 1858-1878*, (The Historical Society of Frederick County, Inc.: 1976).

CHAPTER 2

1. Long, p. 19.

2. Ibid, pp. 45-46.

3. Ibid, p. 46.

4. Myers, ed., *Children of Pride—A True Story of Georgia and The Civil War*, (Yale University Press: 1971), p. 825.

5. Admiral Raphael Semmes, *Memoirs of Service Afloat, During the War Between the States*, (Kelly, Piet & Company: 1868), p. 284.

6. Lewis Leigh Collection, USAMHI, Carlisle, PA.

7. Duncan, ed., *Blue-Eyed Child of Fortune—The Civil War Letters of Robert Gould Shaw*, (University of Georgia Press: 1992), pp. 168-169.

8. Miscellaneous Collection, USAMHI, Carlisle, PA.

9. Letter quoted by permission of relative Elizabeth Wooldridge Haven.

10. Silver, ed., *A Life For the Confederacy as Recorded in the Pocket Diaries of Pvt. Robert A. Moore*, (Broadfoot Publishing Company: 1987), p. 90.

11. James M. Holloway letter, Manuscript Collection, Virginia Historical Society.

12. J. W. Reid, *History of the Fourth Regiment of S.C. Volunteers, From the Commencement of the War Until Lee's Surrender*, (self-published: 1891), reprinted by Morningside Bookshop: 1975, pp. 63-64.

13. Dowdey, ed., *The Wartime Papers of R. E. Lee*, (Little, Brown and Company: 1961), p. 95.

14. Ibid, p. 103.

15. Lewis Leigh Collection, USAMHI, Carlisle, PA.

16. William Child, M.D., *A History of the Fifth Regiment New Hampshire Volunteers, In the American Civil War*, (R. W. Musgrove: 1893), reprinted by R. Van Sickle Military Books: 1988, pp. 41-42.

17. Lewis Leigh Collection, Book #2, folder 48, USAMHI, Carlisle, PA.

18. Folmer, ed., *From That Terrible Field—Civil War Letters of James M. Williams, Twenty-first Alabama Infantry Volunteers*, (University of Alabama Press: 1981), pp. 13, 15-17.

19. Donald, ed., *Gone For a Soldier—The Civil War Memoirs of Alfred Bellard*, (Little, Brown & Company: 1975), p. 37.

20. Blackburn, ed., *With the Wandering Regiment—The Diary of Captain Ralph Ely of the Eighth Michigan Infantry*, (Central Michigan University Press: 1965), p. 26.

21. *Memoirs of—, Company B, 7th Tennessee*, by John A. Fite, Confederate Collection, Tennessee State Archives and Library, Nashville, TN.

22. Bob Wommack, *Call Forth the Mighty Men*, Bessemer, Alabama, 1987.

23. *Robert Mockbee Reminiscences*, William McComb Papers, Museum of the Confederacy, Richmond, VA.

24. Marcus B. Toney, *Privation of a Private*, Nashville, 1905.

25. John Beatty, *The Citizen Soldier: Or, Memoirs of a Volunteer*, (Wilstach, Baldwin & Co.: 1879), Reprinted by Time-Life Books: 1983, pp. 88-89.

26. Lewis Leigh Collection, USAMHI, Carlisle, PA.

27. Ibid.

28. Lester L. Kempfer, *The Salem Light Guard—Company G 36th Regiment Ohio Volunteer Infantry*, Marietta, Ohio 1861-1865, (Adams Press: 1973), pp. 35-36.

29. Flower, ed., *Dear Folks at Home—The Civil War Letters of Leo W. and John I. Faller*, (Cumberland County Historical Society and Hamilton Library Association: 1963), pp. 41-43, 45.

30. *Robert A. Browne Papers*, Miscellaneous Collection, USAMHI, Carlisle, PA.

31. J. B. Jones, *A Rebel War Clerk's Diary at the Confederate States Capital Vol. I*, (J. B. Lippincott & Co.: 1866) reprinted by Time-Life Books: 1982, p. 102.

32. Laas, ed., *Wartime Washington—The Civil War Letters of Elizabeth Blair Lee*, (University of Illinois Press: 1991), pp. 93-94.

33. Woodward, ed., *Mary Chestnut's Civil War*, (Yale University Press: 1981), pp. 269-270.

34. *The Orpheus C. Kerr Papers*, (Blakeman & Mason: 1862), p. 158-159.

35. Myers, pp. 826-827.

36. Cole and McDonough, eds., *Witness to the Young Republic—A Yankee's Journal 1828-1870,* (University Press of New England: 1989), pp. 383-384.

37. *Dansville Advertiser,* (Dansville, New York: January 1862).

38. *Richmond During the War; Four Year of Personal Observations, by A Richmond Lady,* (G. W. Carleton & Co.: 1867) reprinted by Time-Life Books: 1983, pp. 87-89.

39. Davis, *The Orphan Brigade—The Kentucky Confederates Who Couldn't Go Home,* (Doubleday & Company, Inc.: 1980), p. 57.

CHAPTER 3

1. *Harper's Weekly,* Vol. VII, No. 314 Saturday, January 3, 1863, p. 2.

2. *Harper's Weekly,* Vol. VII, No. 314, Saturday, January 3, 1863, p. 14.

3. James Lee McDonough, *Stones River—Bloody Winter in Tennessee,* (University of Tennessee Press: 1980), p. 56.

4. W. J. McMurray, *History of the Twentieth Tennessee Regiment of Volunteer Infantry, C.S.A.,* (Nashville: 1904), p. 224.

5. Larry J. Daniel, *Soldiering in the Army of Tennessee—A Portrait of Life in a Confederate Army,* (University of North Carolina Press: 1991), p. 96.

6. Ibid, p. 90.

7. McDonough, p. 51.

8. Ibid, p. 51.

9. Kirwan, ed., *Johnny Green of the Orphan Brigade—The Journal of a Confederate Soldier,* (University of Kentucky Press: 1956), pp. 58-59.

10. *The Civil War Diary of Captain J. J. Womack, Company E, Sixteenth Tennessee Volunteers,* (McMinnville, Tennessee: 1961), p. 76.

11. *Civil War Times Illustrated,* December, 1961, Elden E. Billings, "Diaries & Letters," p. 7.

12. McDonough, p. 62. Also see *Ninetieth Ohio Infantry* by H. O. Harden, Stoutsville, Ohio, copyright 1902, p. 38.

13. Ibid, p. 62. Also see *Fifteenth Ohio Infantry* by Alexis Cope, Columbus, copyright 1916, p. 228.

14. Ibid, pp. 62-63. Also see *The History of the Fifty-Ninth Regiment Illinois Volunteers,* Indianapolis, copyright 1865, p. 186.

15. Lewis Leigh Collection, "George" Book 46 #21 1st Wisconsin Infantry Regiment, USAMHI, Carlisle, PA.

16. Henry V. Freeman, *Some Recollection of Stones River,* MOLLUS, Illinois Commandery, 1895, p. 229.

17. *Soldier of the Cumberland: Memoir of Mead Holmes, Jr., Sergeant of Company K, 21st Regiment Wisconsin Volunteers; By His Father,* (American Tract Society), pp. 145-125.

18. Peter Cozzens, *No Better Place to Die,* (University of Illinois Press: 1990), p. 44.

19. Ibid, p. 44.

20. Diary of B. Francis Nourse of the Chicago Board of Trade Battery, under the title *Worrell's Diary.* Lewis Leigh Collection, USAMHI, Carlisle, PA.

21. Beatty, pp. 197-198.

22. *Confederate Veteran Volume XIII, Vivid War Experiences At Ripley, Mississippi,* 1905, Reprinted by Broadfoot Publishing Company: 1984, p. 264.

23. Jenkin Lloyd Jones, *An Artilleryman's Diary,* (Wisconsin History Commission: 1914), p. 21.

24. Hess, ed., *A German in the Fatherland—The Civil War Letters of Henry A. Kircher,* (Kent State University Press: 1983), p. 41.

25. Capt. S. T. Ruffner, *Confederate Veteran Vol. XX, Sketch of the First Missouri Battery, C.S.A.,* copyright 1912, p. 418, reprinted by Broadfoot Publishing Company: 1984, p. 418.

26. Letter and Diaries of David Humphrey Blair, Miscellaneous Collection, USAMHI, Carlisle, PA.

27. Thomas Wentworth Higginson, *Army Life in a Black Regiment,* (Fields, Osgood & Co.: 1870) reprinted by Time-Life Books: 1982, pp. 34-35.

28. Burr, ed., *The Secret Eye—The Journal of Ella Gertrude Clanton Thomas, 1848-1889,* (University of North Carolina Press: 1990), pp. 213-214.

29. Mumper, ed., *I Wrote You Word, The Poignant Letters of Private John Holt, 1829-1863,* (H. E. Howard, Inc.: 1980), pp. 121-122.

30. Austin C. Dobbins, *Grandfather's Journal, Company B Sixteenth Mississippi Infantry Volunteers Harris' Brigade Mahone's Division Hill's Corps. A.N.V. May 27, 1861-July 15, 1865,* (Morningside House, Inc.: 1988), p. 116.

31. Pearce, ed., *Diary of Captain Henry A. Chambers,* (Broadfoot Publishing Company: 1983), p. 78.

32. Lewis Leigh Collection, Book #11, USAMHI, Carlisle, PA.

33. Diary of Samuel Pickens Company D 5th Alabama Regiment. Copy of unpublished diary in author's collection.

34. Durkin, ed., *Confederate Chaplain—A War Journal of Rev. James B. Sheeran, C.SS.R. 14th Louisiana, CSA,* (Bruce Publishing Company: 1960), p. 38.

35. Lowell Reidenbaugh, *27th Virginia Infantry,* (H. E. Howard, Inc.: 1993), p. 76.

36. Louis H. Manarin, *15th Virginia Infantry,* (H. E. Howard, Inc.: 1990), p. 36.

37. David F. Riggs, *13th Virginia Infantry,* (H. E. Howard, Inc.: 1988), p. 28.

38. William Henderson, *12th Virginia Infantry,* (H. E. Howard, Inc.: 1984), p. 43.

39. *Civil War Times Illustrated,* December 1961, Elden E. Billings, "Diaries & Letters," p. 8.

40. Dowdy, p. 353.

41. Frederick L. Hitchcock, *War From the Inside—1862-1863,* (J. B. Lippincott Company: 1904), pp. 148-149, 151.

42. Sears, ed., *For Country Cause & Leader—The Civil War Journal of Charles B. Haydon,* (Ticknor & Fields: 1993), p. 301.

43. Silliker, ed., *The Rebel Yell & the Yankee Hurrah—The Civil War Journal of A Maine Volunteer,* (Down East Books: 1985), pp. 63-64.

44. Thomas M. Aldrich, *The History of Battery A First Regiment Rhode Island Light Artillery 1861-1865,* (Snow & Farnham, Printers: 1904), p. 167.

45. John C. Williams, *Life In Camp,* (The Claremont Manufacturing Company: 1864), p. 56-57.

46. Richard Moe, *The Last Full Measure—The Life and Death of the First Minnesota Volunteers,* (Henry Holt and Company: 1993), p. 217.

47. Gavin, ed., *Infantryman Pettit—The Civil War Letters of Corporal Frederick Pettit,* (White Mane Publishing Company, Inc.: 1990), pp. 44-45.

48. Longacre, ed., *From Antietam to Fort Fisher—The Civil War Letters of Edward King Wightman, 1862-1865,* (Fairleigh Dickinson University Press: 1980), p. 63.

49. Henry Kyd Douglas, *I Rode with Stonewall,* (University of North Carolina Press: 1940), pp. 254-255.

50. Walter Phelps, Jr. Papers, USAMHI, Carlisle, PA.

51. McHenry Howard, *Recollections of a Maryland Confederate Soldier and Staff Officer Under Johnston, Jackson and Lee,* (Morningside Bookshop: 1975), pp. 185-186.

52. Randolph H. McKin, *A Soldier's Recollections—Leaves From the Diary of a Young Confederate,* (Longmans, Green, and Co.: 1910), p. 123.

53. George Grenville Benedict, *Army Life In Virginia; Letters of the Twelfth Vermont Regiment and Personal Experiences of Volunteer Service in the War For the Union 1862-63,* (Burlington Free Press Association: 1895), pp. 100-101.

54. Drickamer & Drickamer, eds., *Fort Lyons To Harper's Ferry-On the Border of North and South with "Rambling Jour,"* (White Mane Publishing Co., Inc.: 1987), pp. 68-69.

55. Edwin Franklin Palmer, *The Second Brigade; Or Camp Life, by a Volunteer,* (Montpelier: 1864), p. 87.

56. Ford, ed., *A Cycle of Adams Letters 1861-1865,* (Houghton Mifflin Company: 1920), Volume I, pp. 215-216.

57. Williams, ed., *The Wild Life of the Army: Civil War Letters of James A. Garfield,* (Michigan University Press: 1964), p. 203.

58. Lewis Leigh Collection, Book #16, USAMHI, Carlisle, PA.

59. *Diary of Isaac W. Scherich,* Washington County Free Library, Western Maryland Room.

60. Laas, pp. 218-220.

61. Cole and McDonough, p. 415.

62. Gwin, ed., *Cornelia Peake McDonald, A Woman's Civil War—A Diary, With Reminiscences of the War from March 1862,* (University of Wisconsin Press: 1992), pp. 101-104.

63. Jones, pp. 224-225.

64. Carleton, pp. 201-202.

65. Katherine M. Jones, *Ladies of Richmond*, (The Bobbs-Merrill Company: 1962), p. 147.

66. *Confederate Veteran Volume XIII*, (1905), reprinted by Broadfoot Publishing Company, p. 572.

67. Myers, p. 1003.

68. Summersell, ed., *The Journal of George Townley Fullam—Boarding Officer of the Confederate Sea Raider Alabama*, (University of Alabama Press: 1973), p. 68.

69. Davis, p. 148.

CHAPTER 4

1. *Harper's Weekly*, Volume VII, No. 365, December 26, 1863, p. 818.

2. Burr, pp. 220-221.

3. Woodward, pp. 514-515.

4. Myers, p. 1130.

5. Carleton, pp. 267-268.

6. Phoebe Yates Pember, *A Southern Woman's Story—Life in Confederate Richmond*, (McCowan-Mercer Press, Inc.: 1959), reprinted by Broadfoot Publishing Company: 1991, pp. 178-179.

7. Jones, pp. 199-120.

8. Jaquette, ed., *South After Gettysburg,—Letters of Cornelia Hancock Civil War Nurse, 1863-1865 Quaker Teacher, 1866-1868*, (Thomas Y. Crowell Co.: 1956), p. 37.

9. Carleton, *The Orpheus C. Kerr Papers, Third Series*, (Carleton: 1865), p. 180.

10. Lee, p. 332

11. Cole & McDonough, pp. 442-443.

12. W. P. Conrad and Ted Alexander, *When War Passed This Way*, (Beidel Printing House: 1982), pp. 230-231.

13. Ibid, p. 229.

14. Ibid, p. 232.

15. Turner, ed. *Prisoner of War Letters 1863-1865 From Johnson Island*, (McClure Printing Company, Inc.: 1980), p. 25.

16. Douglas, pp. 254-255.

17. Lieut. Colonel F. F. Cavada, U.S.V., *Libby Life: Experiences of A Prisoner of War in Richmond, Va., 1863-64*, (J. B. Lippincott & Co.: 1865), reprinted by University Press of America, Inc.: 1985, pp. 99-103.

18. John Ransom, *John Ransom's Andersonville Diary*, (Paul S. Eriksson: 1963), pp. 22-23.

19. Lewis Leigh Collection, James W. Bartlett Papers, Book # 3-26, USAMHI, Carlisle, PA.

20. Gavin, p. 132.

21. Sears, p. 347.

22. Blackburn, ed., *With the Wandering Regiment—The Diary of Captain Ralph Ely of the Eighth Michigan Infantry*, (Central University Press: 1965), p. 70.

23. Miscellaneous Collection, Diary of Abram Fulkerson, 114th Illinois Regiment, Co. C, USAMHI, Carlisle, PA.

24. Walton, ed., *A Civil War Courtship—The Letters of Edwin Weller from Antietam to Atlanta*, (Doubleday & Company, Inc.: 1980), p. 63.

25. Lawrence Van Alstyne, *Diary of an Enlisted Man*, (New Haven, Conn.: 1910). Also see *The Civil War Christmas Album*, selected and edited by Philip Van Doren Stern, (Hawthorne Books, Inc.: 1961), p. 25.

26. Daniel, p. 103. John Farris Letter to his wife, December 26, 1863, Farris Letters, Emory University.

27. Ibid, p. 96. Brown Diary, December 24, 1863, Greenwood, Mississippi Public Library.

28. Davis, ed., *Diary of a Confederate Soldier, John S. Jackman of the Orphan Brigade*, (University of South Carolina Press: 1990), p. 102.

29. James H. M'Neilly, *Confederate Veteran, Volume XXVIII*, "Christmas in Camp," 1920, reprinted by Broadfoot Publishing Company: 1984, pp. 182-183.

30. Capt. Richard Beard, *Confederate Veteran, Volume XXXVI*, "Christmas Dinner In 1863" 1928, reprinted by Broadfoot Publishing Company: 1984, p. 545.

31. E. Polk Johnson, *Confederate Veteran, Volume XV*, "Christmas and the Result of Volunteering" 1907, reprinted by Broadfoot Publishing Company: 1980, p. 545.

32. Jones, p. 157.

33. Adam, ed., *On the Altar of Freedom—A Black Soldier's Civil War Letters From the Front—Corporal Henry Gooding*, (University of Massachusetts Press: 1991), pp. 94-96.

34. Blackburn, ed., *"Dear Carrie..." The Civil War Letter of Thomas N. Stevens*, (The Clarke Historical Library: 1984), pp. 209-210.

35. Pearce, p. 160.

36. Dobbins, pp. 173-174.

37. Jones, ed., *The Civil War Memoirs of Captain William J. Seymour, Reminiscences of a Louisiana Tiger*, (Louisiana State University Press: 1991), pp. 103-104.

38. Captain Theodore Garnett, Trout, ed., *Riding with Stuart—Reminiscences of an Aide-de-Camp*, (White Mane Publishing Co., Inc.: 1994), pp. 30-31.

39. Lewis Leigh Collection, Philip H. Powers Papers, Book #19, USAMHI, Carlisle, PA.

40. *Southern Historical Society Papers, Volume XXVI, Diary of Captain Robert Emory Park*, 1898, reprinted by Broadfoot Publishing Company: 1977, p. 27.

41. Runge, ed., *Four Years in the Confederate Artillery—The Diary of Private Henry Robinson Berkeley*, (Virginia Historical Society, 1961), p. 64.

42. *Unpublished Diary of Samuel Pickens of Co. D, 5th Alabama Regiment.* Copy in the author's collection.

43. Dowdey, pp. 644-645.

44. Silliker, p. 231.

45. Barber and Swinson, eds., *The Civil War Letters of Charles Barber, Private, 104th New York Infantry*, (Gary E. Swinson: 1991), p. 153.

46. Rhodes, ed., *All For the Union—The Civil War Diary and Letters of Elisha Hunt Rhodes*, (Orion Books: 1985), p. 136.

47. Kohl, ed., *Irish Green & Union Blue—The Civil War Letters of Peter Welsh*, (Fordham University Press: 1986).

48. James I. Robertson, Jr., *Soldiers Blue and Gray*, (University of South Carolina Press: 1988), p. 80. Also see *The Sixteenth Maine Regiment in the War of the Rebellion, 1861-1865*, by Abner R. Small, Portland, 1886, p. 159.

49. Drickamer & Drickamer, p. 152.

50. *A Cycle of Adams Letters 1861-1865*, p. 110.

51. Donald, p. 247.

52. Summersell, p. 169.

53. Davis, p. 206.

CHAPTER 5

1. Stern, ed., *The Civil War Christmas Album*, (Hawthorn Books, Inc.: 1961), pp. 115-118, and the *Diaries of Gideon Welles*, Allan Nevin, ed., 1961.

2. *Harper's Weekly*, December 31, 1864 Vol. VIII, Vol. 418, p. 2.

3. Letter from John Anderson (McGowan) to his father. Miscellaneous Collection, USAMHI Carlisle, PA.

4. Adin B. Underwood, A.M., *From Three Years Service of the Thirty-third Mass. Infantry Regiment 1862-1865*, (A. Williams & Co.: 1881) reprinted by Blue Acorn Press, p. 122.

5. Burk Davis, *Sherman's March*, (Random House: 1980), p. 122.

6. Bauer, ed., *From Soldiering: The Civil War Diary of Rice C. Bull, 123rd New York Volunteer Infantry*, (Presidio Press: 1897), pp. 201-202.

7. Kirwan, pp. 184-185.

8. Davis, ed., *Diary of a Confederate Soldier—John S. Jackman of the Orphan Brigade*, (University of South Carolina Press: 1990), p. 152.

9. Robertson, p. 145. *Also see* original source, Charles E. Belknap, "Christmas Day Near Savannah In Wartime," *Michigan History VI*, 1922, pp. 591-596.

10. Brown, ed., *One of Cleburne's Command—The Civil War Reminiscences and Diary of Capt. Samuel T. Foster, Granbury's Texas Brigade, CSA*, (University of Texas Press: 1980), pp. 158-159.

11. Letter of Lieutenant William McAdams to his wife, Lewis Leigh Collection, USAMHI, Carlisle, PA.

12. Diary of David Humphrey Blair, Miscellaneous Collection, USAMHI, Carlisle, PA.

13. Diary of John Quincy Adams, 95th Illinois Infantry Regiment, Company H, Miscellaneous Collection, USAMHI, Carlisle, PA.

14. Jenkins Lloyd Jones, *An Artilleryman's Diary,* (Wisconsin History Commission: 1914), pp. 291-292.

15. Private W. H. Bird, *Stories of the Civil War,* (Advocate Print), p. 42. This very small memoir was probably self published in a very limited printing for family and friends. Miscellaneous Collection, USAMHI, Carlisle, PA.

16. Blackburn, pp. 269-271.

17. Longacre, pp. 222-224.

18. Ransom, pp. 237-238.

19. Diary of Michael Dougherty, 13th PA Cavalry, Miscellaneous Collection, USAMHI, Carlisle, PA.

20. *Southern Historical Papers Vol. 11—Diary of Capt. Robert E. Park, Twelfth Alabama Regiment,* (Southern Historical Society: 1876), reprinted by Broadfoot Publishing Company: 1977, pp. 237-238.

21. Swank, ed., *Confederate Letters and Diaries 1861-1865,* (Burd Street Press: 1988).

22. Menge and Shimrak, ed., *The Civil War Notebook of Daniel Chisholm,* (Orion Books: 1989), p. 100.

23. Diary of Orrel Brown, 16th Maine, Company C. Miscellaneous Collection, USAMHI, Carlisle, PA.

24. Dobbins. p. 225.

25. Unpublished diary of Samuel Pickens, 5th Alabama Regiment, Company D. Used by permission.

26. John B. Gordon, *Reminiscences of the Civil War,* (Charles Scribner's Sons: 1903), reprinted by Time-Life Books: 1981.

27. Camille Baquet, *History of First Brigade, New Jersey Volunteers From 1861-1865,* (State of New Jersey: 1910), reprinted by Stan Clark Military Books, p. 363.

28. Diary of Albert H. Artman, 4th Pennsylvania Cavalry, Company H, Miscellaneous Collection, USAMHI, Carlisle, PA.

29. Rhodes, pp. 202-203.

30. Letter of H. E. Sears to his sister, 4th Regiment New York Heavy Artillery, Lewis Leigh Collection, USAMHI, Carlisle, PA.

31. Jaquette, p. 99.

32. Sylvanus Cadwallader, *Three Years With Grant,* (Alfred A. Knopf, Inc.: 1955), pp. 279-280.

33. Pearce, ed., *Diary of Captain Henry A. Chambers,* (Broadfoot Publishing Company: 1983), pp. 235-236.

34. Runge, ed., *The Diary of Private Henry Robinson Berkely,* (Virginia Historical Society: 1961), reprinted 1991, p. 113.

35. Gwin, p. 221

36. Durkin, pp. 150-151.

37. Douglas, pp. 307-308.

38. Letter from John M. Bell to his best friend, Lt. George O. Manning of the 1st Mass. Light Battery, dated December 25, 1864, Washington, D.C., Lewis Leigh Collection, USAMHI, Carlisle, PA.

39. Jones, pp. 354-365.

40. Hammond, ed., *Diary of a Union Lady 1861-1865,* (Funk and Wagnalls Company, Inc.: 1962).

41. Lee, pp. 453-454.

42. Quynn, ed., *The Diary of Jacob Engelbrecht, Volume* III *1858-1878,* (The Historical Society of Frederick County, Inc.: 1976), p. 94.

43. Burr, pp. 249-251.

44. Carleton, pp. 340-341.

45. *Confederate Veteran,* Volume XXIII, June 1915, p. 269, Alice West, "The Tree Was a Lovely Holly," "Recollection of the War in Virginia."

46. *New York Sunday World,* December 13, 1896, Mrs. Jefferson Davis, "Christmas In the Confederate White House" and *Ladies of Richmond—Confederate Capital,* Chapter VII, "Never Cry for Quarter," Katherine M. Jones, ed., (Bobbs-Merrill Company, Inc.: 1962), pp. 247-253.

CHAPTER 6

1. *Harper's Weekly,* Volume IX, No. 470, p. 818.

2. Burr, p. 278.

3. Cole, p. 492.

4. Hammond, pp. 381-382.

5. McGee & Lander, eds., *A Rebel Came Home: The Diary & Letters of Floride Clemson 1863-1866,* (University of South Carolina Press: 1989, 1961), pp. 196-197.

6. Foley, p. 117.

7. *The Atlantic Monthly Press,* 1922, p. 149, M. A. DeWolfe Howe, "Memories of a Hostess—A Chronicle of Eminent Friendships." James T. Fields was the editor of *The Atlantic Monthly* during the Civil War.

8. J. M. Golby and A. W. Purdue, *The Making of the Modern Christmas,* (B. T. Batsford, Ltd.: 1986), p. 48.

9. Mrs. Hale, *Manners; Happy Homes and Good Society All the Year Round,* (J. E. Tilton and Company: 1868), pp. 363, 367-370.

10. Wilber F. Hinman, *Corporal Si Klegg and His "Pard,"* Chapter XXVIII, (Williams Publishing Company: 1887), pp. 379-381.